本书得到江西师范大学外国语言文学学科建设经费的资助

江西师范大学外国语言文学学术文库

A Discursive-psychological Study of Judges' Judicial Behavior

Zhong Caishun

中国社会科学出版社

图书在版编目（CIP）数据

法官司法行为的话语心理学研究 = A Discursive-psychological Study of Judges' Judicial Behavior：英文 / 钟彩顺著．—北京：中国社会科学出版社，2017．12

（江西师范大学外国语言文学学术文库）

ISBN 978-7-5203-1648-4

Ⅰ．①法…　Ⅱ．①钟…　Ⅲ．①法官-法律语言学-研究-英文　Ⅳ．①D90-055

中国版本图书馆 CIP 数据核字（2017）第 299456 号

出 版 人　赵剑英
责任编辑　李庆红
责任校对　沈丁晨
责任印制　王　超

出　　版　中国社会科学出版社
社　　址　北京鼓楼西大街甲 158 号
邮　　编　100720
网　　址　http：//www. csspw. cn
发 行 部　010-84083685
门 市 部　010-84029450
经　　销　新华书店及其他书店

印　　刷　北京明恒达印务有限公司
装　　订　廊坊市广阳区广增装订厂
版　　次　2017 年 12 月第 1 版
印　　次　2017 年 12 月第 1 次印刷

开　　本　710×1000　1/16
印　　张　15. 25
插　　页　2
字　　数　236 千字
定　　价　66. 00 元

凡购买中国社会科学出版社图书，如有质量问题请与本社营销中心联系调换
电话：010-84083683

Preface

This book is a recent adaptation of my PhD dissertation submitted to Guangdong University of Foreign Studies in 2009. I was enrolled in its PhD program in forensic linguistics in 2006. Before that, my academic training was mainly on critical discourse analysis (CDA), a theory and method for social research. This aroused my interest in institutional discourses such as law, education and business. That was the main reason I chose judges' discourse practice as my PhD research project. This topic was borne out of a prevalent observation that, despite the speeding-up of law-making in China over the past few decades, the public trust in judicature is lower than expected. Since judges are the gatekeepers of law, looking into their judicial behavior (JJB) shall be an essential juncture to gain insight into Chinese judicature.

This book consists of 7 chapters. Chapter 1 maps out the backdrop to this research. Over the past four decades, much endeavour has been made to institute and reform the judicial system in China. However, the public have not yet placed sufficient trust on it. Among the critiques raised against it, there arises a strong voice to attribute the conundrums of current judicature to judges' qualification. This is, however, not entirely fair since such criticism is out of a prescriptivist rational model. Judicial decision making is indeed more complex than rational principles can address. This book intends to offer an alternative discursive psychological account of JJB, which will show how judges account for their own judicial discourse practice.

In Chapter 2, relevant literature is reviewed to establish the niche for this research. Judges' role is variously defined under different legal systems. In China, judges are not only legal professionals but also *Guan*, (an incumbent of the officialdom) holding legal, social and political accountability. Such multiple roles are unlikely to be addressed by the reductionist cognitive psychological approach. This book argues that discursive psychology (DP) can provide an ethnomethodological understanding of judges' folk knowledge.

Chapter 3 firstly constructs a theoretical framework for this research. By drawing on Discursive Action Model, Speech Act Thoery, Exchange Structure Theory and Linguistic Anthropology, this book develops an analytical framework to construe judicial discourse order. It is argued that framing and categorizing are the main judicial functions judges' discursive actions aim to fulfill. How such functions are achieved interactionally can be revealed by attending to either structure-generated or category-implicated identities. Secondly, the dataset for this research is elucidated and the steps taken to analyze the data are explained.

From Chapter 4 to Chapter 6, the results of data analysis are discussed. Chapter 4 presents the construction and function of judges' decision constituting discourse. Correspondent with China's judicial trial frame, judges are found to perform four types of discursive actions, i. e. coordinative, inquisitive, representative and attributive. However, each of them is diversely reified due to thetension between structure and contingency in judges' discourse activities. This dynamism is reflected in the sequential unfolding of judges' discourse practice.

Chapter 5 examines how identities are evoked by the judges as a strategy to hold accountability for their judicial behavior. It is found that discourse, situated and transportable identities are all occassioned as the linguistic, institutional and socio-cultural resources by the judges to rationalize their discursive actions. The judges are institutionally situated as the procedure organizer, fact investigator and order maker. In performing these situated identities, two discourse identities are frequently made relevant: interaction initiator and participation controller. The specific forms and their distribution of discursive actions are also shaped by the transportable identities they oriented to.

Chapter 6 aims to provide a theoretical account for contingency and idiosyncrasy of JJB. It is shown that JJB can vary along three dimensions.Firstly, it can be either prodedure-oriented or substance-oriented con tingenton its stake or interest. Secondly, judges can assume a role of authority or solidarity in their discourse style. Thirdly, they can be either paradigmatic or narrative in their mode of thinking. By drawing on Heideggerian Theory of Being, this book argues that JJB is the manifestation of judges' Being or care structure. In this vein, judges' personal order shall be the ontological structure for us to comprehend JJB.

Finally, Chapter 7 concludes the book by summarizing its major findings and its theoretical and practical implications. The limitations of this research are also discussed with suggestions for further studies.

The debts I have incurred in drafting this book go back over many years, and I am fully aware that I cannot acknowledge them adequately enough. I want to mention, however, a few specific contributions. I would like to express my deepest gratitude to my PhD supervisor, Professor Du Jinbang, who gave me tremendous support, constant encouragement and professional guidance throughout my doctoral candidacy. It was he who awoke me to all the wonders that I could enjoy in pursuing forensic linguistics studies. Whenever I foundered or became powerless in my research, he would be the one I could rely on. Most of the ideas in the book emerged in our weekly"academic hill hikes", an informal forensic linguistics forum served as an arena for both phsycial and intellectual training.

I am also deeply grateful to those professors whose inspiring lectures sparked my interest in academic research. Professor Qian Guanlian and Professor Huo Yongshou guided me through a philosophical tour of language. Professor Liu Jianda provided me with necessary training in statistics. Professor Shen Sanshan helped me to make out an outline of semantics.

My heartfelt thanks should also go to my PhD committee members, Dr. Zhang Xinhong, Professor Xu Zhanghong, Professor Mo Aiping and Professor Yuan Chuanyou. Their valuable comments and suggestions on my research significantly influenced and shaped what the book now is.

My sincere thanks are also extended to my MA supervisor, Professor Wu Zongjie in Zhejiang University. He kindly read my PhD research proposal and offered me insightful suggestions which greatly inspired me to continue this research work.

During the three years in Guangzhou, I also reaped great friendship. Huang Yongping, Cheng Jinshi and Xu Youping were the best companions in times of solitude, confusion and depression. The traces of their ideas can also be found throughtout the books, as we had numerous conversations on this topic.

A huge thank-you is due to my wife (Cheng Weizhen), my son (Zhong Yuxuan), my parents (Zhong Yongshu and Huang Xuanxian) and my brother (Zhong Caifang). Without their love and support, I could not have gone through the enduring ordeal of PhD research.

Finally, I have to acknowledge that the publication of this book is under the auspice of the Academic Excellence Program in Foreign Languages College at Jiangxi Normal University.

Contents

Chapter 1

Introduction

1.1 Background to the Study

Since the late 1970s, a comprehensive program for judicial reform has been implemented in the Chinese judicial system with a view to accommodating the political philosophy of "rule of law". It is claimed that the establishment of a new judicature in China has been marked by 13 major judicial and political events (Shen 2004). Among them, the formulation and enactment of the three procedure laws① are the most remarkable accomplishments, and thereby new procedures of trial have been prescribed, the roles of judges, litigants and other participants in courtroom trial have been redefined and the rules governing evidence determination and judicial decision making have been reformulated. Within this endeavor, there seems to be a propensity to capitalize on the strengths of both the Common Law and the Civil Law traditions, which is manifested in the existence of some hybridity in the current Chinese judicial system. However, this reform is a complex social project that can not be achieved at a strike. So far, reform experiments are still going on at different levels of judicature. The following quotation represents a critical view about current reform of Chinese

① They are Civil Procedure Law (1982/1991), Criminal Procedure Law (1996) and Administrative Procedure Law (1989).

judicature:

> *Much evidence has shown that the judicial reform in China has not been effective in enhancing public confidence in courts and judges and promoting judicial independence, as was expected by the decision-makers, but on the contrary, has aggravated in certain aspects the existing problems, and even brought about new ones.* (He, 2002: 17)

Apart from the criticism that has been leveled at current Chinese judicial system, constructive suggestions have also been proposed as to what and how to reform. Xiao Yang (2002), the former Chief Justice of China, points out that there are three major problems to address: the localization of judicial power, the bureaucratization of judicial institution management, and the under-professionalization of judges. These problems all have much to do with the role of judges. In this vein, there has emerged a strong call for respecification of judge's identity (Qu, 2006; Tian, 2013; Yang, 2014; Yu, 2012). Research that resonates with the call has canvassed judges' independence (Zhang, 1999), professionalization (Lin, 2006), qualification (Qu, 1999), Knowledge (Cai, 2003), selection and appointment (Xia, 2001), etc. As a result, laws and regulations (e. g. the evidence rules, Civil Procedure Law, Criminal Procedure Law, etc.) have been formulated to regulate judges' judicial behavior.

However, the empirical evidence has shown that judges' professional performance can not be berigorously monitored by existent legal rules or codes of conducts. The process of judges' judicial decision making is far more complex than what procedure laws or judicial codes can capture. This is well illustrated in sentencing disparity. It is quite common that different judges may arrive at different judicial decisions on the same case. This suggests that rules and codes can not predict judicial behavior and judicial justice can not be guaranteed merely by law alone. The legal realists argue that law is drafted and exploited by human beings and is, thus, subject to human foibles, frailties and imperfections. In this light, the study of law shall pay closer attention to the nature of judges' judicial behavior (JJB) in order to explicate how justice is enacted and lived out in judicial process.

However, research into JJB is still in its infancy in China (e. g. Su, 2004; Wu, 2008; Li, 2013; Xu, 2012; Zhang, 2014). The existent literature is mostly concerned with the putative norms of judges' judicial behavior. Quite few empirical studies have examined the actual behavior of judges.

In the western scholarship, judicial behavior has been an important research topic in political science in the past few decades (Schubert and Danelski, 1969; Gibson, 1983; Baum, 1997; Baum, 2006; Klein & Mitchell, 2010). Efforts have particularly been made to address judges' discretion in sentencing (Thomas, 2003) by modelling their judicial decision making (Lovegrove, 1989) or documenting the affecting variables. For example, in researching juvenile court sentencing, Sanborn (1996) identifies three types of variables:

(1) legal-severity of offense and previous record,

(2) administrative-particular court or judge, and

(3) social-race, class, gender, and age.

These variables have also been drawn on to account for JJB in other types of case (e. g. Pratt, 1998; Steffensmeier and Britt, 2001; Manning and Carroll et al., 2004; Becker-Lindow, 2007; Staley, 2007; Wu, 2007). However, no consistent results have been pooled so far. For example, in St. Louis's (2000) research of juvenile court judges, the assumed correlation between the potential variables and the judicial decisions is rejected by the statistical result of empirical data. This indicates that those specified variables are not always reliable predictors for JJB. The conflicting results from academic research also suggest that a critical re-evaluation is essential to justify a theoretical account of JJB.

Among the existent research, a rational model is assumed by many people regardless of whatever variables they are concerned with. This model is driven by a prescriptive interest, aiming for a unified account of judicial practice (Wu 2008) . However, such a model has its inherent limitation as is manifested in the inconsistency or disparity of JJB. It fails to address how judges deal with contingencies.

Moreover, previous judicial behavior studies have used limited empirical data to extract variables that underpin judges' decision-making. Theorization about judicial behavior is made "without ever setting foot in a trial court or encountering a trial court judge face to face" (Philips, 1998: xi) . They do not rely on "data based on direct observation of judicial behavior (Tate, 1983: 62) but on given written documents or surveys. In other words, the existent judicial behavior theories are putative in nature. They do not reflect the real situation in which JJB occurs.

In short, previous studies of JJB provide only a limited or partial insight into the ways judges figure in the judicial process. In the milieu of China's judicial reform, JJB has become a perplexing issue for judges who need to find orientation in their professional life and for policy makers who need to steer the direction for legal and judicial development. Therefore, further exploration into JJB will be of apparent practical and theoretical significance.

1.2 Purpose of the Study

The purpose of this study is to provide an alternative perspective to shed light on the nature of JJB. The traditional research on JJB is dominated by cognitivism, an approach focusing on the "black box" of judges. This has resulted in some model-theoretic descriptions and explanations of judges' decision making. Some psychometric models (e. g. Segal & Spaeth, 2002) , for example, have characterized judicial behavior in terms of personal, social and cultural attributes. However, research along this line heavily relies on researchers' personal erudition and unjustified theoretical assumption (e. g. Gao & Jiang, 2006) , or on the myth of statistical or experimental tools (e. g. Tiede, 2007) .The theoretical categories and principles it has given rise to have little to do with judges' actual judicial behavior.

Recently, an alternative sociological approach has been advocated to address the contingency and complexity of judicial behavior. For example, Su (2004) conducts a contextual analysis of JJB. Wu (2008) applies a sociology of narrative to the case study of some judges in the local courts. Both of them recognize the discursive nature of JJB. Their objective is to describe how judicial behavior is enacted and lived out as accountable patterns of meaning, inference, and action. By focusing on the recorded discourse of judges, they try to cut across the basic problems associated with the gap between what they observe and what they generate as the theoretical account about judicial behavior. But as we can see, both approaches may be skewed by the researchers' theoretical preoccupations in interpretation. Either the contextual analysis or the sociology of narrative (Ewick & Silbey, 1995; Fleury-Steiner, 2002) is by no means free from the researchers' presumed ideology. Findings of these methods are in essence the researchers' etic claims.

Given these problems with previous judicial behavior research, this study aims to offer a new perspective into JJB so that judges' personal and practical knowledge can be properly accorded with. Such a concern entails development of a better fit between theory and data. A theory will be constructed out of rather than imposed on judicial behavior. By doing so, we can hopefully gain access to the authentic knowledge that informs JJB.

1.3 Theoretical Assumptions of the Study

This research proposes a discursive-psychological approach to JJB, which is premised on our ontological and epistemological commitment to the researched object. Building on the current knowledge about JJB as mentioned in the previous two sections, the present study subscribes to a discursive view of judicial behavior. This orientation is in line with the discursive turn in social sciences and, particularly, in legal studies (Liao, 2006) . In this vein, it is argued that "the trial system is constructed entirely through linguistic performances of various kinds, both spoken and written" (Luchjenbroers & Aldridge, 2008: 191) . Therefore, discourse shall be a reasonable juncture for JJB research.

Underlying the discursive view of JJB is a constructionist epistemology which takes a dialectic stance to overcome the unproductive division between "macro" and "micro" or between "structure" and "agency". In other words, it highlights a holistic understanding of judicial behavior and avoids the one-dimensional view of structuralism or subjectivism.

Given this theoretical orientation, judicial behavior research shall adopt a trans-disciplinary way, taking into consideration both the dynamicism of discourse process and the structural constraints from psychological, institutional, social and cultural systems. The discursive nature of JJB suggests that linguistics, and discourse analysis in particular, shall occupy a central place. Meanwhile, judicial behavior as a social phenomenon is necessarily subject to the constraints of social psychology①. In this light, this study will draw on discursive psychology (DP) , an approach which integrates discourse and social psychology. It emerges from distinctive, but converging, lines of investigation in psychology, sociology, anthropology, and linguistics (e. g. Potter & Wetherell, 1987, Edwards & Potter 1992; Potter, 1996; Edwards 1997; Harre, 2001) . There are three central tenets, which differentiate DP from the traditional cognitive approach (see Table 1-1) :

---

① Social psychology can be simply defined as "the study of certain kinds of interaction between people" .

Table 1-1 Two Psychological Approaches to Judicial Behavior Research

A discursive-psychological approach	A cognitive-psychological approach
Focusing on discourse, the dynamics of real-life social Process	Exploiting data from experiments, surveys or judicial documents
Taking psychological topics as discursive constructions and resources	Regarding cognition as the determinant
Adopting the agentic framework	Subscribing to the cause/effect metaphysics

From this comparison, we can find that DP is by nature a grounded theory. Following it, JJB theories shall be extracted through rigorous discourse analysis. However, this form of research shall be better regarded as a complement to more traditional cognitive methods of dealing with the same issue (Bavelas, 2005). The validity of the discursive approach will be enhanced if its findings can also endure the experimental tests.

In sum, this study will utilize DP as the lens to examine judges' discursive practices. It aims to show what insights DP can yield into JJB in the judicial process. Thus, it echoes the call for diversity in theoretical approaches to "facilitate progress toward good explanations of judicial behavior" (Baum, 1997). We also hope that this study may help to consolidate the role of forensic linguistics in the legal scholarship.

1.4 Research Questions

DP draws on the literal use of the concept of "conversation" as a guide to building working models of psychological phenomena (Harre, 2001). Conversation is a complex social episode, with its own rules and conventions. Thus, DP's major task is to discover the aims and norms of collective joint actions that constitute the episodes. In this light, the practical DP research shall focus on episodes that people participate in and come up with dynamic models of their joint actions. To achieve this, we need to know what acts people perform to accomplish the overall project of episodes. In order to capture the unfolding of those episodes and sequence of acts, close attention must be paid to the dynamics of the participants' positioning, a momentary assumption or ascription of a certain cluster of rights, duties, and obligations with respect to what participants, in that position, can say and do. In short, a discursive psychology is "to bring out the' semantics' of actions and the' syntax' of their building up into intelligible episodes" (Harre, 2001: 703). Following this paradigm, this study will be centered on the following three questions:

1) What do judges do when they participate in the judicial process?

A discursive psychology of JJB moves beyond the inner mind of judges to the interactional, social and cultural dimensions of the discursive process in which all the components of JJB are constituted. This suggests that judicial behavior research shall take a fine-grained look into how judicial behavior is constituted and constructed within the "everyday" talk at the localised and situated level of the judicial proceeding. That is, empirical analysis must first accomplish the task of identifying and describing some of the detailed discursive strategies and activities deployed by judges to achieve judicial undertakings. The discourse analysis for DP can address what discourse practice judges are engaged in and what tools (i. e. discursive resources) they make use of to accomplish them.

2) What enables judges to behave the way as they do?

In order to understand the unfolding of those episodes in which judicial justice is sealed, close attention must be paid to the dynamics of judicial interaction. In accordance with the agentic framework of DP, we need to understand what judges must know to produce a sequence of acts that accomplish the judicial activities and how judges' decision making is linked to such knowledge. In DP, the notion of "identity" (Antaki & Widdicombe, 1998a), "role" and "positioning" (Harre, 2001) are introduced to describe how actions are associated with certain persons as role holders. That is, the knowledge that participants utilize is attributable to their identity. Different from cognitive psychology, identity is treated in DP as the "tool" and "achievement" in discourse practice (Antaki & Widdicombe, 1998b). DP emphasizes the ephemeral character of identity which can be challenged, transformed, repudiated, exploited, expanded, and so on. This suggests that a discursive psychology of JJB shall reveal how judges orient to particular identities to perform their specific tasks. By addressing judges' identity, we shall also be able to show the stake or interest that judges display in JJB.

3) How is judges' behavior held accountable?

One remarkable feature of people in social interaction is that they do not only act on others but also attend to the accountability of their own agency. The latter has been a major theme in DP. DP assumes that the way discursive accounts are constructed is significant to our understanding of the concerned social behavior, for they embrace interpretive and justificatory elements. By investigating the accountability of JJB, we are able to see how judges claim about the meanings of their discursive actions and their assertions of the relevant norms and how the legitimacy and warrantability of their behavior is managed.

However, accounting is itself a form of hierarchical social action (Harre, 2001), for it always implies another level of accountability. Put in another way, the participants also hold accountable for their act of accounting. This raises the question of the closure of accounting hierarchies. For this, Taylor's (1989) answer is the participants' "existential" declarations while Wittgenstein (1997) reduces it to the form of life that the participants inhabit. In this light, the discursively oriented social psychological study of social behavior shall be expanded to incorporate social, cultural and biographical information about the participants. In our case, we need to understand judges' way of life so that their judicial behavior can be construed.

Chapter 2

Literature Review

This chapter is devoted to reviewing the literature relevant to this research. We will firstly examine the various ways of defining judges' roles in different legal systems. Secondly, a general survey will be made of the various research approaches to and current knowledge about judicial behavior. Finally, an introduction to DP will be made and its relevance for judicial behavior research will be discussed.

2.1 Judges' Institutional Roles

This section will provide an overview of the institutional roles that different judicial systems ascribe to judges. We will begin with a snapshot of the two main legal systems in the world. Following that, we will discuss how judges' roles have been defined in different schools of jurisprudence. Finally, the role and behavior of judge in current Chinese judicial system will be examined.

2.1.1 Judges' Varying Roles Under Different Judicial Systems

Different legal systems specify different roles for judges. Within the current world, there are two main legal systems. An examination of them shows that judges are differently institutionalized.

2.1.1.1 The Common Law system

The Common Law system is currently in practice in countries such as the

United States, the United Kingdom (excluding Scotland), Australia, India, South Africa, Canada (excluding Quebec), and so on. It is also current in Hong Kong. This legal system is characteristic of its judicial laws (established by judicial precedents, decisions, or reviews), its adversary system in the trial and its jury trial. In a jury trial, the judge plays the part of (Foley, 1993):

1) taking charge of the trial proceedings and maintaining the order;

2) deciding the admissibility of evidence;

3) determining the laws to be applied;

4) directing a verdict;

5) passing judgment if found guilty by the jury.

Judges normally make decisions based on the rules of law or the principle of "stare decisis". When there is no law or precedence applicable, judges are entitled to create a law guided by precedents. They may also choose to ignore precedents if necessary.

In the common law system, judges seldom actively investigate the case. They only decide the admissibility of evidence based on the reasonability of case accounts. Its adversary system requires that the one who claims has the responsibility to prove.

Instead, people who are not legal professionals are entitled to make judicial decisions in the jury trial. However, jury trial is not the only means to solve disputes in the common caw system. Actually, most civil cases are heard by the judge alone. Some cases are even settled without trial. Resolutions are reached through negotiation, mediation, or arbitration, with trial being the "ultimate weapon" in the battle. In this case, judges merely play the role of mediator.

2. 1. 1. 2 The Civil Law System

The Civil Law, also known as the European Continental law, is the most widespread system of law in the world (Merryman, 1985). Just like the Common Law system, there is no unified practice for Civil Law system. According to comparative Law research, the Civil Law can be subdivided into three distinct groups: French Civil Law, German Civil Law, and Scandinavian civil law. What they have in common is that the source of law is codifications in a constitution or statutes passed by the legislature, the Civil Law gives little leeway to judges' independence and discretion in the judiciary, and that judges are required to follow the enacted laws in the absence of an order from the constitutional court, even if the judge personally believes those laws are unconstitutional.

However, judges under the Civil Law have inquisitorial mandate to investigate the case facts. Serious matters are almost always co-decided at the trial level by at least three judges, and sometimes in combination with lay persons in serious criminal cases, with one of those judges taking the lead in gathering evidence in a case. Small claims and misdemeanors are handled by a single trial judge.

2.1.2 Jurisprudential Definitions of Judges' Role

The relation between law and judge is an aged issue in jurisprudence. Correspondent with the three major schools of jurisprudence①, judges' role has been defined in three distinctive ways, which has been characterized by Simon (2001) with three metaphors.

2.1.2.1 Judges as "Scientists"

This is a conception held by the formalists, who regard law as a science of rules or principles. When applying the law, judges need only opt for clear-cut "black-letter" or "bright line" of the legal text. Judicial decisions shall not be tainted by judges' personal or political tastes. This conception is underscored by the assumption that the justice of law is grounded on the logical integrity of the legal system or that law is a system of reason, which is built on principles of ethics or admitted axioms (Hart, 1994). In this sense, judicial decision is a

① This categorization is made in Simon (2001). We can find different labels for the jurisprudential schools for different scholars.

matter of invoking and applying relevant legal rules and proper reasoning process.

However, reducing JJB to application of rules and principles is obviously contestable, considering the contingency and complexity of varying case facts. Few judicial opinions can simply be justified by resorting to rules and logic.

2.1.2.2 Judges as Policy Makers

In the later 19th century, the criticism of formalism led to the emergence of realism in law, a school of jurisprudence which stresses the discretion of judges. It is argued that judges do not confine themselves to the legal rules but take advantage of them to meet their personal or social interests. Holmes (1880), the leading figure of legal realism, argues that "the life of the law has not been logic: it has been experience". This tradition of law runs counter to the dictates of logic in formalism by considering itself as an empirical science.

In line with this sociological view of law, judges are held responsible to redress social malfunctions. As Cohen (1935) points out, the application of law shall involve an empirical as well as a prescriptive (ethical) concern. That is, judges are supposed to play the role of policy makers. They should on the one hand empirically examine the cause and effect of their judicial decisions and on the other hand ethically assess the social values at stake in their judicial opinions. Their objective is to quest for an intelligible account of the social order in which they live.

When dealing with judicial cases, judges are encouraged to turn to resources in the extra-legal worlds to rationalize their judicial decision. Motives, individual histories and social opinions can all be taken into account. It is argued that judges' behavior can not be divorced from their social concerns. Laws and judicial decisions shall be couched in the moral, ethical and ideological norms.

The main problem with legal realism is that the boundary between legal and extra legal worlds is blurred and the integrity of law is deconstructed. Competing rationalities originated in both the legal and extralegal worlds are appropriated to justify legal reasoning. This will certainly complicate the nature of law and justice.

2. 1. 2. 3 Judges as Ethicists

Similar to the policy-maker view of JJB, the ethicist also stresses the social nature of judicial justice. But it recognizes the moral and political limits placed on judges' judicial behavior. Dworkin (1977), the main advocate of this philosophy, argues that judges do not have total freedom to make laws. They must surrender themselves to the value system of a community which the members share. What distinguishes Dworkin from others is that he tries to salvage the integrity of law as undermined by realists and recognizes the discretion of judges as neglected by formalists. Dworkin argues that when encountering hard cases judges shall dig deeper into the law to find the strongest moral and political principles behind the legal ethics that could justify their decision. It is emphasized that this political morality is not something transcendental but internally embedded within the integrity of legal practice. While judges can and do differ in their views on certain proposed judicial decisions within their community of practice, they will treat and experience the proposed judicial decisions as having moral authority.

The ethicist obviously presupposes the existence of some universal moral and political principles. However, the tenability of this presupposition is questionable in reality. We cannot guarantee that judges will try to and can reach such principles in practice.

2. 1. 3 Judge under China's Constitution

According to the Constitution of the People's Republic of China (2004), the judicial organs of the state consist of the people's courts and the military courts. It is stipulated in the Constitution that the source of the judicature power is the People's Congress[①]. The judges are nominated by the country's President or provincial governors and are subject to the approval from the congresses of the equivalent levels. Chinese judges are distinctive in at least three ways:

Firstly, they are identified with *Guan* (an in cumbent of the officialdom).This is not only manifested in the address name for them (*Faguan*, Chinese for judges), but also built into the institutional operations such as judge recruitment. In fact, it was an established practice throughout the Chinese history that *Guan* played both the role of administration and that of adjudication. Now the enrollment of judges requires passing the same examination as those intending to be civil servants.

Secondly, the sociopolitical interest is explicitly recognized. For example, after the advent of the worldwide economic depression in 2008, a lot of businesses were shut down and workers laid off. Consequently, more cases concerning labor contracts than before were brought to the court. For the sake of sociopolitical stability, the SupremePeople's Court launched an appeal for the judges to take care of the interest of the disadvantaged.

Thirdly, judges are highly institutionalized. This can be illustrated in the way an individual judge is related to the institutional hierarchy:

As we can see, an individual judge is often a member of a collegial panel when trying a case. They act in cooperation and strive for a consensus in final opinions. Their opinions are subject to the scrutiny by trial committee which is in turn subject to the dual leadership of higher court (s) and the respective levels of congress. Research has shown that the membership of the institution has a significant impact on JJB. Judges normally consider their professional work as the fulfillment of their duty to the institution (Wu, 2008). Their judicial behavior is normally attributed to the institution rather than their

① "The Supreme People's Court is responsible to the National People's Congress and its Standing Committee. Local people's courts at different levels are responsible to the organs of state power which created them." (Article 128)

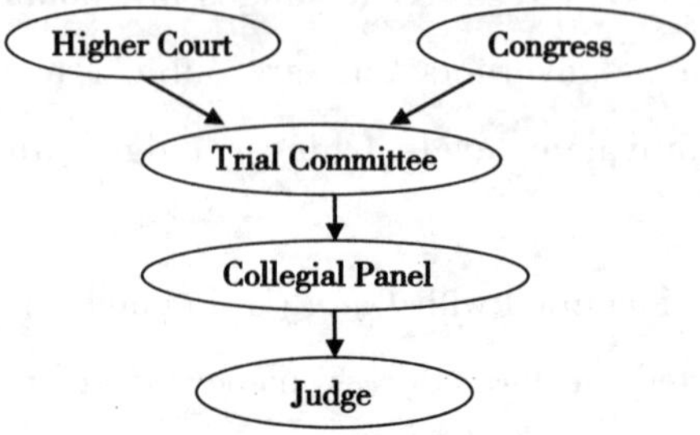

Figure 2-1 The Institutional Hierarchy of Judicature

individuality.

According to the background or training experience, there are three types of judges within current judicial system:

• Experience-based judges

They are those who received little or no formal training in law. They were recruited because of lack of specialized talents at the time when the judicature was just set up and Chinese legal education was still in its inception. Their judicial behavior has taken shape mainly out of their experience.

• Veteran judges

These judges are former military officers who were relocated from the army and appointed through the administrative actions. They mostly had no previous experience or training in law.

• Academic judges

They are the graduates from colleges of law.

These abovementioned features of judges' institutional role have direct bearings on JJB. For example, although the basic judicial principle is unambiguously stipulated that "when trying civil cases, the People's Courts must base themselves on facts and take the law as the criteria" (Article 7 in Civil Procedure Law of the People's Republic of China by the National People's Congress, 2007), findings from empirical research show that JJB is often susceptible to the influence from the following factors (Wu 2008):

1) the social status of the litigants

The judges may subconsciously balance the power relation between the litigants through their own influence in pursuit of justice. They may fall into a "converse thinking", deciding who "the good egg" is before looking for the factual and legal ground.

2) the opinions of the higher court

Judges in China hold accountability for their own behavior and decision-making in the judicial process. Misjudged cases have to undergo investigation, which may result in serious consequence for their career. With these concerns in their mind, judges are inclined to value the documentary evidence and hard evidence while looking down upon witness testimony in order that the judges in the appeal court might not pick out "reasonable doubts".

3) the personal relation between the judges and the litigants (agents)

Judges are vulnerable to their concerns of interpersonal relations and social connections.

4) the public opinions

The courts show particular respect to the public opinions in the stage of social transition.

5) the influence from supervisors

The representatives from the People's Congress often give their personal attention to cases or even express their judicial opinions to the courts. Comments and instructions from the superior can shape the trial process and judgmental decision.

These factors do not all conform to or even go against the codes of conducts for judges as stipulated in statutes such as Judges' Law of the People's Republic of China (the National People's Congress, 2001), Organic Law of the People's Courts of the People's Republic of China (the National People's Congress, 2006), Civil Procedure Law of the People's Republic of China (the National People's Congress, 2007) and the Behavior Codes for the Judges (the National People's Congress,

2005). This indicates that judges have both legal as well as extralegal concerns. Judicial behavior is more complex than what is stipulated in the law.

In sum, there is no consensus over either the role of judge or the behavioral codes the judge shall observe, although judicial justice is almost universally valued. It is this uncertainty that makes judicial behavior an important agenda for legal research.

2.2 Judicial Behavior Research

2.2.1 Cognitive-psychological Approach to Judicial Behavior

The focus on JJB was seen as early as in Langdell's case book method for realist legal study in the later 19th century, when judge-made law attained high stature. This began the redirection of jurisprudential concern from general questions about the nature of law to particular studies of judicial behavior. During the past half century, JJB has primarily been a concern for political scientists (Baum, 1997). Since the most consequential forms of judicial behavior typically consist of judicial decisions, judicial behavior research has been confined to judicial decision making or sentencing. But judicial behavior is defined in a broad sense to include preliminary actions, courtroom interactions and final decisions (Baum, 1997). When a social conflict or dispute is brought to the court, the judicial justice system is invoked and the judges may be confronted with the following issues:

- Should the case be accepted?
- What pretrial preparation should be made?
- How should the trial process be conducted?
- What information should be explored?
- What legal attribution should be attached to all the facts presented?
- What should be the sentence?

• Any special conditions?

These are but a few decisions[1]the judges need to make. Judicial behavior research aims to account for the actions that judges undertake to deal with these issues and the reasons for which judges choose to take their particular actions. In short, judicial behavior is concerned with the explanation or prediction of these actions.

Among the existent judicial behavior theories, the cognitive psychological approach (CPA) has dominated the literature so far. CPA has produced diverse theorizations about judicial behavior. As Back (1961: 16) notes:

> *Explanations range from models that rationally postulate zones of indifference and the subjective difference between objectively equal gains and losses, through models that acknowledge differences in taste, to those that explain single impulsive acts.*

Influenced by analogies to computers and conceptions of information processing, CPA basically aims to reveal the programmatic mechanism through which judges' decisions can be generated. Based on this cognitive assumption, CPA attends to the factors that might impact on the operation of judges' judicial cognitive psychology. The focus of judicial behavior research is on the perception, transmission and creation of information that is relevant to judicial decision making. This suggests judicial behavior involves: 1) identifying relevant information, 2) determining its value, and 3) working out the result with a formula. In addressing these issues, scholars, however, differ in their views, basically due to their various perspectives on the rationality of judges. They can be roughly categorized into three types (Back, 1961) .

2. 2. 1. 1 The Legal Models

The legal models are formulated after the belief that law is in essence a

---

① By judges' decision-making, we mean more than the process of reaching judicial opinions. It is broadly understood as what judges undertake in the judicial process.

set of rules. According to them, judicial decision is made "in light of the facts of the case vis-à-vis precedent, the plain meaning of the Constitution and statutes, and the intent of the framers" (Segal & Spaeth, 2002). The theoretical assumption of this model is possibly best reflected in Dworkin's (1999) "right answer thesis" and "law as integrity". It is argued that there is always a best solution to any legal issues within the framework of law. This model can be simplified into three steps:

- retrieving the case information
- finding applicable laws
- working out the legal answer either deductively or inductively

For each step, there are rules to follow. Analytical models of justificatory reasoning are formulated to capture the paradigm of legal reasoning. It is held that any judicial decision shall meet in relatively highest degree expectations of a certain, impartial, and objective legal rules which can lead to conclusions from the premises through reasoning. Wroblewski's (Figure 2-2) theory of justificatory reasoning can serve as an illustration of this model:

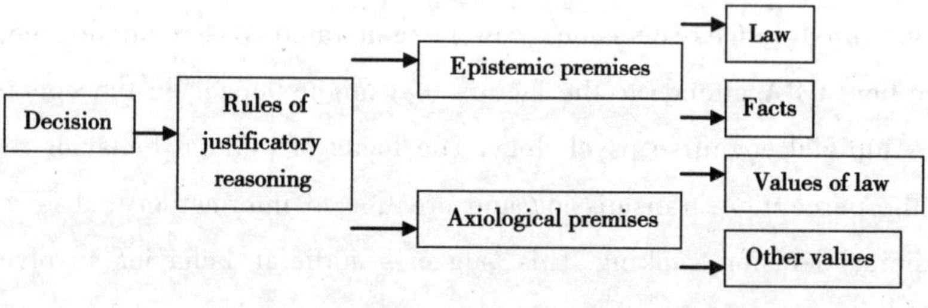

Figure 2-2 Justificatory Reasoning for Legal Decision-making (Wroblewski, 1988)

Such a modeling construes judicial decision as a set of rules which are either derived from epistemic or axiological sources. A judge subscribing to epistemic premises is one who gives a true verdict only according to the evidence and law without fear or favor while one who makes judicial decisions on the basis of axiological premises is to find the fulcrum of judicial decisions from ethnic principles and value system.

The influence of the legal model on judicial behavior is immense. In fact, the value of modern judicial justice system is founded on the ideology underlying this model that law and only law can provide solutions to all social problems. The legal model has been widely institutionalized in current legal systems. Its reification in China's judicial system is best represented in the judicial principle, "when trying civil cases, the People's Courts must base themselves on facts and take the law as the criteria" (the National People's Congress, 2007).

Nevertheless, the legal models are generally considered over-simplistic. Judicial practice shows that legal rules can hardly account for the complexity of judicial behavior. Although the judicial policies and guidelines are implemented for judges (Sharples, 1972), the legal frameworks (Lovegrove, 1997) can not capture the whole reality of judicial process. One illustration is the common phenomenon of judicial disparity. There are three obvious causes for the limitation of the legal model. Firstly, laws are neither plain in meaning nor comprehensive in coverage. The recognition of the open texture of laws (Hart 1994) represents one jurisprudential insight into this issue. In practice, there are often cases in which there are no unequivocal legal rules to apply. Secondly, the information that judges can obtain about case facts is often inadequate or partial. Judges' perception may not reflect the circumstance which stimulated the judicial proceeding. If the premises are not solid, how can the conclusions stand? Thirdly, judges do not always work out the fittest rules or take in all the information for their decision making. Black (1997: 52) argues that "rules are themselves shot through with discretion; they will not act as constraints." This suggests that the legal models do not conform to the actual psychology underlying judicial behavior.

2.2.1.2 The Attitudinal Models

As the legitimizing symbolism of mechanical jurisprudence lost its force as a causal explanation of judges' decision-making process, people started to turn their attention to judges' personal attitudes and values (Gibson, 1983).

This brings about the attitudinal models. The thrust of them is that judges have their policy preferences and when they make decisions they want the outcomes to approximate as nearly as possible their policy preferences. Or to put it simply, judges make their decisions"in light of the facts of the case vis-à-vis the ideological attitudes and values of the justices" (Segal & Spaeth, 2002: 86) .

Prichett (1948) marks the emergence of the attitudinal approach to the study of judicial behavior. He analyzes the distribution of the judges' ideology based on a systematic survey of the non-unanimous decisions rendered by the justices in the Roosevelt's Court from 1937 to 1947. After that, the correlation between the judges' ideology and their voting habits has been established.

The first well-delineated theory of attitudinal model is documented in Schubert (1965) . According to him, there are two affecting factors. One is a multidimensional, ideological space in which justices have ideal points (i-points) . These points represent the justices' "own syndrome of attitudes". The other is the case stimuli (j-points) , which are presented to the justices for approval or disapproval and can be measured in the same multidimensional space. Thus, "the decision of the Court in any case will depend upon whether the case dominates, or is dominated by, a majority of i-points" (Schubert, 1965: 38)

In line with Schubert's attitudinal model, to account for judicial behavior is to determine the dimensions of the ideological space. In this regard, varied arguments are made in existing literature. Some take the case-related factors as the attitudinal predictors such as offensive characteristics, criminal record, the biography of the accused, and behavioral manners. Others focus on judges' individual features such as political preference, philosophies of sentencing, socioeconomic background, age, personality traits, and so forth (e. g. Diamond, 1981; Ebbesen & Kone, 1981) . Based on existing research, we can roughly sketch the dimensions of ideological space as follows:

Table 2-1 Dimensions of Ideological Space

Levels	Some attitudinal stimuli found in existent literature
Institutional	institutional hierarchy of courts (Zorn & Bowie, 2007), collegial court (Hettinger & Lindquist et al., 2006), mandatory sentencing efficiency (Ashworth, 1982; Kunselman & Vito, 2002), judicial discretion (Gottfredson & Gottfredson, 1988), judicial guideline (Kempf-Leonard & Sample, 2001)…
Socio-cultural	race (Steffensmeier & Britt, 2001; Mitchell, 2005), economic status (Spiegel & Templeman, 1989; Betsey, 2005), ethics (Everett & Wojtkiewicz, 2002), public opinion (Tomaino, 1997), religion (Miller & Bornstein, 2006; Gilzer-Katz, 2007)…
Individual	subjectivity (McKnight, 1981), education and background (Bond & Lemon, 1981), psychology (Fitzmaurice & Pease, 1986; Pennington and Lloyd-Bostock et al., 1987), gender (Hedderman & Gelsthorpe et al., 1997), emotion (Sigler, 2000), age and occupation (Loeffler & Lawson, 2002), goals (Baum, 2006), personal characters (Wu, 2007), personal appearance (Staley, 2007), demographics (Becker-Lindow, 2007)…

One problem with the attitudinal models is that all these ideological dimensions are hypothetical rather than empirical. That is, they are either contrived by the researchers or worked out through one of the two means: 1) inference from the judicial opinions judges passed; 2) surveys and questionnaires (Segal & Cover, 1989). However, all these methods do not function as the effective independent measure of judges' attitudes. They heavily rely on the researchers' own erudition or judges' introspection of their behavior which may not reflect judges' real attitudes operating in their decision making.

The vulnerability of the attitudinal models is best manifested in the conflicting results that are often reported. For example, St. Louis (2000) does not observe obvious relationship between the legal as well as extra legal factors and judicial decisions made by the judges. Similarly, Annus & Tavits (2004) find that there are no statistically significant effects between case outcomes, the experience of the judge, and the ethnicity of the suspect. Gibson (1978) reports that attitudes only account for 14% of the variation in the decisions in a study of Iowa trial court judges. Nardulli et al. (1984) find that there is a negative bivariate relationship between a judge's belief in punishment and plain-bargained sentence. Contrary to the above findings, in a study of Supreme Court justices Segal & Cover (1989) find a correlation efficient of 80 between judicial values (as measured by newspaper editorials) and votes in civil liberties cases for justices appointed between 1953 and 1988.

Comparative studies of data from judicial process show that the judges' attitude orientation is context sensitive. It depends upon the particular judicial proceedings. This is well illustrated in the studies of judges' judicial role orientations (Gibson, 1978; e. g. Scheb, Bowen & Anderson, 1991; Scheb, II, & Hayes, 1989). For example, the ideological and policy-related effects on federal judges' decisions are found to be larger at higher levels of the judicial hierarchy, while legal and case-specific factors dominate at lower levels (Zorn & Bowie, 2007). All these indicate that the attitudinal models fail to address this contingency of judges' attitude orientation.

2. 2. 1. 3 The Strategic Models

The strategic models seek to elaborate how judges behave in a purposive and forward-looking fashion by sorting out the various competing interests faced by judges. It is based on three theoretical assumptions (Segal & Spaeth, 2002):

1) The judges' behavior is policy oriented. In line with the attitudinal model, the strategic model also holds that judges will try to maximize their policy preference in their behavior.

2) The judges' behavior is strategic, in that judges have to take into account the policy preferences of other concerned parties when pursuing their own.

3) The strategic behavior is constrained by the institutional context in which judges interact with other parties.

Different from attitudinal models, the strategic models do not exclusively focus on judges' personal preference. They shift their attention to how the institutional context impacts on JJB. For example, they study judicial behavior by examining the relations between the court and other political institutions. They focus more on the dynamic process of judicial behavior such as the case discussion, the judicial opinion draft, etc. The strategic models may be divided into two camps: an internal camp that focuses on the interactions among the justices and an external camp that focus on constraints imposed on the Court by other political actors (Segal & Spaeth, 2002: 100). One classic judicial behavior study in the strategic model is Murphy's (1964) *Elements of Judicial Strategy*, which examines both the internal interaction between the justices and the external interaction between the court and the congress. This study suggests that the integrated model has more explanatory power.

The strategic models focus on the way judges deal with the competing policy preferences of different participants in the judicial process. This may be true to the judges in the Federal Court (as judicial behavior research mostly focuses on) who mainly decide on cases which are politically influential and legally controversial. However, the policy preference in judicial behavior of judges at lower levels may not carry such weight.

2.2.1.4 A Critique of CPA

The CPA approach reviewed above reflects a trend of judicial behavior research which started to gain its momentum in the 1960s. It was motivated by the cognitive psychology. It aims for formulation of theoretical constructs by embracing the most explanatory aspects (Segal & Spaeth, 2002). A common theme in CPA theoretical construct is rationality. The legal models emphasize the formal rationality while the attitudinal and strategic models emphasize the instrumental one. To put it simply, the CPA is underwritten with the assumption that human beings are rational. This assumption is, however, controversial in terms of real-life judicial practice. Contradictory evidence has often been observed. For example, judicial judgments and decisions are found to be made without exhausting the relevant information that is available from the circumstance. Judges may go with the very first response that enters their mind. That is, judicial behavior can result from a subjective feeling, a spontaneous idea, or an intuitive response. It is reported that people's intuitions can outperform their deliberate thinking processes under specific conditions (Plessner, Betsch & Betsch, 2007) .

According to Gottfredson (1987) , rationality in criminal justice can not be achieved for three reasons. Firstly, the specific objectives of legal apparatus can not be rendered with adequate operational definitions for implementation. Secondly, it is not likely to identify or adequately describe all the decisional options at each step. Thirdly, the information necessary for rational decision making is often insufficient. These three factors can severely undermine the validity of the CPA approach. As Segal & Spaeth (2002) point out, all the rationality-based models only represent reality in a simplified way and ignore certain aspects of reality. The explanations provided in these models are reductionist in that the context and meaning of judicial behavior are idealized. We can not expect any rational models to address the richness and complexity of judicial reality.

Besides rationality, JJB research also needs to address the irrationality and nonrationality inherent in judges' behavior (Back, 1961) . We need to make allowance for the errors judges commit, the poor analysis judge make and the inappropriate heuristics judges use. That is, the rationality-based CPA shall be complemented with theories that incorporate judges' personal values, thinking patterns, skills and habits as well as the limited information available. Back (1961: 16) points out that "the rational model derives the decision from the structure of the situation while the irrational model derives it from the structure of the person". This understanding of JJB has propelled JJB researchers to shift their attention to the dynamics of the judicial context and the social constraints.

2. 2. 2 Sociological Approach to Judicial Behavior

In modern psychology, as the conduit metaphor of human cognition has become an increasingly less satisfactory model, there emerges a call for a humanistic view of psychology (Fuchs & Milar, 2003). Similarly, judicial behavior research has found that only very rare situations can meet the canonical cognitive models. More often than not, judicial behavior is unprogrammed, with no fixed patterns to follow. Judges have to deal with situations which are novel, unstructured and consequential. This observation engendered the sociolegal work (Black, 1997) in JJB research. Different from the traditional approaches which build their theorizations on cognitive psychology, this sociological approach focuses on the"interactive decisions" (Raiffa, 1994). It is interested in the real, complex, ill-defined world and aims to account for the differences in the situation, the person and the decision.

Following this sociological perspective, judicial behavior research shall be rooted in empirical analysis and seek explanations for the actual judicial behaviors of individuals or groups of people by describing them as their personal or institutional life (Back, 1961). It shall turn to "look at the many and varied practice and behaviors we call ' legal' and seek, in a somewhat piecemeal way, to build our understanding of law from below in a gradual and accumulative way" (Murphy & Coleman 1990: 35). In this line, Baum (2006), for example, points out that we shall pay attention to judges' response to their audience, for it is primarily judges' desire to be liked and respected that influences their judicial behavior.

This redefinition of the object for judicial behavior research entails a requirement of some new methods. One consequence is that the ethnographic data is highly valued and several sociological tools are introduced for data analysis:

2.2.2.1 Contextual analysis

The sociological approach to the law aims to address the relationship between the law and the society (Su, 2004). Contextual analysis is one way to account for the pervasive context dependency of judicial behavior. Among the existing literature, we can find various methods are drawn on to measure and evaluate the contextual constraints for judicial behavior. For example, the analysis of micro context can be done through case-based ethnomethodology while macro context can be construed with sociological models.

In a study of the mode of judicial judgment in the context of Chinese local judicial courts, Gao & Jiang (2006) undertook field work, observing and participating in the activities in a local court for over three months. They visited villagers and local government officials. They conducted in-depth interviews with some judges. They also participated in all the judicial activities in the court during the period. They found in one case study of a judicial trial concerning a neighborhood dispute that the judge had already formed his judgment before the trial. But the judge still made utmost efforts to conciliate the two litigant parties during the judicial proceeding. It turned out that the judge did not care much about the litigants' concerns. He was unconscious of what justice to achieve. During the trial the judge was instead concerned with what benefits the judicial process would bring to him-his professional good repute. What the judge did was simply to demonstrate how he"adjudicates for the people".To him, it was a positive act to persuade the litigants into conciliation by exploiting even nonlegal means. He did all this simply to act out a"dedicated"judge in the presence of the experts.

The contextual analysis is concerned with the specific contextual elements that affect the judicial behavior. Among the complexity of judicial context, only some take effect. For example, in a study of the relation between judges' decision making and the affecting factors (Konecni & Ebbesen, 1984), the judge is found to simply follow the psychiatrists' recommendation when deciding whether the suspects are mentally disordered sex offenders. The contextual analysis may also focus on the interaction of different contextual elements. For example, Murphy (1964) examines how the judges in the Federal Court of U. S. interact with other judges and the congress.

The abovementioned study reveals the particularity of judicial context. There are also studies which focus on general accounts of judicial context for judges. The goal-based model (see Figure 2-3) proposed by Baum (1997) is one best known theory which elaborates the overall contextual constraints on JJB. He argues that JJB is goal driven. There are three contextual sources that goals are originated in: the judges' recruitment, court situations and individual characteristics.

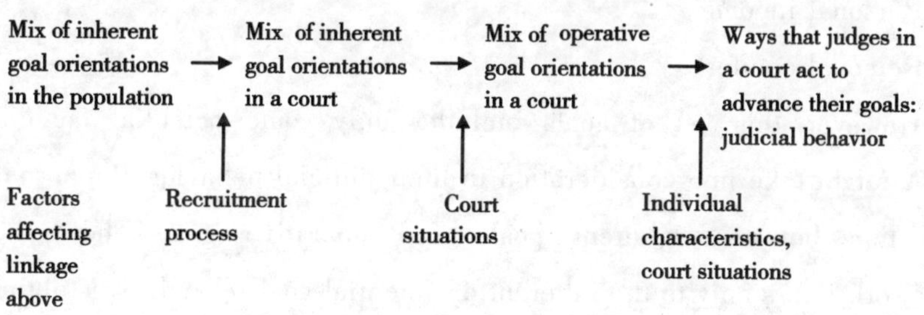

Figure 2-3 A Framework for Analysis of Judicial Behavior (Baum, 1997: 14)

This framework has expanded the scope of contextual analysis to include both the external social world and the internal psychological world. The inclusiveness of contextual analysis is further specified in Baum's typology of possible goals for judges as follows:

Ⅰ. *Content of Legal Policy*

Accurate interpretation of the law ("legal accuracy")

Clear and consistent interpretation of the law ("legal clarity")

Good policy as gauged by the judge's policy preferences ("good policy")

Ⅱ. *Personal Standing with Court Audiences*

Popularity and respect in the legal community

Popularity and respect in the community as a whole

Power outside the court

Ⅲ. *Career*

Continued tenure in the current judicial position

Promotion to a higher court securing attractive nonjudicial positions

Ⅳ. *Life in the Court*

Good relations with other judges and with participants in the courts who have other positions

Power within the court

Limited work loads

Court resources

Ⅴ. *Standard of Living*

Personal income

Personal comfort

However, this list of goals includes only some potential factors that judges might take into consideration in their judicial behavior. Baum makes a distinction between inherent goals and operative goals. The proposed framework refers only to the inherent or potential goals of judges as defined in their personal and contextual characteristics. His theory does not give an adequate account of how the inherent goals are converted into the operative goals for judicial behavior.

Moreover, research shows that "working to achieve legal and policy goals does not serve judges' self-interest as conventionally defined" (Baum, 2006: 11). Few justices are motivated exclusively or even primarily by a desire to make good legal and political policy. There has been increasing evidence which indicates that the intersubjective meaning experienced by the judges is more fundamental to their behavior (Gottfredson & Gottfredson, 1988).

Context sensitivity has been recognized to be critical for judicial behavior (VonDoepp, 2008). However, we still know very little about the contextual forces that motivate JJB. Judicial behavior research has traditionally foundered due to the inability to provide systematic tools or methods to identify the operative contextual factors. In the extensive literature on judicial decision making, the analyzed data are obtained either through interviews and questionnaires, final judicial opinions or experimental simulation (Conley & O'Bar, 1990). The relevant research themes are identified through content analysis. One problem with this method is that what is revealed with statistics-based content analysis is only the scholastic hypothesization about judicial behavior. It calls for a more theoretically informed and a more rigorous method to link the data and theory.

2. 2. 2. 2 Narrative Sociology

To pinpoint the forces that shape JJB, legal scholars usually rely on one or more of three informing sources: the researchers' observation or recording of judges' judicial activities, the judges' account of their behavior, and the account by some other independent observers. One nascent research interest concerning judicial behavior is to examine critically how the different informing sources pertain to the nature of JJB. Narrative, a fundamental sociological concept, has thereby been appropriated to capture the nature of those informing sources and the narrative sociology has been introduced into sociolegal scholarship (Ewick & Silbey, 1995; Fleury-Steiner, 2002; Maines, 1993).

As a method of inquiry, narrative sociology differs from other sociological approaches in its focus on the conditions of narration that produces the social actions and the accounts for them. In other words, this approach does not aim to draw theoretical conclusions about social phenomena based on the content of the narratives but focuses on the forces that underlie the narratives by investigating their construction. For example, in a study of the consciousness of jurors in death penalty trials (Fleury-Steiner, 2002), jurors are solicited to tell about important moments during the trial, deliberations, and their impressions of the defendant. This study reveals not only the racialized discourse by the jurors but also investigates how a hegemonic tale of racial inferiority is built on the jurors' social class or relevant biographical experiences.

One major methodological assumption of the narrative sociology is that the sociological understanding of social behavior can be revealed through the analysis of the emplotment and temporal structure of the narratives. In this light, narrative is assumed to be the form we interpret and make sense of

JJB. Looking into the narrative representation of JJB such as the biographic stories of individual judges (e. g. Wu, 2008) can provide a new perspective into the judicial mechanism.

In a study of judicial rendering of case facts, Baldwin (2005) examines the case of P, C & S vs. United Kingdom to see how a narrative of a dangerous mother was constructed in the judgment in the absence of fact and due process. It is found that the narratives in the judgment rely on the narrative trajectory, the presentation of consensus, the incorporation of supportive discourses, and the smoothing over of contradictory evidence. This is known as"anchored narrative" (Wagenaar & van et al., 1993; Wagenaar, 1995) in which truth is "anchored directly to the belief structure, without any intermediate level of evidence" (Wagenaar, 1995: 270).

The narrative sociology has opened up a new opportunity to look into judicial behavior by highlighting the verbal behavior of judges as the object for study. It charts the role and significance of narrative as a lens to look into JJB. By examining the linguistic and cultural resources that judges draw on to make their stories appropriate, reasonable, or persuasive, the concerns and tactics of JJB can be specified. However, the narrative analysis alone is not sufficient to identify all the variables that constitute the judicial behavior. To determine the operant linguistic and cultural resources, we need theories and methods that can better address the nature of the narratives and the relationship between narratives and judicial behavior.

2. 2. 3 The Discursive Turn in Judicial Behavior Research

In the latter half of the 20th century, a discursive turn emerged in the social sciences including jurisprudence. The main feature of this turn is that the function of language becomes the focus of the academic interest. The emphasis on discourse and the law has opened a new perspective on the judicial justice. The narrative sociology, for example, is one manifestation of the discursive turn in judicial behavior research.

The discursive turn is underwritten by two theoretical postulates. Firstly, it is relativist or constructivist in epistemology, rejecting the deterministic view of optimal final decision. It holds that judicial behavior is co-determined by the situational conditions, individual predisposition, and conscious commitment. Secondly, it draws on linguistic analytic methods in construing JJB. Judicial behavior is considered as constituted and represented in legal discourse. In this light, the focus of analysis is on the discursive features and what implications they have on the law. However, the way to approach discourse and law is still in the bud.

2. 2. 3. 1 Conceptual Analysis

Hart (1994) is probably the first jurist who draws people's attention to the linguistic analysis of legal language. In *The Concept of Law,* he argues that the jurisprudential issues lie fundamentally in the ambiguity of some legal concepts such as "law", "obligation", "right", etc. Legal issues could be clarified through conceptual analysis.

Although Hart does not specifically address JJB, his theory has illuminated the discursive nature of judicial behavior by pointing out the "open texture" of law. Obviously, it is often the judges' responsibility to fill the void left by the open texture. Hart argues that this normally requires a semantic analysis of legal concepts. This suggests that judicial behavior implies not only a psychological process but also a discursive action. So any endeavor to theorize JJB shall be able to elucidate how judicial discourse is produced, transmitted, perceived and transformed. However, probably due to their academic interest, legal scholars following Hartian approach have not developed a systematic and rigorous method for conceptual analysis.

2. 2. 3. 2 Discourse Analysis

The study of JJB from the discursive perspective can be subsumed under the academic discipline of discourse analysis in its broadest sense. Although language has long been recognized as a key element in the law, serious academic study of language and the law did not come to the fore until 1970s when the functional, social and pragmatic perspectives began to gain weight in linguistics (Kurzon, 1994). Motivated by linguistic, social and legal interest, the language in the legal setting has attracted attention from linguists, sociologists, anthropologists as well as legal practitioners and theorists (Kurzon, 1994). Among them, we can identify three views of language and the law (Levi, 1990, Kurzon, 1994):

1) Legal language as a style

This perspective aims to describe the linguistic features of legal language. Explorations have been conducted into the lexical, syntactic, semantic, sentential, discoursal, pragmatic and stylistic features of legal language (Mellinkoff, 1963; Bhatia, 1983; Bowers, 1989; Tiersma, 1999; Liao, 2003). However, one challenge against this structural approach is whether there is an essential structural distinction between everyday language and legal language. So far, there is still no consensus over the identification of legal language (Kurzon, 1997). Potentially, every genre of everyday language can be drawn into the legal practice. Thus, legal discourse is defined not by structure but by function. Despite the fact that much structural description has been provided in the literature, this approach has shed little light on the nature of law and the judges' actual judicial behavior.

2) Language as an issue in law

As language mediated practice becomes the norm of social life, a lot of judicial issues actually revolve around language. Two major linguistic issues often arise in judicial processes: linguistic production and linguistic comprehension (Gibbons, 1994). One typical example of the former is voice or author identification, i. e. determining "who said that" or "who wrote that" (Solan and Tiersma, 2005). Problems with linguistic comprension may be obvious when people of different linguistic backgrounds are engaged in the same litigation. In cases of this kind, linguists or interpreters are often called in to appear in the court as the experts or assistants (Coulthard, 2005; Shuy, 2006; Coulthard and Cotterill, 2007).

3) Law as discourse practice

Law is not only coded in language but also reified in discourse practice. Take judicial practice for example, whatever evidence is presented to the court has to be translated into legal discourse. Given the discursive nature of law, discourse analysis becomes a basic method to gain a heuristic or critical understanding of law. So far, the topics addressed in this approach include interactional order, power, ideology, gender, age, race and culture. These studies aim to show how discourse practice bear in one way or another upon the legal activities such as evidence presentation and determination, witness testimony, (cross-) examination, juror instruction, legal interpretation, and so on (Atkinson & Drew, 1979; O'Barr, 1982; Drew, 1985; Berk-Seligson, 1990; Conley & O'Bar, 1990; Levi and Walker, 1990; Matoesian, 1993; Gibbons, 1994; Conley & O'Barr, 1998; Philips, 1998; Matoesian, 2001; Cotterill, 2002; Cotterill, 2003; Gibbons, 2003).

Among all these studies of legal discourse, two main methods of discourse analysis have been applied to JJB:

- Linguistic anthropology

Conley & O'Bar (1990) report an anthropological study of small claim courts in which they find five types of judges in terms of decision making styles through an analysis of the judgments passed by them. Another similar study is done by Susan (1998) who reveals how judges' diverse ideologies are constituted in their discourse structure.

- Discursive psychology

MacMartin and his colleague have done a series of research on JJB through discursive psychology (MacMartin, 1999; MacMartin & Wood, 2005; Wood & MacMartin, 2007). They explore how judges draw on various discursive resources to establish the facticity in their judgment.

2.2.3.3 A Critique of Current Discursive Approaches to Judicial Behavior

The discursive approaches to JJB assume that discourse is the substantial form of JJB. By attending to the details of judges' discourse practice, they aim to gain a heuristic understanding of the dynamism of their judicial practice. One major credit of discourse analysis is that it can be a transdisciplinary approach which can flexibly draw on and combine theoretical and methodological insights from various other disciplines such as psychology, sociology, philosophy, anthropology and ethnomethodology. It is this elasticity that enables discourse analysts to address the complexity of judicial behavior.

However, this flexibility of discourse analysis can also be problematic when we attempt to propose a working model, since no fixed paradigm can be found to address different judicial issues. In other words, the discursive approach lacks an internal integrity. Moreover, we also have to make allowance for the limitations of different discourse theories.

Within current discourse studies of JJB, the focus has mostly been on judicial judgments or opinions rendered by the judges (MacMartin, 1999). This type of discourse is only the final product of the dynamic judicial process. To understand JJB, it is also essential to construe what transformation it has gone through before its final form comes into being. This is not likely if we only focus on "the written residue of actual behavior" (Philips, 1998). Studies on the interactional dynamism of the judicial process (e. g. Liao, 2009) will be more illuminating in terms of judicial behavior.

Over the last three decades, the increasing interest in legal discourse has been evidenced. However, this work is imbalanced. Gonzâlez (2006: 392) notes that:

> *These studies [of courtroom interaction] have focused almost exclusively on the dynamics of courtroom discourse in English-speaking countries, whose common legal system requires evidence to be presented and scrutinized in court through the oral examination of witnesses and defendants by counsels.*

Moreover, most studies are concerned with the interaction of the (cross-) examination between litigants and witnesses. Judges' discourse seems to have attracted little attention from researchers so far (Hu, 2004). This is probably due to the fact that judges have a low involvement in the court interaction. The judges' discourse is often formulaic and less robust. It is the interaction between litigants and witnesses that takes the center stage in the courtroom debate and becomes the central interest of most researchers (e. g. Danet & Kermish, 1978; Wodak, 1980; Penman, 1990; Winiecki, 2008).

Going through the extant literature, we can find that the discourse approach to law and JJB is still problematic. Some research deals with the linguistic features of legal discourse, taking law as the sole explanator. For example, Liao (2009) investigates interruption (both by judges and litigant parties) in the Chinese criminal courtroom discourse and explains its features by referring to the Chinese judicial system and legal culture. There is an unexamined assumption about the nature of law and JJB. There are other studies which basically aim to address judicial behavior as a legal issue from the discursive perspective. Philips (1998) is one example which explores through an analysis of discourse how judges are ideologically oriented when dealing with procedural and judgmental issues on the trial. But this analysis is not guided by a coherent and systematic linguistic theory or method. Our literature review shows that a better theoretical integration between discourse and judicial behavior is required before the discursive turn in judicial behavior research can be advanced.

2.3 Discursive Psychology

Discursive psychology (DP) is a tradition of study which addresses the psychological topics that are managed in discourse. It was motivated as a reaction to problems inherent in the traditional social cognition paradigm which regards human behavior as produced on the basis of information processing. Its direct theoretical and analytic antecedents were developments in sociology of scientific knowledge, ethnomethodology and conversation analysis and a range of notions from post-structuralism and particularly the work of Foucault and Barthes. There are three major strands that DP works on (Edwards, 2005; Edwards & Potter, 2005): (i) respecification and critique of psychological topics and explanations; (ii) investigations of how everyday psychological categories are used in discourse; (iii) studies of how psychological business (motives and intentions, prejudices, reliability of memory and perception, etc.) is handled and managed in talk and text, without having to be overtly labeled as such. The main theoretical assumptions of DP can be summarized as follows (Potter & Edwards, 1999; Potter & Edwards, 2001; Potter & Edwards, 2003):

1) Discourse is action performative. Discourse is considered as the means to perform social actions rather than represent the mind or reality. DP emphasizes the primacy of practices.

2) "Reality" and "mind" are constructed in language as part of the interactional business;

3) Social life is basically the normative and rhetorical product rather than the outcomes of the consequence of an interplay of some permanent factors;

4) Norms are treated as orientated to rather than governing action;

5) Norms and rhetorics only make sense in relation to the context of practices;

6) Cognitive entities and processes are approached empirically as participants' ways of talking rather than as the analytic resource;

7) The focus for analysis is how psychological notions are constructed and employed in discourse to achieve specific pragmatic objectives;

8) DP practitioners share a methodological preference to rigorous empirical analysis of records of natural interaction rather than experiments, surveys and interviews;

9) The data for analysis are often conversations and talks in the natural settings, or documents of various kinds;

10) DP analysis focuses on the specific details of interaction and how that details are precisely related to the activities that are being performed rather than looking beyond the apparent messiness of interaction to discover general patterns and laws lying beyond it;

11) All details of interaction, whether it be pauses and repairs, the selection of particular words, or the placement of interruption and overlaps, should be assumed to be relevant to interaction;

12) The range of revealing features of discourse include turn taking, hesitations, repair, lexical choice, adjacency pairs, repair, preference organization, rhetorical organization of discourse, etc. ;

13) A dynamic relationship is established between talk, interaction and social structure;

14) The validity of analytic claims is justified by revealing participants' own understanding as they display in interaction.

From these theoretical assumptions, we can see DP differs significantly from traditional psychology. 1) -6) reflect the constructivist view of discourse, reality and cognition in DP. It questions the representationalist view of language and rejects the "conduit metaphor" of communication (Maynard & Perakyla, 2003). It takes social structures and cognition as the discursive construct rather than as the explanators. For DP, discourse is the focus for understanding the discursive action and the reality in which discourse is produced. In this light, DP deviates from the traditional social psychology (see 7) -13)) which seeks explanations for discourse from the social and cognitive constructs. DP also shifts from Logical Empiricism to Hermeneutic-Dialectic Mode (Zajacova, 2002) by focusing on the interactions in natural settings to see how discursive actions are occasioned to do particular things, such as blaming, justifying, explaining, and so on. DP establishes its epistemological claims on the discursive evidence that participants actually orient to in interaction (see 14). There are three major agendas for DP research (Maynard & Perakyla, 2003).

2. 3. 1 Accounts of Course of Action

One main topic for DP research is participants' accounts of action. The reason to focus on accounts of actions is thatthey are meanwhile a way to make the action accountable. "Accounts of actions are invariably, and at the same time, accounts for actions" (Edwards, 1997). Accountability of action is managed via the selection of alternative descriptions. The could-have-been-otherwise quality is one of the most important features of descriptions in dealing with accountability. Descriptions have to attend to actions in terms of what is normal, expectable, and proper and what is the describer's own responsibility in the reporting of action. This characterization is called script① formulation in DP. The formulation or breach of a script involves a rhetorical, argumentative quality with regard to the potential other alternatives. This rhetorical nature of discourse opens up the possibility of looking to see what moral and normative issues of appropriateness, responsibility, and blame are at stake in the way actions are articulated. For example, the following extract, which is taken from Edwards (1997), can illustrate how script formulation can help us to make sense of the way blame is toned down in a report of marital problem to the counselor.

1 Mary: I went out Friday n ↑ i ↓ ght (.) and (.) Jeff was
2 ↓ work ↑ ing (.) on call (.) and (.) um (2. 2) the
3 place That I went to (.) like (.) closed at half
4 past twelve and I got home about one o' clock

Mary is recounting what happened before she and Jeff, her husband, had an argument over her late arrival home. The accounting consists of a simple narrative. A script which is projected is a sequence of three events: she went out on Friday night, the place she went to closed at half past twelve and she

① The script used here refers to features of how events are Describe-d. It is called script-d in contrast with script-w (features of the World, of events themselves) and script-p (features of Perception and cognition) in script theory (Edwards, 1994).

got home at about one o' clock. This is recognizably produced with regard to our expectation of a social life. However, what has not been mentioned is what "went out Friday night" might mean, what kind of "place" Mary is probably referring to, and what kind of thing "working on call" might be. Neither did she indicate that, as the rest of the transcript shows, she had recently had an extra-marital affair with a man who she met at the place she went to. Her account is simply an externalizing, situational kind of description. Such an orientation makes her reported action accountable and implicitly attributed the marital problem to her husband.

2.3.2 Accounts of Mind

Attribution to the emotional and cognitive states is another common discourse phenomenon in everyday language. Cognitive states are constructed through the ways in which statements, stories and reports are designed and received in conversation. The following four cognitive topics are often brought to the fore by discursive psychologists:

1) Knowledge

In the existent discourse theories, communication is prevalently regarded as a transactional act to alter the participants' knowledge status. Speakers will not only construct a picture of their own knowledge but also manifest their assumption about the recipients' prior knowledge. Research in pragmatics (Sperber & Wilson, 1995) and functional linguistics (Halliday, 1994) have explored how "shared knowledge", "mutual knowledge", or "information status" can be indexed by grammatical, lexical and intonational devices such as deixis, anaphora, definiteness, presupposition and implicature. But behind this approach is cognitivist determinism. It holds that there is a correspondence between cognitive status and the use of language. The use of linguistic devices can reflect speakers' actual cognition.

This view is, however, challenged by DP advocates, as Edwards (2004: 43) argues that "Treating something as given, definite, new, or newsworthy, is a way of talking and of doing things by talking, rather than the expression of speakers' best guesses at what each other actually knows". That is, rather than conceiving of talk as the means of sending and receiving information or knowledge the speaker possesses, DP treats talk as a domain of social action in which cognitive states are at stake in talk and are attended to, implied, made relevant, etc., as part of whatever business talk is doing. The crux of DP criticism is that the psychological assumption does not situate discourse in context as performative.

With this practical concern of knowledge, DP regards it as one type of analytic categories (e. g. given, new, agreed, contextual, contentious, or common knowledge) which participants use to perform interactional work. The following extract, which is a dialogue of police interrogation, is found in Edwards (1997) as an illustration of how knowledge is formulated to perform institutional work:

P: How long did you have that job?
S: (...) the last job I had now we can take ((P: Mm)) it was at Lights
Limited with the Ekbergs ((P: I see)), then I had both my hands in
plaster, after an accident
P: Mm, we can leave that, I will just write what you have said
S: Yes
P: Mm: Ah healthy and fit for work we usually write, you know.
You have no illnesses?
S: Noo, I hope not... No, illnesses, I have had a cold since last autumn
but ah ah ((P: Mm)) ((pause)) well, that counts as an illness, I guess
P: Well, this is, they' re referring to more serious illnesses

(Linell and Johnson, 1991: 82, cited from Edwards, 1997: 129)

Edwards (1997) points out how a written factual statement is produced jointly through the reciprocal work between the police and the suspect. The police first explained the requirements of the ready-made boxes on the bureaucratic report form and then asked the question about the suspect's health (lines 8). The answer was not directly to the point (line 9). They had to negotiate the meaning of illness before the police fixed the information for the record (lines 10—11). In this conversation, the knowledge about health was invoked as the conversational topic but the point was to build up a version of fact for the legal purpose.

2) Disposition

Disposition is often made inferentially available when a breach from the script occurs. An extraordinary or abnormal action can be attributed to specific dispositions of the actor. Formulations of disposition are often achieved by describing the intention, personality or moral character of the actor. Again, what distinguishes discursive psychologists from cognitivists is its emphasis on the discursive nature of disposition, i. e. how it is invoked and employed as resources for speakers to pursue their local interactional goals. Conversations on personal actions, events, and responsibility often provide the juncture for dispositional analysis. For example, in a study of the use of the modal word *would* in police interrogation, Edwards (2006) explores how it is used as a generalized dispositional formulation to handle accountability. "S" is a suspect being interrogated by the police for his involvement in the theft of cigarettes from a shop.

P: But she said (0. 2) that she was pushed backwards
by yourself. = Now I' ve been to see this lady
yesterday. . hhh And at the (.) bottom: r: ight hand
side of her back (0. 4) she's got a (.) brui: se
about the size about a fifty pence piece. =
S: =Well then somebody else has done that mate.
→ I wouldn' I ↑ wouldn' t do that. No I' ll admit to
stealin the ciggies, right . hh but they were on the
counter, . h I did not jump over no counter for them.
(0. 3)
P: NO I [DIDn' t say you jumped over a count[er.

S: [I- [I didn'
even go <u>be</u>hind the counter for them. = I didn' push
the woman or nothin, (0. 5) I really did not do
→ that. = I' m not that type of person y' know what I
me: an. . h Fair enough I stole the ciggies, (0. 9)
→ I wouldn' hurt an old lady.
(0. 5)
P: [Right.]
S: [No.] (.) Not a chance. =

(Edwards, 2006: 479)

Preceding the extract was an account of the fact given by S. It was objected by P in lines 1-5. At line 6, S immediately denies his accuser's account, first by suspecting some other unknown perpetrator and then producing the first person generalized dispositional expression "I wouldn't do that". The emphasis of this disposition was further marked by its repetition with raised pitch. This can be seen as an explicit orientation to his own character within a moral order. In the following lines, S continued this argument by showing his honesty through admitting stealing the cigarettes (lines 7 and 8). He also reiterates his personality (line 15) and morality (line 17) to emphatically deny the accused offence that he pushed the woman. Clearly, S is at pains to offer a generalized disposition to justify his version of his actions. One interesting point is that P does not challenge S's dispositional would-based self-assessments (lines 11 and 19). This seems that dispositional formulations are sometimes hard to attack in disputation.

In the legal context, intentionality is the one of the dispositional features that is often broached and handled in detail. It pertains to the identification of legal facts or legal consequences of offence. Particularly in police interrogations, there is a pervasive concern with the intentionality of case accounts (Edwards, 2008). Police need to identify the possible intentional status of a suspected crime so that a proper accusation can be made. The way that the police approach it is discursive reconstruction. The current findings in DP (Jayyusi, 1993; Edwards,

2008; Stokoe & Edwards, 2008) suggest that the attribution of intent and the description of actions in legal contexts is a more programmatic than psychological or cognitive issue. So it is necessary to explore how participants assign intention to speakers bears on the accountability of judicial decisions.

3) Emotion

Emotion is another important phenomenon related to psychology, although it is normally associated with irrational subjective feelings. Emotion categories are often appropriated to account for human actions and interpersonal relations. Emotion discourse is one important resource to assign causes and motives to actions such as blaming, making excuse, and giring accounts. For example, anger is often invoked to signal problematicity in an account.

The discursive psychology of emotion investigates how emotional states become the objects to be accounted for and also as explanators for events or actions that precede or follow them (Edwards, 1997) .Discursive psychologists are interested in how speakers avow their own emotions and ascribe them to others. The focus is the rhetorical organization. In line with other social constructionist approaches (Harre, 1986), DP approaches emotion discourse by explicating the link between emotions and cognitive scripts and disposition. They can be both cause and effect. That is, speakers can explain away emotional states by resorting to cognition:

e. g. *When I learned the news, I was very excited.*

Emotion can also be conceived as the stimuli of cognition and action:

e. g. *She was too worried to think about her English paper.*

DP aims to explore how emotion discourse is evoked to perform communicative acts such as describing the origin of events and managing the accountability of a narrative.

4) Memory

DP views memory as the participants' concern as exposed in their situated uses of words such as "remember", "forget", and so on. The discursive psychology of memory can be characterized in five ways (Reavey and Brown,

2006): a) concerned with "remembering" as discursive actions; b) emphasizing the social constructive nature of memory; c) interested in the inconsistency and contradiction in memory; d) appealing to the effect of a version of past events on the present; e) focusing on issues of responsibility, accountability or morality involved in remembering as action.

As we can see, rather than exploring how knowledge was acquired, retained, and retrieved, DP is interested in the purposive use of memory. For example, in a study of conversational joint remembering, Edwards and Middleton (1986) find that memory discourse can serve three functions:

> *(1) framing and orientation-the establishment of criteria for joint recall, and the ways in which individuals accordingly locate themselves vis-a-vis the unfolding account;*
>
> *(2) correspondence functions-including a "semantic function" through which experiences are put into words, and a "continuity function" which concerns the ordering of things recalled; and*
>
> *(3) validation function-a variety of means by which the joint account is constructed as a mnemonic consensus, jointly agreed.*

From this research, two implications can be drawn: One is that remembering is context sensitive. The occurrence of remembering is triggered and constructed within the specific interactional setting. The other is that the interactional function of past experiences in current activities is generally of greater importance than accuracy and completeness of the account of the past events. For this, studies of courtroom interaction have produced some good illustrations. For example, Lynch and Bogen (1996 as quoted in Edwards (1997)) notes "I don't remember" and "I don't recall" are used as a strategy in witness examination to avoid both an incriminating confession and a potentially troublesome denial if later evidence and testimony should undermine it.

2. 3. 3 Accounts of Identity

The third central theme in discursive psychology is identity. The conceptions of the term "identity" are varied ranging from an agentive, psychological self, to a label of social membership, and then to a product of the social (Benwell & Stokoe, 2006). DP does not entangle itself in the disputes over the ontological status of "identity". Both the structural and emergent nature of identity is recognized. That is, identity is treated both as an achievement of and as a tool for talk in interaction (Antaki & Widdicombe, 1998).

The focus of DP theorization of identity is the use of identity categories in everyday talk. Their research basically addresses the question of "*construction*" (how the identity discourse is constructed) and "*function*" (what it is interactionally designed for) (Edwards & Potter, 1992). The former is about how identities are occasioned in discourse. Its theoretical assumption is that identity "is inextricably dependent on the linguistic practices used in everyday life to make sense of our own and others' actions" (Potter & Wetherell, 1987: 95). The second question is concerned with the interactional consequence of identities. DP practitioners are interested in the way how identities fit into the interactions and practices.

In analyzing identities, DP heavily draws on conversation analysis and membership categorization analysis (Antaki & Widdicombe, 1998; Edwards, 1998). It is argued that identities can be either turn-generated or indicated through the use of identity-implicated categories. That is, the mobilization of identities can be shown in the actual instances of interaction. DP's objective to analyze identity discourse is not to reveal the nature of identities or to categorize them but to see how interactional tasks are accomplished thereby. Edwards & Potter's (1992) analysis of Lawson's letter of resignation illustrates how the discursive psychology of identity is put into work. Lawson was the Chancellor of the Exchequer in Margaret Thatcher's cabinet. He resigned by quoting the reason that there was a disagreement over the economic policy between the Prime

Minister and himself. He also argued that the occurrence of such a situation was a violation of the "essential requirement" of being a minister and also explicitly stated that he resigned regretfully to the interest of the government. In analyzing his resignation letter, Edwards and Potter note that Lawson obviously embedded his action within the requirement of his role as a cabinet member. He attributed his resignation to his political obligation to support the government. He did not quote other possible reasons like leaving for a better paid job (which he actually did later). This construction projected his political identity rather than his individual identity with personal interest. By doing so, he made his resignation morally accountable. If he chose a personal psychological account, his action would be hardly laudable.

All the three themes of research in discursive psychology are incorporated to show how the design and reception of discourse contributes to particular social actions. Since DP mainly bases its analytical framework on ethnomethodology and conversation analysis, they jointly subscribe to a policy of "ethnomethodological indifference" (Garfinkel & Sacks, 1970). That is, they reject prior theories as resources for understanding the social world. Instead, they try to construe what participants orient to in interaction. Such a methodological approach is pioneered by CA proponents.

> *...what informs the analysis is what is relevant to the participants in its target event, and not what is relevant in the first instance to its academic analysts by virtue of the set analytic and theoretical commitments which they bring to their work.*
>
> (Schegloff, 1992: 196)

Based on this principle, CA has developed rigorous analytical systems. However, this method has also its inherent weaknesses. As we know, not all cognitive processes are manifested in our discursive expressions. In actual interaction, there is often more assumed contextual information than what is put into words. To incorporate this broader contextual information into theorization, CA often finds itself in a strained circumstance. In this case, DP extends its analytical toolkits beyond CA. There are at least two signs of development along this direction. One is the inclusion of written texts for analysis (Edwards & Potter, 1992; Edwards, 1994). The other is the emergence of argument for synthetic approaches (known as critical discursive psychology) to do discourse analysis (Wetherell, 1998).

DP is developed as an effort to handle methodological problems in the science of social studies, aiming to deal with participants' accounts of their own practices (Edwards, 1994). A major contribution of DP is to celebrate the action-orientation as a feature of psychology in everyday talk. It reformulates cognition as a feature of participants' practice and moves cognition from being an explanatory resource to a topic of study (Potter & Edwards, 1999).

2.4 Summary

The overview of research on judges' judicial behavior shows that the focus has been shifted from exploration of unified models to gaining insights into the contingency of judges' discretion. This goes along with criticism of the model-theoretic approach for failing to address the flexibility and contingency of judicial behavior. We observe that over the past few decades, more and more attention has been attracted to factors other than law in legal behavior theory. Some new lights have been shed on judges' judicial behavior. One major breakthrough is that nonrational and irrational judicial behavior, which is more common in reality, has been theorized as a complement to the formal decision theory. In line with this new trend, some heuristic decision theories have been acclaimed and a discursive turn has emerged in current legal scholarship. As a result, discourse analysis has been incorporated as an important tool for empirical judicial behavior research.

Following this academic trend as we observed, this chapter has devoted a separate section to examining existent work on linguistics and the law, with special attention to the discursive perspective on legal decision-making. It is found that existing research lacks a coherent theory and method in relating discourse to judicial behavior.

In the final part of the review, a snapshot of discursive psychology is made to show how it can shed light on social psychology research. DP has found that the evocation of a cognitive or psychological category in interaction is always functional. Psychological and cognitive discourse is often managed to perform actions or negotiate accountability. The most significant insight we can draw from this is that an alternative approach to judicial behavior is possible. If we subscribe to the action-oriented view of discourse, judges' judicial discourses must fulfill certain interactional purposes. However, this purpose-oriented nature on the part of judge is often ignored or even denied. Therefore, it will constitute an exciting area for future research into JJB.

Following DP, this research is designed to provide a new perspective into judges' judicial behavior and enhance our understanding of this social phenomenon. Particularly, we aim to show how discourse analysis can contribute to our knowledge of judges' judicial behavior which has more significant bearings on social life than ever before. We recognize and appreciate that a lot of work has already been done on this topic (Huang, 2002; Wang, 2005; Li2005; Zhan, 2005; Huai, 2006; Qian, 2008; Wu, 2008). However, we also notice that their approach is dominantly prescriptive. That is, they aim to formulate decision-making models and determine the affecting variables. This approach is fit for the purpose of institutional administration. However, the judicial practice (for example, judicial disparity) has indicated that no prescriptive model can successfully predict judges' judicial behavior. As we can observe, making and implementing rules for judicial behavior (The Supreme People's Court, 2005) is one thing, and the actual practice of judges' judicial behavior is another. This divergence awaits further exploration.

Chapter 3

Theoretical Framework and Method

JJB is a topic falling within the field of psycholegal studies. Built on the discursive turn in jurisprudence, this study will respecify JJB as a discursive phenomenon and propose a discursive psychological approach to it. In this chapter a theoretical framework will be formulated for our empirical JJB study by drawing on DP. To be specific, we will elaborate how the discursive action model, which encompasses a set of principles for DP, can incorporate speech act theory, exchange structure theory, and linguistic anthropology to operationalize a DP study of JJB. Finally, in line with the aforesaid theoretical position, we will formulate a method for an empirical study of JJB in Chinese judicial system.

3.1 Respecifying Judicial Behavior

Our literature review shows that traditional judicial behavior research has mainly subscribed to the CPA which focuses on judges' cognitive process in judicial behavior and the factors that may influence it. The following model captures how judicial behavior is construed within the tradition of CPA.

This model specifies four factors operative in judicial decision making: role orientation (the belief about proper behavior within the institutional position that judges hold), attitudes (expectations about how they should behave as judges), facts (the circumstance of the case concerned) and decisional formula (the cognitive psychological process). According to this

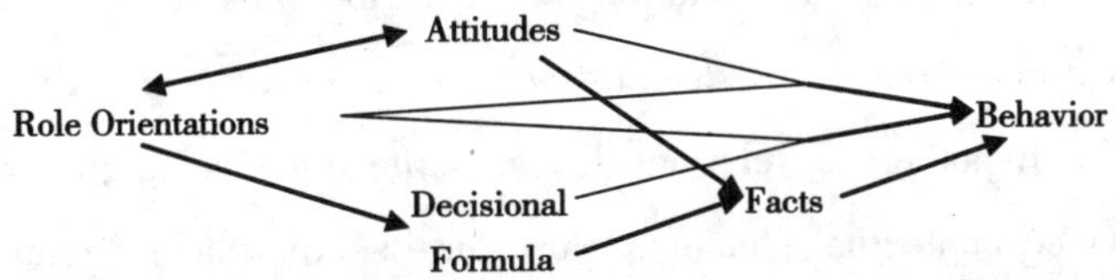

Figure 3-1 An Integrated Model of Judicial Behavior in Gibson (1983)

model, no single factor can account for JJB. Judicial behavior is construed as "a function of what they [judges] prefer to do, tempered by what they think they ought to do, but constrained by what they perceive is feasible to do" (Gibson 1983: 32). This model deconstructs the cognitive process of JJB into several internal as well as external contextual variables. However, no theory so far can give an adequate account on how the different factors interact given the complexity of judicial behavior. As we know, the CPA is by nature an analytical rather than synthetic method. It provides no effective tool or method to mediate different contextual forces in its theoretical construct. To address the complexity of judicial behavior, we need a theory which can explicate the dynamicism of judicial process. This suggests that judicial behavior theory shall shift from normative prescription of general cognitive process to descriptive account of dynamism underscoring judges' individual behavior. In this vein, a study of judicial behavior shall be:

- empirical in terms of research object

It shall focus on the behavior of individuals rather than the hypothesization of the rationality of decision makers or optimality of decisions.

- descriptive in terms of paradigm

The method of JJB research shall be able to describe how the judicial behavior is enacted in the context of judicial process.

- holistic in the terms of epistemology

The judicial behavior shall be construed by considering all the relevant contextual forces.

In short, judicial behavior theory shall capture the ecological environment of the judicial behavior, i. e. the relation between judicial behavior and all the relevant contextual forces. The existent research in the CPA tradition focuses on establishing the hypothetical relations between the outcome of judicial behavior and the perceived contextual elements. However, its experiment-oriented paradigm tends to miss out on the dynamicism of judicial process.

Another problem with current behavioral research is that it mostly relies on linguistic data (which is obtained through such empirical methods as psychological experimentation, field observation and survey) but there is no ensured method to read off the cognitive and psychological process from them. No matter what specific research methods are adopted, judicial behavior research is indispensable from the analysis of language. The judicial decision making process can not be fully captured without taking language into consideration. The formulated decisional patterns or models are elicited or inferred from the discursive accounts of decisional process through researcher's observation or judges' self-reflection. But the problem with CPA is that it takes for granted the relationship between the language used to represent judicial behavior and the actual behavior. Only quite recently has attention been paid to the discursive nature of JJB (e. g. Ewick & Silbey 1995; Wu 2008).

In line with the discursive turn in law, judicial behavior is now considered as discourse practice (MacMartin, 1999). This discursive view is underscored with the perception that judges do not only perform their judicial tasks through discourse but also account for their behavior in discourse. It is this accountability that is neglected in traditional CPA studies of judicial behavior. Within the CPA approach, judges are generally cast as information processors, sifting and computing informational input and generating a range of outputs (Sales, 1981). However, scarce attention has been paid to the information sources and contents as well as the context in which it is processed. For example, when judicial behavior research builds its theorization on judges' introspective information, it normally does not examine how the introspective information was produced by the judges.

In line with the discourse theory after the philosophy of ordinary language, any instance of discourse is a social action which is contingent on the relevant context. That is to say, the introspective information about JJB is not a statement about the objective reality of judicial decision making but a discursive product contingent on the socio-cultural, historical and situational context the concerned judges are embedded in. We shall not ignore possible pragmatic concerns underlying judges' discursive action. In this vein, to explore JJB, we need first of all reveal the"discursive formation" (Carbaugh, 1995) of the accounts for their behavior.

The discourse theory that pertains to this discursive view of judicial behavior is discursive psychology which deals with the psychology of social behavior as a discursive topic. During the past half century, research into judicial sentencing or decision-making is copious and multifarious models have been produced. But they mostly follow the dominant social cognition paradigm which considers judicial behavior as produced on the basis of information processing based on perceptual input. Such modeling often oversimplifies or homogenizes actual processes of judges' information processing. It is often based on the postulation of judicial rationality. However, judges do not always display the same degree of adherence to rationality. It is now recognized that the perception of input information is not immune from the values judges may personally embrace or interactionally negotiate in the trial process. It is this mediated nature of cognition and psychology that DP can address.

3.2 Concept and Assumption

3.2.1 Discourse

DP is premised on the theoretical assumption that discourse is central to social life. For DP practitioners, discourse is both an object and a practice. That is, discourse is on the one hand taken to be talk and text of any kind, including all the semiotic media produced in lifeworld (Edwards, 2005) and on the other hand a social process in which interactional tasks are discursively performed. There are three key features inherent in the use of the term"discourse"by the DP practitioners (Potter & Edwards, 2001; Potter & Hepburn, 2005):

1) Action orientation

For advocators of DP, discourse is a symbolic tool articulated to perform actions. By"action", it means the performance of personal and social tasks in daily life. The action-oriented sense of"discourse"is the central difference between DP and standard cognitive psychology. For cognitive psychology, discourse is the means which we use to represent the world. This mapping metaphor is criticized by DP advocators in that the cognitive psychologists treat discourse as unproblematic in expressing or reflecting the world and as a result the inconsistency or breakdown of communication is often ignored. DP argues that all these are also inherent parts of the discourse practices and takes them as equally important junctures for analysis.

2) Situation

DP relates discourse to situation in two ways. First, discourse is occasioned only in a given context. DP adopts a relativistic rather than deterministic approach towards the relation between discourse and context. Second, DP conceptualizes discourse as having rhetorical and argumentative purposes. So when one discourse category is mobilized to account for a judicial decision, DP won't simply attribute the former to the case situation in issue. Instead, DP will examine the contextual factors such as institutional activities and identities to see how they are made relevant. Situation is a necessary frame to capture how discourse is managed in the interaction.

3) Construction

This refers to the constructivist view of discourse. There are also two senses of it. First, discourse is constructed by drawing on linguistic, interactional and transactional resources. This is an issue concerned with the order of discourse. DP research will address how certain discourse is produced or what motivates the discourse production. Second, discourse constructs versions of the world. An articulation of discourse will have a certain practical implication, either sustaining, changing or removing a state of reality.

The constructionist view of discourse is another key theoretical departure from traditional social cognition. As we know, discourse in cognitive psychology is an index of speakers' mind. For DP, discourse is an interactional device evoked to fulfill certain social functions.

3.2.2 Discursive Action Model

The Discursive Action Model (DAM) is an overall scheme formulated as a DP framework for research of practical interest (Edwards & Potter, 1992; Edwards & Potter, 1993; Potter & Edwards et al., 1993). This model does not provide an operational framework for empirical study. It consists only of three general principles of DP (Potter & Edwards et al., 1993: 389):

Action

1. *The research focus is on action rather than cognition or behavior.*
2. *As action is predominantly, and most clearly, performed through discourse, traditional psychological concepts (memory, attribution, categorization, etc.) are reconceptualized in discursive terms.*
3. *Actions done in discourse are overwhelmingly situated in broader activity sequences of various kinds.*

Stake and Interest

4. *In the case of many actions, there is a dilemma of stake or interest, which is often managed by doing attribution via*

factual reports and descriptions.

5. *Reports and descriptions are therefore constituted/displayed as factual by a variety of discursive devices.*
6. *Factual versions are rhetorically organized to undermine alternatives.*

Accountability

7. *Factual versions attend to agency and accountability in the reported events.*
8. *Factual versions attend to agency and accountability in the current speaker's action, including those done in the reporting.*
9. *Concerns 7 and 8 are often related, such that 7 is deployed for 8, and 8 is deployed for 7.*

From these three principles, we can find that DAM marks a totally different approach to social psychological issue.

Firstly, the DAM is a model of action, not of cognition. It is concerned with what people do rather than the mental constructs, representations or processes as cognitive psychology does. It recasts psychological and cognitive topics as discursive actions. It focuses on how psychological themes are managed in discourse to perform specific actions. This theoretical re-orientation is premised on the assumption that everyday language use involves accounts of and for action (Edwards, 1997). It is argued that discourse is not a window to the stable underlying representations of the world. Instead it serves the rhetorical argumentative functions. In this sense, psychological topics involved in discourse such as memory, attribution, categories and knowledge are treated not as the objective representation of cognitive state but more primarily as the constructions that are invoked to perform social activities. Thus, the account of case information processing in the judgment, for example, does not reflect the legitimate way that a case is dealt with. A

DP account will probably see it as a way the judges develop a theory for the case.

Secondly, DP emphasizes the goal-oriented nature of discourse. The choice of a specific discourse form is related to the actant's particular stake or interest. Let's take the attributional discourse for example. Cognitive psychology treats it as a matter of competency (accuracy, capacity and so on). However, in DAM this is reformulated as a *dilemma of stake or interest* in social activities. It is argued that attributional inferences are an integral part of communicative actions and participants always have a rhetorical discursive stake or position as the starting point of their action. That is, the dilemma of stake or interest is an inherent feature of the content and organization of the discourse. The management of the dilemma in action is manifested in the use of specific discursive devices. It could be revealed by examining the possibility of could-have-been-otherwise in discursive actions. For example, the group membership categories are employed to establish the killing as a group act rather than personal interest (Watson, 1983); the role and trait talk is found as the excuses and mitigations of police violence (Wetherell & Potter, 1989). Edwards & Potter (1992) present a summary of factual-accounting devices which include: category entitlement, vivid description, narrative, systematic vagueness, empiricist accounting, rhetoric argument, extreme case formulations, consensus and corroboration, lists and contrasts.

Thirdly, DAM is concerned with the accountability of a discursive action from the social point of view. The accountability can be directed towards both the reported event and the reporting act. These two facets of accountability are in a relation of mutual manifestation. That is, a facet of accountability can allow inferences about another. From the perspective of source, accountability can be attributed to discourse participants of different "footings" (Goffman, 1983). However, the participant's footing is not treated as the motivator for but a product of the constructive and rhetorical discourse practice.

In summary, DAM is proposed as a complementary approach to address the limitations in the current research into cognitive and psychological issues (Edwards & Potter, 1993; Edwards & Potter, 1999). The thrust of DAM is that cognitive entities and processes are not regarded as the analytic resource but as the construction of discourse practice. It rejects the factor-and-outcome model which aims to identify the regular patterns of social life (Potter & Edwards, 2001). It instead focuses on the norms and rhetoric strategies which the organization and production of social life rely on. The norms do not govern discourse practice, but function as the participants' resources for action and understanding. In line with this argument, the study of psychology shall shift its focus from the "blackbox" to the instances of social activities.

3.3 Theories of Discursive Actions

Based on DAM, a discursive psychology of JJB shall be grounded on a theory of discursive actions. DP finds its theoretical sources in Wittgenstein's (1997) philosophy of ordinary language and Garfinkel's (1967) ethnomethodology. In practice, DP mainly resorts to CA as the analytical tool. The methodological strength of CA is that it can address how discursive actions are unfolded in the sequence of social interaction through the detailed and systematic analysis of conversational structure. However, JJB is not solely accomplished in conversations. Actually the most common discursive form of judges' is written judgment. In the study of judges' judicial behavior, MacMartin and his colleagues (MacMartin, 1999; MacMartin & Wood, 2005; Wood & MacMartin, 2007) have exclusively focused on the written judicial judgments. CA alone obviously can not address the complexity of judges' judicial discourse. Judges' discursive actions also need to be illuminated by referring to other discourse resources such as textual structure, generic styles and semantic features. A too strict adherence to CA has been criticized as a theoretical defect of DP (Wetherell, 1998; Wetherell, 2007). It is agreed that other linguistic theories and methods shall also be drawn on to develop a more comprehensive theory of discursive actions. But before we we do that, some relevant theories on discursive actions will be discussed.

3.3.1 Speech Act Theory

Speech Act Theory (SAT) is a philosophy of language which deals with "how to do things with words" (Austin, 1962). Social actions performed through language are the focal object of "speech act research" (Kasper, 2004). SAT holds that when issuing an utterance, we perform three kinds of actions simultaneously: locutionary, illocutionary and perlocutionary. The execution of speech acts needs to satisfy four felicity conditions: propositional, preparatory, sincere and essential (Searle, 1969). Based on these four conditions, five basic types of speech acts are identified: representatives, directives, commissives, expressives and declaratives.

The relevance of SAT to judicial decision research has been demonstrated in a recent study by Charnock (2009) who reveals how judges present their overruling decisions not as new legislation, but rather as declarations of the true state of the unchanging common law to avoid assuming a legislative function. This research has shown the performative functions of implicit speech act in overruling judicial decisions. However, there are some problems with the application of SAT to judicial decision discourse. It is pointed out that "the legal validity of overruling declarations depends to a large extent on their perlocutionary effects" (Charnock, 2009: 401). But SAT deals mainly with illocutionary act, leaving perlocutionary effects as the indeterminate residue of the context.

There are also some other problems inherent in SAT when applied to the analysis of discourse practice. For example, there is no fixed taxonomy for classifying speech acts in discourse. The one provided by Searle (1969) is criticized for not being built on "a principled basis" and failing to live up to the four felicity conditions (Levinson, 1983: 210). It is admitted by the main advocates of SAT (Austin, 1962: 150; Searle, 1969: 23) that the actual number of speech act types is indeterminate. There are often instances of speech act whose classification is in dispute (Trosborg, 1995; Zhang, 2000). One discourse action can play two or more acts simultaneously. Although SAT holds that "speaking a language is engaging in a rule-governed form of behavior" (Searle, 1969: 22) and that there are specifiable constitutive rules for speech acts, we can not reliably recover speech acts based on given theoretical rules. Neither the illocutionary force indicating devices nor the constitutive rules can accurately predict speech acts in context. The indirect speech act is one particular challenge for speech act classification.

These problems with SAT are related to the insufficient recognition of the context dependency of discursive social actions (Sbis, 2002). Speech acts are the interactional phenomena emerging within particular social settings. However, philosophers and linguists of speech acts generally fail to properly take into account the contextual information (Sadock, 2006). They are mainly concerned with the conceptual analysis of speech acts (Kasper, 2004). That is, "speech-act pragmatics was developed from considerations of idealized sentences-originally construed as occurring in a 'null context'" (Drew & Heritage, 1992: 12). This is reasonable given the philosophical interest underlying SAT. However, without embracing contextual information, speech act theory can not address the actual discourse in social interaction. This deficiency has been recognized, for example, in Kryk-Kastovsky's (2009) "speech act network", a notion developed from the historical pragmatic perspective to capture the interrelated nature of illocutions and their corresponding perlocutions in the courtroom discourse.

3. 3. 2 Exchange Structure Theory

Exchange Structure Theory (EST) is an approach to discourse analysis, originally developed by Sinclair & Coulthard (1975) for the study of classroom interaction. Sharing much of the theoretical basis of systemic functional linguistics,

EST sets out to model the hierarchy of discourse structure and specifies the functions of discourse components of various ranks. EST might not be the first to pay attention to the discourse structure above sentential level. But it is EST that first provides a set of rigidly defined categories of discourse structure. According to EST, classroom discourse is modeled as an ordered structure of a 5-scale rank: lesson, transaction, exchange, move, and act. They are related to each other in a"consist of"relation. The basic unit for analysis is exchange. It is found that a lesson typically consists of boundary exchange (preliminary and terminal) and teaching exchange (medial). Different exchanges consist of different moves. The boundary move is realized in framing and focusing moves while the teaching move is typically comprised of opening, answering and follow-up moves. Acts are the units at the lowest rank of discourse. They correspond most closely to the grammatical unit clause. According to the tagging scheme in Sinclair & Coulthard (1975), 22 acts are identified in their data:

Table 3-1 The Structural System for Analyzing Classroom Discourse

<table>
<tr><th>Lesson</th><th>Exchange</th><th>Move</th><th>Act</th></tr>
<tr><td rowspan="5">Lesson</td><td rowspan="2">Boundary</td><td>Framing</td><td>marker, silent stress</td></tr>
<tr><td>Focusing</td><td>marker, starter, system at head; choice from metastatement or conclusion, comment</td></tr>
<tr><td rowspan="3">Teaching</td><td>Opening</td><td>marker, starter, system operating at head; choice of elicitation, directive, informative, check; system operating at post-head; choice from prompt and clue; nomination</td></tr>
<tr><td>Answering</td><td>acknowledge, system operating at head, choice of reply, react, acknowledge, comment</td></tr>
<tr><td>Follow-up</td><td>accept, evaluate, comment</td></tr>
</table>

The most important finding of EST is that a teaching exchange consists of three moves in a linear sequence: Initiation-Response-Feedback (IRF). This finding has also been extended to the analysis of discourse other than the classroom teaching genre (Stubbs, 1983; Tsui, 1994; Eggins & Slade, 1997).

EST also argues that an exchange structure can be expounded by construing its situation and tactics. Situation refers to the context of situational, social and personal constraints while tactics is meant here for"the syntagmatic patterns of discourse" (Sinclair & Coulthard, 1975). This suggests that exchange of conversation is dependent on the external and internal context of discourse.

> *In identifying formal categories for the original analysis much reliance was necessarily placed on assumed contextual meanings which derived from apprehensions about what goes on in classrooms.*
>
> (Coulthard & Brazil, 1992: 68)

EST differs from SAT in their foci on discourse context. The felicity conditions in SAT are presupposed or pregiven while EST addresses the emerging localized contextual elements (Sinclair & Coulthard, 1975). The actual structure and element that are evoked are contingent on the interactional context. Sinclair & Coulthard have particularly made it clear that their categories for the structure of classroom discourse may not be appropriate for other types of discourse.

Nevertheless, EST was originally motivated by the grammar theories and aims to be developed as a discourse grammar. This orientation consequently restricts its view of context. What is actually taken into account is only the sequential development of interaction. A closer examination of context is necessary to address the panoply of the situational, social and historical backdrop.

3.3.3 Linguistic Anthropology

Linguistic Anthropology (LA) also studies language use as action (Duranti, 1997). In fact, linguistic anthropology has found its theoretical source in speech act theory. It shares the basic view of ordinary language philosophy and takes a praxisoriented view of language. In contrast to the pragmatic analysis of SAT, however, LA has displayed:

> *a stronger concern for the socio-cultural context of the use of language, with the specific relationship between language and local systems of knowledge and social order, and a lesser commitment to the relevance of logical notation to the strategic use of speech in social interaction.* (Duranti, 1988: 213).

As a subdiscipline of anthropology, LA regards discourse actions as social behavior. It assumes that understanding the form and content of discourse in its various manifestations can contribute to our understanding of the social activities in which the discourse is produced. Specifically, there are three theoretical concerns in LA (Duranti, 1997):

Performance LA takes linguistic performance as the starting point for the study of social life. Performance is originally used by Chomsky as "the use of linguistic knowledge" and by Austin as "doing things with words". But the former emphasizes its biological nature while the latter its social aspect. This suggests that performance can be approached from varying theoretical perspectives. Performance in the LA sense refers to the domain of human actions where special attentions are attached to the ways in which communicative acts are executed. There are three analytical foci of performance. The first is the form of performance, i. e. the semiotic resources of social behavior. The study of performance aims to show what social meaning is conveyed and how it is achieved. The second is the dimension of accountability. Performance implies an exposure to the judgment, reaction and collaboration of the audience. LA deals with how the interactive accountability is unfolded in social contexts. The third is the aesthetic and creative dimension of performance. Different from the dominant interest of other performance theories in the cognitive or social norms, LA has particular interest in the creativity manifested in performance in relation to concrete settings.

Indexicality Language in use is connected to or index the context, either real or imaginary. It is with this assumption that LA places linguistic performance or action within the focus of anthropological research. Linguistic anthropologists hold that language is on the one hand the important resources employed by the participants to construct the reality and is on the other hand the contextualization cue which can enable us to know what is going on in a given situation and how the social activity proceeds. The differentiation of performance is marked in the varying accesses to the linguistic resources. Through linguistic analysis, we can see how the individuals' interests and social dynamics interact and shape performance.

Participation This notion is served as an alternative to "communicative event", "speech event" and "speech activity". Central to it is the relationship among the components of the speech event, including setting, participants, and genres. By focusing on participation, LA enjoys "the advantage of preserving information about the social system as a whole while at same time allowing the researcher to get into the details of personal acts" (Duranti, 1988: 128-129). This suggests that LA stresses both the interactional and socio-cultural contexts of human behavior.

In analyzing participation, LA displays particularly "a concern for speakers as social actors" (Duranti, 1988: 120). LA has incorporated several socially-implicated categories such as "footing" (Goffman, 1981) and "conversational sequence" (Sacks, 1992). It is argued that the nature of participation is defined by the participants. Participants assume different statues and stances with respect to their own as well as others' discourse. They together configurate the participation framework. The participant status is related to the distribution of linguistic resources. In this light, we can see how the three key notions of LA constitute the systematic linguistic-anthropological perspective on social behavior:

Among the three notions, performance is used to capture the nature of social actions, participation the anchors for the distribution of interactional roles and

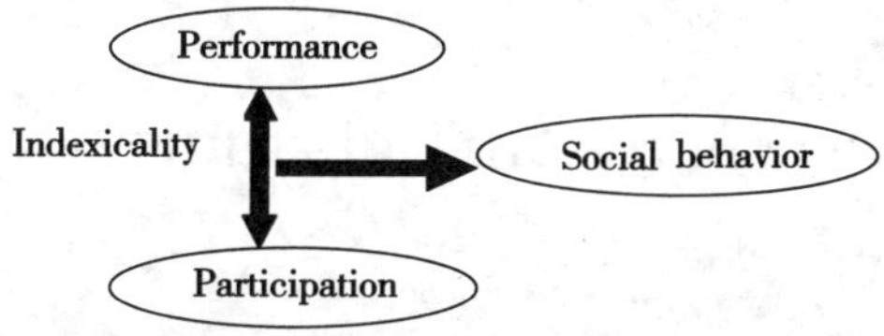

Figure 3-2 Linguistic-Anthropological Perspective of Social Behaviors

indexicality the semiotic resources for reflection and construction. The revolutionary idea of this framework is the incorporation of a social unit of analysis, i. e. participation. The gist of the anthropological theory of social action (Duranti, 1997) can be summarized as: First, social behavior is produced as the achievement of multi-party joint activities. Second, one participant can represent the voices and social personae of different individuals or institutional roles. Third, linguistic methods which can provide the sequential and structural descriptions of discourse are accommodated to address the interactional organization. Finally, besides discourse, other (e. g. material) resources are incorporated into the analysis of social behavior.

Compared with other theories of discursive actions such as SAT and EST, LA obviously appeals more to a systematic theorization of context. LA is considered as the only school of academic study that has paid close attention to context.

> *Anthropology and, especially, the ethnography of speaking and linguistic anthropology are the only directions of research that have now for a period of decades been paying explicit attention to the study of context. … . Until today these are also the few approaches that have produced (edited) books on context and contextualization.*
>
> (Van Dijk, 2008)

With these theoretical strengths, the pertinence of LA to research on praxis-oriented human behavior is obvious.

3.4 A Theoretical Framework

In line with DP, this study is initiated as a reaction to the cognitivism in judicial behavior research. This study will lay particular stress on the contingency of judicial behavior that is often neglected in CPA. Our discursive respecification of judicial behavior suggests that research into JJB can be reformulated as an endeavor to construe judges' professional discourse practice. Our discursive approach consists of two analytic tasks:

3.4.1 Characterizing Discursive Actions

Based on the existent literature, discursive actions can be categorized in two ways: one is framing which explicates the interrelations between actions and the other is categorizing which explores the design features and taxonomy of discourse actions.

3.4.1.1 Framing

Framing represents the relational thinking of discursive actions. That is, a discourse action will not mean anything unless related to other discourse actions. Discursive actions are structured in two ways:

1) Sequence

By sequence, we mean the linear development of discursive actions. The best known theory for sequential analysis is conversation analysis (CA), in which turn-taking is the basic unit of social interaction. The turn-taking system consists of two components: the turn constructional component and the turn allocational system. There are two rules operating on the turn-units (Levinson, 1983: 298):

Rule 1-applies initially at the first TRP of any turn

(a) If C [current speaker] selects N [next speaker] in current turn, then C must stop speaking, and N must speak next, transition occurring at the first

TRP after N-selection.

(b) If C does not select N, then any (other) party may self-select, first speaker gaining rights to the next turn

(c) If C has not selected N, and no other party self-selects under option (b), then C may (but need not) continue (i. e. claim rights to a further turn-constructional unit)

Rule 2-applies at all subsequent TRPs

When Rule 1 (c) has been applied by C, then at the next TRP Rules 1 (a)-(c) apply, and recursively at the next TRP, until speaker change is effected.

The basic unit of sequence organization is adjacency pair, which is (Schegloff, 2007: 13):

(a) composed of two turns;

(b) by different speakers;

(c) adjacently placed; that is, one after the other

(d) relatively ordered; that is, the two turns of an adjacency pair are differentiated into "first pair parts" (FPPs) and "second pair parts" (SPPs,).

(e) pair-type related; that is, not every second pair part can properly follow any first pair part. Adjacency pairs are typologized into particular pair structures.

Through the analysis ofadjacency pairs, we are able to reveal the conditional relevance in the social interaction. However, the FPP and SPP are not in one-to-one correspondence. One FPP may be followed up with more than one SPP. The different SPPs are in different preference organizations, i. e. some are preferred while others dispreferred. Within an adjacency pair, some other sequences can also be inserted.

Besides the use of turn-taking, talk-in-interaction also has an overall organization which contains some sequential locations. Generally, there is the opening section which is comprised of some pre-sequences, the main body with side sequence such as repairs and the closing sections. An adjacency pair can be expanded by presequences, insertion sequences and post-expansions. For these issues, we will draw on EST, another branch of discourse analysis which takes interest in the sequential element of discursive actions. EST is characterized for the two criteria Coulthard and Brazil (1992: 71) in defining exchange structure:

(1) *does the element generate constraints which amount to a prediction that a particular element will follow; and*

(2) *has a preceding element predicted the occurrence of the element in question?*

Different from CA, EST does not simply rely on the temporal sequence such as turn taking in characterizing discursive actions. It also takes into account thesocial knowledge such as routines to accomplish the involved interactional business.

The combination of CA and EST is intended to give a fuller account of the sequential dynamism underscoring judges' discursive actions.

2) Hierarchy

Hierarchy is complementary to the description of sequence in discursive actions. Besides sequence, discursive actions are also structured hierarchically. This view is most systematically developed in Sinclair & Coulthard's (1975) exchange structure theory. In EST, the interrelationship between discursive actions is presented in terms of rank scale after Halliday's systemic-functional linguistics. It is argued that one social activity such as a lesson consists of some exchanges, each of which, in turn is comprised of some moves. Each move is performed by means of one or more discursive acts. For example, a move may contain a head act with some auxiliary pre-and post-acts. By examining the hierarchy of exchange structure, we are able to know in what a discursive action is functionally embedded.

However, EST does not specify how each component of the exchange structure is defined. For this, we find that it is fruitful to draw on van Dijk's

(1977) macro-structure, Brown & Yule's (1983) topic framework and Swales' (1990) genre analysis. All these discourse theories share some basic conceptions of the interrelation between discursive actions in one way or another. For example, in genre analysis, we can find some categories (such as *move*) which are already used in EST. However, these different theories illuminate the nature of discursive actions from different perspectives. They can all contribute to our understanding of judges' discursive actions.

3.4.1.2 Categorizing

The other way of characterizing discursive actions is categorization. Categorizing is an essential way we make sense of the world. Categorization enables us to identify and differentiate received information. Our knowledge and theories are indispensable from categorical representation. Austin's (1962) speech act theory proposes a best known categorization of discursive actions. He first categorizes discursive actions into constatives and performatives and then into locutionary, illocutionary and perlocutionary. The later development of discursive action theories has also been largely centered on the issue of categorization. The difficulty in categorization lies in the fact that categories are something not to be discovered but created. Amsterdam & Bruner (2000) set out the following rules as admonitions for exploring the "category game".

- Categories are made not found;
- Categorizing is an act of meaning making
- Categories imply a world that contains them
- Categories serve particular functions
- Categories become entrenched in practice
- Categories are never final

The relevance of these admonishments to our research is dual. When we explore judges' discursive actions in making judicial decisions, we need to categorize what judges do. Again, the judicial behavior by judges is also an act of categorizing the legal world. In this sense our research is to categorize categorizing work. But before we elaborate our categorizing framework, it will be instructive to make a critical comparison among SAT, EST and LA. SAT sets out with the philosophical concern of utterance meaning. So its categorization is basically semantic as it relies mainly on the different meanings of performative verbs. EST instead approaches discursive actions from the grammatical perspective by modeling the structure of language above the level of sentence. LA addresses discursive actions in terms of cultural practices such as telling a story, asking for a favor, greeting, showing respect, praying, giving directions, reading, insulting, praising, arguing in court, making a toast, or explaining a political agenda:

Table 3-2 The Comparison of Three Discursive Action Theories

	SAT	EST	LA
Perspective	Semantic	Structural	Cultural
Purposes	Philosophical understanding of language use	Grammatical description of discourse	Social account of human behavior

The comparison indicates that categorizing is theory-specific. Discursive actions can be approached from different perspectives and consequently different criteria are involved. Given our interest in judicial behavior, an anthropological perspective will serve our purpose best. However, the relevance of SAT and EST to our DP study of judges' judicial discourse is also immediate, for they provide the necessary theoretical reference for a linguistic account of judicial discourse. This linguistic analysis makes it possible to construe the judicial behavior since both "performance" and "participation" is indexed through language.

Following LA, there are two central issues concerned with the characterization of discursive actions:

(1) How is a discursive action functionally related to the institutional setting in which it occurs?

For LA, the nature of a discursive action is defined by the interactional and structural slot it occupies. Such a slot can be conceived as, in Bourdieu's

(1985) term, the location in the field. It is the field that provides the reference frame for a discursive action. This frame is not such as is stipulated in laws or proposed by the theoretical analysts. Instead it is a product of the discourse actions. So the first step for our analysis is to see what frames judges are oriented to in their discursive actions. This often relies on our understanding of the structure of the whole discourse. In this regard, EST can provide a useful tool in identifying how the participants take part in the transaction by negotiating exchanges, moves and acts.

(2) What discursive resources are available to judges in terms of their participant roles?

Our study of JJB is by nature to characterize judges' habitus (Bourdieu, 1985) in the judicial setting. Habitus is the function of peoples' disposition which is in turn the inculcation of objective social structure of the field into the subjective, mental experience of agents. The participants' habitus is manifested in their accessibility to specific discourse resources. Thus, examining the categorization and distribution of judges' discursive actions is essential to gain insights into their habitus. To do so, we can find much theoretical support from SAT and EST. For example, directive is a type of speech act which is often found in judges' judicial discourse. When it is used to coordinate the courtroom interaction, the authoritative role is made relevant by the judge. In this way, judges' habitus can be revealed by examining the distribution of the speech acts they use.

3.4.2 Identifying Identity

3.4.2.1 Conceptualizing Identity

Identity is a keyword appearing in various social sciences and humanities. However, there is no unified way to conceive it. In cognitive psychology it is treated as "the project of the self". In constructivist social theories, identity is considered as a discursive construction intersubjectively produced in social activities. In researching social behavior, DP also focuses on identity. However, DP takes a dialectic view of identity. That is, identity is both the tool for and achievement in social practice (Antaki & Widdicombe, 1998). That is, identity links both the distal and proximate contexts (Antaki & Widdicombe, 1998) and addresses both the structure and agency of social behavior. As Bucholtz & Hall (2005) points out, "identities encompass macro-level demographic categories, temporary and interactionally specific stances and participant roles, and local, ethnographically emergent cultural positions". In this light, identity is a key concept that enables us to capture the dynamism of social behavior. It locates identity in the social activities as a public phenomenon (Benwell & Stokoe, 2006).

With this theoretical assumption, DP does not try to reveal the "real" identity of the participants through experiment or retrospective think-aloud. Instead, it studies the social interaction to see how people describe, negotiate and challenge their images and mental states to accomplish social interaction. What it highlights is the rhetorical and political interest in the construction of particular identity. This theoretical orientation also promotes discourse as a central theme in DP. This is the reason why DP heavily draws on discourse analysis for its analytic method. It is held that identities are linguistically indexed through labels, implicatures, stances, styles, or linguistic structures and systems. Generally, there are two discursive approaches to identity in DP (Benwell & Stokoe, 2006): one is based on ethnomethodology/conversation analysis which examines how identity is indexed in linguistic details of interaction and made relevant in the local settings. The sequences of conversation and the membership categorization devices are the major linguistic cues. The other approach attends to wider macrostructures and cultural-historical contexts after the poststructuralist paradigm in social sciences (Potter & Wetherell, 1987). Discourse is connected with the wider systems through identity as the "interpretative repertoires" and "subject positions" (Wetherell, 1998). This approach is typically practiced in the school of discourse studies known as critical discourse analysis (Fairclough, 1995).

We argue that these two discursive approaches to identity are in fact complementary. CA-based approach can not purely rely on the identity categories that participants explicitly refer to in discourse and CDA can not come up with an identity category out of the blue. The two approaches can work in combination to address different levels of identity. CA can illuminate the analysis of identity performance with linguistic delicacy while CDA can expand our scope by bringing in a broader socio-cultural context.

3.4.2.2 Taxonomizing Identities

According to the association with discursive resources, identity can be generally categorized into two types:

1) Structure-generated identities

Structure-generated identity is a discourse property related to the structural development of social activities. A participant involved in a discourse activity will inhabit one or more roles, such as questioner-answerer, requester-replier and so on. Any stretch of talk is uttered as a response to what has come before and as anticipation for what will come next. This suggests that the structure orientation typically displays the sense that the participant makes of his or her own status in the participation framework. Therefore, close attention to this structural development provides one important juncture for examining identities.

Within the slot of each structural position, there is also a minute distinction of identity that discourse participants orient to. This is well captured in the concept of "footing" of participants in Goffman's (1981) frame theory. Footing is a concept to capture the positioning or alignment that the participant takes in performing a discursive action. According to the participation status, three distinct participant roles are identified: author, animator and principal. This distinction is significant in construing the nature of a discursive action, for it suggests the ideological stance that the participant takes.

2) Category-bound identities

Discursive approach to identity generally holds that participants' orientation to their identities is manifested in the details of their verbal conduct. Linguistic categories such as person reference, lexical choice and grammatical choice are often associated with the participants' identity orientation (Drew & Sorjonen, 1997). A given identity category in turn conveys certain beliefs, feelings and obligations normatively. According to Sacks (1992), much of the knowledge that people deploy in social actions is stored in these categories. Therefore, through an examination of those category-bound identities, the epistemological ground of discursive actions can be revealed.

3. 4. 3 Configurating Judicial Discourse Order

Our DP approach to judicial behavior is to explore how such judicial issues as facticity, justice, rationality and legitimacy are managed by analyzing judges' judicial discourse. The central issue is"order of discourse" (Fairclough, 1992), i. e. how different discursive actions are structured in a specific way to accomplish a legal activity. To explicate this, we need to address two issues: what discursive actions are articulated and how. The characterization of discursive actions will be further elaborated by an analysis of judges' identity performance. According to Zimmerman (1998: 88), "participants' orientation to this or that identity-their own and others'-is a crucial link between interaction on concrete occasions and encompassing social orders. "Thus, identity opens a channel to understand the judicial order underscoring JJB. Following this theoretical insight, the theoretical framework proposed for our research can be fashioned in the following diagram:

According to this framework, an exploration into judges' judicial behavior begins with the characterization of discursive actions. This involves explicating the framing and categorization of actions. Specifically, the questions to address include what discursive categories are employed and how discursive actions are sequentially and hierarchically structured. With these characterizations, we will

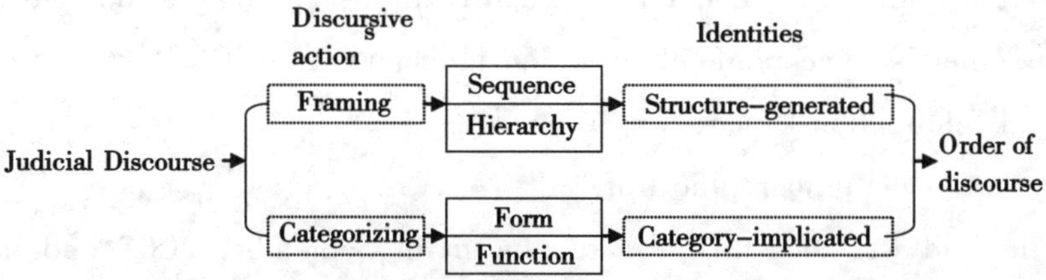

Figure 3-3 A DP-based Framework for Exploring JJB

further explore the identities that judges assume as indexed in their discursive actions. The configuration of these identities will help configure the "order of discourse" (Fairclough, 1992) which constitutes the knowledge for judges' judicial behavior. To summarize it, our discursive approach to judges' judicial behavior is to examine how judges exhibit their reflexive understanding of the judicial process in which they are engaged.

3.5 Method

This book conducts an empirical DP research of JJB. The three ethnometho-dological principles are observed (Wooffitt & Clark, 1998: 107):

> *First, the data are naturally occurring, not artifacts of contrived laboratory arrangements. Second, analysis focuses on the socially organized inferential processes through which people themselves orient to the relevance of categorizations of self and others. Thirdly* [sic], *these studies are rigorously empirical, in that analysis is not motivated by theory, intuition or a priori assessments of significance of events represented in the data.*

3.5.1 Dataset

This research uses triangulated data which come from two sources. One is the ethnographic data collected through field observations in the courtroom and the other is some randomly-sampled judgments from CLIPS (the Corpus for Legal Information Processing System①).

3.5.1.1 Ethnographic Data

The field work for this research began in September 2007 and lasted until September 2008. During this time, 19 civil trials were observed with permission from the court. They took place in two courts of different levels. One was local and the other intermediary in two different cities of Guangdong province. These court trials were totally convenience sampled, i.e. our participation depended only on the permission arrangement with the judges.

The observations were made by the author as an audience. The proceedings were recorded with permission. Restricted by the courtroom disciplines, the author only kept retrospective notes after each observation.

Due to the limited information we could have about the case proceedings and the emergent nature of the judicial process, not all the cases we chose to observe were of much academic significance. Among the 19 trials, 9 were only partialy observed. That is, they were the continued sessions of previous trials that I had not observed or were adjourned in the half, with no follow-up information available. This was due partly to the complexity of the cases and partly to the institutional management. We noted that judges, particularly those sitting in the intermediary courts, were often appointed to sit in several courts during a day and they had to set strict time limit for each case. It was often the case that the time ran up while disputes were still going on and the judges had to cram or adjourn the trial in the midway. These patched trials were mostly excluded from my detailed transcription and analysis (only few were used as the complementary data). So altogether 10 cases consisted of the

① This corpus was developed in Guangdong University of Foreign Studies, consisting of various genres of legal discourse.

main body of our ethnographic data[①](for general information about the case, please refer to Appendix 1).

3.5.1.2 Corpus Data

Our research also extracted 10 trial judgments from CLIPS. As is already mentioned in the Introduction, DP prefers ethnographic data. DP practitioners normally situate themselves in the ethnography of communication framework, collecting, transcribing, analyzing, and presenting only recorded social interaction. The reason for us to use corpus data arose out of two considerations. Firstly, judgments, particularly final judgments, were not available in our ethnographic observations. It was more often than not that judges passed delayed judgments. This posed a big challenge for the researchers to trace the following-up development of the cases. We only observed two cases in which the judgments were passed right after the hearing on evidence presentation. Secondly, judgments constitute a rather independent juncture of JJB which can be examined on its own. In fact, the traditional study of JJB has almost exclusively focused on the judgments. Although written discourse is rarely taken as the objects for research in DP, it is not exceptional. For example, the study of written judicial judgments has already been done into judges' judicial decisions on child sexual abuse (MacMartin, 1999; MacMartin & Wood, 2005; Wood & MacMartin, 2007). It has also been noted that the construction of monologues relies on the same linguistic resources as those used in conversational turns (Antaki, 1994).

Among our data, 5 cases were concerned with torts, 2 intellectual property, 2 contracts and 1 divorce (see Appendix Ⅰ for general information).

3.5.2 Data Analysis

There is no standard format for data analysis in DP. It depends on the

---

① However, the retrospective notes were not limited to the eight cases.

data and questions being asked (Potter & Hepburn, 2005). Since our research is exploratory in nature, and we aim to offer a new perspective into JJB, we set off our research agenda with an ethnographic observation of the judicial process. The data analysis was executed in two stages: firstly, the ethnographic data was analyzed to gain an initial understanding of the features of judges' judicial discourse. Our focus will be on the categorization of discursive actions; secondly, the identities that are manifested in judges' discursive actions will be identified. The relation between discourse and identity will lay down the basis for the ontological construal of JJB.

3.5.2.1 Transcription

Transcription of the recorded courtroom interaction was carried out by the researcher directly from the digital record. We made use of the software Total Recorder Editor 8.5 to facilitate simple repeated listenings and timing of pauses. The transcription system used in this research was developed after that by Gail Jefferson (2004), with some modifications to accommodate Chinese language (See Appendix Ⅱ). For the convenience of representation, the dialects used in the court were translated into standard Chinese, only marked with notations when it was relevant in our analysis.

3.5.2.2 Categorical Analysis

The first phase of analysis was to identify the discursive categories which indexed the frames judges oriented to and the actions that they undertook. We took individual cases as the unit of analysis (Conley & O'Bar, 1990; Wetherell, 2007). An initial conceptualization (or pilot study) of the data was developed by making line-by-line reading of transcriptions of three recorded trials without imposing a priori categories. We then created mini-frameworks, or diagrams that illustrated the relationships among categories and subcategories. These mini-frameworks served as our frame of reference so that we could elaborate and refine our insights and subject the broader collection of data to close intensive reflection and analysis. Since our research was cross-case analysis (Babbie, 2005), we had to map our concepts which emerged from pondering over different cases. The small sample from which the original features were isolated obviously could not contain all discursive features relevant to JJB, and we expected modifications were necessary when further data were compared to the initial frame of reference. Throughout the analysis, the observation notes were also sorted and categorized into themes arising in the analysis of transcribed data.

During the first phase, the features identified were still considered very tentative. However, the findings laid ground for our second phase, the substantive data analysis. Particularly, the coding scheme derived from findings in the first phase could be applied to the whole set of data. In our research, the data were coded along three dimensions: event, action and identity. Event, which was used in a sense similar to transaction in Sinclair & Coulthard (1975), means the type of discursive activities that judges engaged in. There were actually some distinctive discursive events for decision making. For example, Carbaugh (1995) points out there are four discursive junctures relevant to judicial behavior:

> (1) *The event or incident of a breach or violation occurs.*
>
> (2) *This is followed by a discourse which publicizes the violation, thus ratifying it socially as a crisis, with various social relations being formed in the process.*
>
> (3) *The crisis is responded to in some ways, with the responses involving various types of remedial discourses as efforts to redress the violating incident (s).*
>
> (4) *The redressive actions may or may not suffice, resulting in some sort of social reintegration, or a recycling of violations, creating continual social division or schism.*

These four junctures constitute the reference for us to analyze the frame and structure of judicial discourse. With this frame, discursive actions and identities could be classified. Discursive actions were defined in our research in terms of the functions specific to the interactional frame in the judicial process. In so doing, four general types were found: coordinative (relating to the behaviors of managing the courtroom interaction), inquisitive (seeking information), representative (determining the issue of facticity) and attributive (resolving legal consequence). Identity was coded in line with Zimmerman (1998) who holds that there are three levels of identity assumed simultaneously by the interactants: discourse identity, situational identity and transportable identity. In making this categorization, we observe the five general principles that are favored by DP practitioners (Antaki & Widdicombe, 1998), and transformed them into five guiding questions:

1) What characteristics or features are associated with the identity category?

2) How is an identity occasioned or indexed?

3) Is it made relevant or oriented to by the judge?

4) Is it consequential upon the judicial process?

5) How does it fit into the larger discourse structure?

It must be emphasized that our analysis was only concentrated on the features that were palpable in our sampled judges' discourse. We did not attempt to make exhaustive descriptions of judges as a whole. Judges' discursive features from these data could only be used as illustrations of possible strategies and conditions under which judicial justice is performed.

3.5.2.3 Interpretative Analysis

Identifying and categorizing judges' discursive actions was implemented with a view to arriving at an interpretative account of judges' behavior. This was a theme shared with most judges' behavior research. But the way we approached it was different from others. In cognitive psychology, judges' judicial behavior was accounted for by developing models or theories which were postulated to capture the underlying cognitive process in the judges' mind. DP, however, takes a discursive and functional approach by focusing on the way accountability or attribution is managed by the participants. This approach is based on the recognition of the pragmatic nature of all social behavior. That is, we must first of all hold accountable for own actions:

> *Within a discursive psychology of attribution, the current speaker's accountability for what is said, in terms of such talk's occurrence within an interaction sequence, comes before issues of accountability in the report itself.*
>
> (Edwards & Potter, 1993: 25)

This suggest that, for a DP study of JJB, the major issue is how judges account for their own discursive actions rather than the legal issues that judges account for. For example, to address how judges took certain case accounts as legal facts, our focus was on the way judges justify their particular decision rather than the cognitive process that such a decision was derived. To do so, we drew on Goffman's notion of"footing". It is argued that "footing plays a central part in accountability" (Edwards & Potter, 1993). Footing is a configuration of the participants' discourse status or their identity. Therefore, to account for JJB, we need to relate their discursive actions to their identities. Identity is the central concept to unravel the discourse order of judicial process.

Thus, our interpretation of JJB is made by examining judges' identity performance and its implications on judicial consequences. We will explore the potential repertoire of judges' identity in performing different judicial actions. This study also implies a comparison of judges' identity orientation across cases. That is, we will relate judges' identity performance to categories of discursive actions and types of case. We are interested not only in the general patterns of JJB but also in the deviations which are often ignored in traditional cognitive psychology. Deviations often give rise to legal as well as social disputes. We argue that it is these deviations that constitute the junctures where judges' agency plays the most critical role. So they are a fertile area for the research of JJB. In this line, what is construed in our research is not the marco order of the judicial discourse abstracted by the research. Instead, what we present is the personal order (Wetherell, 2007) of judges in particular judicial process.

Finally, the ontological ground of judges' personal order will be discussed in relation to Heideggerian philosophy. The reason for this philosophical account is that our discursive approach to JJB is fundamentally in line with the linguistic turn for which we can find theoretical source in Heidegger's Theory of Being. The whole research will be rounded up with a discussion on how a discursive approach bears on such judicial practice as well as research in JJB.

Chapter 4

Discursive Enactment of Judges' Judicial Behavior

4.1 Introduction

This chapter examines what discursive actions are enacted in judicial behavior. It is concerned with the array of discourse resources that are available to judges. We firstly examine the patterns and categories that judges' discourse falls into. The generic structure of the courtroom interaction is mapped out based on what judges orient to. This offers the frame of reference for our identification of judges' discursive actions. Secondly, the varying discursive realizations of those actions are discussed in terms of their legal consequences.

4.2 Framing Judicial Trial

Research of courtroom discourse has shown that there is "a set of behavioral norms and rules" (Elwork et al., 1981) specific to the courtroom setting. They constitute a "forensic schema" (Liao 2003) or a trial frame. The realness of this frame is manifested in judges' "script formulation"①(Edwards, 1994) which, as we observed, was often explicitly articulated:

Extract 1 (Case 10)

Judge: This court session will proceed at three stages. The first is the court investigation. The second is court debate. After the debate--, the court will try the conciliation > if possible <. If it fails, a judicial judgment will be served according to the law.

The performative effect of this frame, however, lay not just in this pronouncement. Its relevance was more often seen in judges' acts which attempted to maintain the frame throughout the courtroom trial:

Extract 2 (Case 1)

Judge: Now we proceed to court investigation: : . The focus of the court investigation is the facts that both parties are disputing over. The party: : who puts forward claims has the responsibility to produce evidence and shall specify his argument, when raising objections ↑.

Extract 3 (Case 4)

Judge: The court debate is over. Now both parties make your final statements.

Actions like these served to set the boundaries between different phases of the judicial phases. These boundaries framed the judicial interaction. Every segment within the frame was filled with rather distinctive discursive events. From all the cases we observed, judges almost unexceptionally oriented to a frame which consisted of five component episodes: preparation, opening statement, evidence examination, closing argument and judgment/conciliation.

As is shown in Figure 4-1, within each block, there was also a tangible sub-frame. From the perspective of DP, our focus is on how frame setting

---

① It refers to the discourse instances which describe actions and events as routine or expectable.

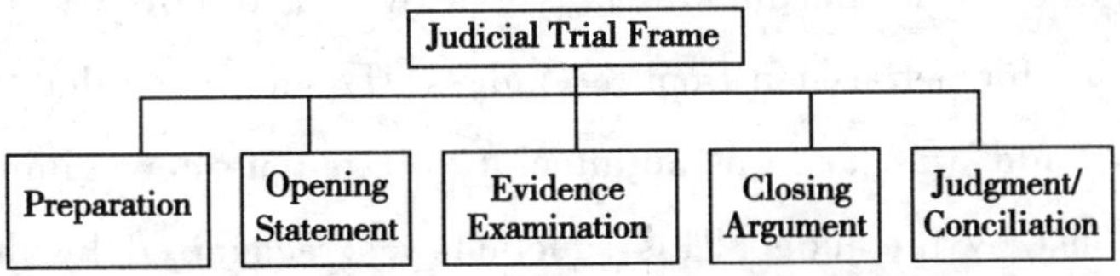

Figure 4-1 Judicial Trial Frame

became an interactional business that was consequential on the judicial performance. For example, in the preparation stage, the judges evoked a "gate-keeping" frame in which who was eligible to appear in the court was negotiated and decided. The declaration frame was offset to introduce the opening statements so that the issues could be brought forward. Evidence examination mainly fell within the frame of demonstration-challenge. The confrontational frame was evident in the closing argument. The verdictive frame capsulated the delivery of final judgment. This observation, of course, is not new or exclusive to our DP approach. What we intend to address is not the deduction of the frames. Such frames are actually explicitly defined in the law (e. g. the Organization Law of the People's Republic of China). What we aim to show is how the orientation to or deviation from the frames became a consequential issue in the judicial process. The focus is on how judges managed it as part of their judicial decision. This can be illustrated in the following example in which the frame became the ground for judges to sanction the contribution of the lawyer:

Extract 4 (C. O. 1)

(1:00)

PL: Judge? °I have one more point to add.

Judge: Now you can ask questions. If you do not have any, you may make your comments later.

PL: =Sure, >I want to ask<Mrs Zhang ** , er, --

...

This exchange took place within the witness examination session. Preceding this exchange was a lapse of one minute after the plaintiff lawyer asked some questions. The plaintiff lawyer in turn 1 ventured to resume her floor by asking for permission from the judges. Her utterance that"I have one more point to add"was taken as an attempt to articulate her opinion and was guarded against by the judge. This sanction was recognized by the plaintiff lawyer in the form of a quick acknowledgment (= Sure) and echoing reformulation (>I want to ask<).This exchange shows that a frame of witness examination was shared and oriented to by both of them. This frame had also a direct impact on the upcoming discourse actions on the part of the PL. The hesitation after PL's echoing reformulation indicates she was adjusting or changing her pursuit in this turn.

The analysis above also shows that it was the judge that enjoyed the dominant power in the negotiation of the frame. He exercised the discretion over what to include/exclude within the frame. It was in junctures like this that judges were prominent as the decision makers. One significant theoretical implication of this initial observation is that the frames oriented to in the courtroom interaction shaped the discursive actions that the participants undertook. Therefore, it is necessary to construe judges' discourse practice by examining the process of frame setting. In the remaining parts of this chapter, we will present our findings on the categories and features of judges' discursive actions in relation to the frames that judges constructed collaboratively with litigants.

4.3 Judges' Discursive Actions

This part examines judges' discursive actions that were constitutive of their judicial behavior. There are two issues involved in categorizing discursive actions. One is what discursive actions were articulated and the other is how. The former is related to the activities that judges participated. According to the frames that judicial trials normally fell into, we find that judges mainly did four things in the trial: coordinating, inquiring, representing and attributing. Therefore, we classify judges' discursive actions into four correspondent categories. The second issue involved in judicial behavior research is how the discursive actions were articulated. This again involves two perspectives: descriptive and interpretative. That is, we shall describe what discursive resources judges used to perform the actions on the one hand and examine how judges accounted for their actions on the other. In this chapter, we will present the descriptive analysis of judges' judicial discourse. The issue of accountability will be treated in the next two chapters.

4. 3. 1 Coordinative

Coordinative was the type of judges' discursive actions which addressed the order of the courtroom. It was physically embodied in the courtroom seating chart-the judge sat behind a raised desk while the plaintiff, the defendant, and their respective counsels were on the two front sides respectively. They formed an isosceles triangle with the judge's seat on the top. The judge assumed the role of intermediary who coordinated and made possible smooth interactions between the litigants. In this research, the discursive actions judges undertook to facilitate the courtroom activities were collectively called coordinatives.

Coordinatives were directive in terms of their illocutionary force (Searle, 1969). That is, they functioned to regulate the behavior of attendants in the court. Since the judicial practice was highly institutionalized, coordinatives were often formulaic in expression, although with variation. We note that the judges in the trial process frequently enacted three forms of coordinatives.

4. 3. 1. 1 Rule Instruction

Judicial trials normally began with rule instruction by the judge, occasionally also done by the court reporter. The dos and don'ts were enunciated to ensure the implementation of a proper procedure for the ongoing trial:

Extract 5 (Case 1)

Judge: According to the Civil Procedure Law, the litigants enjoy the following rights:

1. to present and examine evidence;

2. to argue over the controversial matters and plead for conciliation by the court;

3. to add, relinquish or modify his claims, for the plaintiff, and to rebut or file counter claims, for the defendant;

4. to make final statements.

In the course of trial, the litigants shall also fulfill the following obligations:

1. to abide by the laws and not abuse their litigation rights;

2. to follow the court instructions and disciplines;

3. to state only facts.

The above excerpt was pragmatically a "declaratory act"① (Liao, 2003) to forestall possible disorder in the judicial process. This coordinative action is specified and required in the procedural law. However, it could be performed in various discourse forms. For example, in the following case, the judge implemented a question to check the litigants' knowledge about those rules without bothering with the details.

Extract 6 (C. O. 3)

Judge: Then, have you read about the litigants'rights and obligations? (0. 2) [Are you all clear about them?]

PL: =[We have.]

This confirmatory question was a surrogate for the declaratory act to ensure that those rules were well understood by the litigants. Discursive actions like

① It is translated into English by the author of this thesis from "宣布性的话语行为" by Liao (2003: 94).

this were normally found in those cases in which both parties were represented by the lawyers. We note that judges might well opt to abbreviate or omit this action unless they perceived that it was necessary to implement it. That is, rules could be flexibly introduced to serve specific interactional purposes. For example, in the following excerpt, the judge interrupted the side talk by exercising his role of rule instructor:

Extract 7 (C. O. 2)

(Some audience are whispering.)

Judge: Stop talking. Sit and listen. No talking.

Rule instruction was the main discourse resource for judges to steer or maneuver the course of judicial process. Such actions enabled judges to solicit, guide and sanction the behavior of other attendants in the courtroom. The combination of rule instruction with other actions was an ostensible orientation by the judge to bringing into play rules that justify or support their actions:

Extract 8 (Case 1)

Judge: ① The court investigation is over. ② Now we proceed to court debate. (0. 3)

③ In the debate, both parties shall concentrate your comments on the controversial issues on the basis of evidence and law. ④ No personal or insulting remarks are allowed. Now the plaintiff can express your opinions.

In terms of textual pragmatics, this move was a macro-action (van Dijk, 1977) to facilitate the transition of trial proceedings. We can delineate the extracted stretch of discourse into four micro-actions. Each action was correspondent with one sentence. The first one, which declared the end of court investigation session, was *preparatory*; the second, which started the new session (Now we proceed to court debate.), was *essential*; the third, which was an instruction of rules, constituted an *auxiliary* action; the final was another auxiliary action which selected the turn for the plaintiff. This analysis suggests that rule instruction was not a display of judicial dogmatic formality but a discursive resource that judges can draw on to facilitate their other discursive actions on various substantial issues.

4. 3. 1. 2 Turn Control

Turn control was the most straightforward way for judges to engage the participants in an ordered activity frame. One of the most significant features of courtroom interaction was its turn taking system (Atkinson & Drew, 1979). In our analysis, we find that a mediated turn taking system was dominantly observed in the courtroom interaction. It could be graphed as follows:

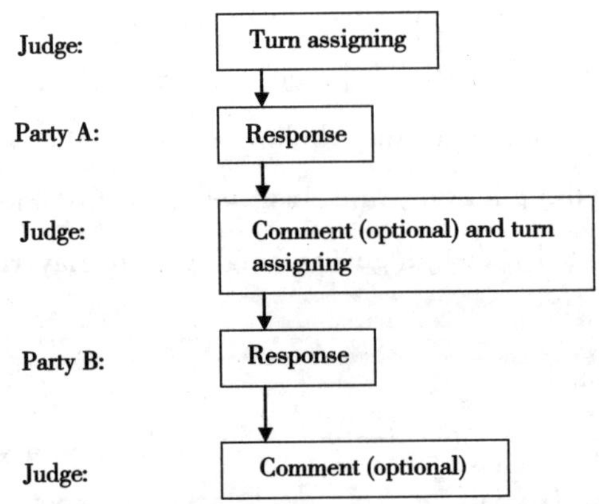

Figure 4-2 Mediated Turn-taking System in the Courtroom Interaction

As we can see, the judge mediated every question or answer by the litigant party. With this system, judges were able to maintain a strict control over the courtroom agenda. This function was made particularly prominent in court debate, the juncture where the litigants were legally supposed to enjoy the greatest freedom to interact with their counterpart.

Extract 9 (Case 1)

1. Judge: The court investigation is over. Now we proceed to court debate. (0. 3)

In the session, both parties shall concentrate your comments on the controversial issues on the base of evidence and law. No personal or insulting remarks are allowed. Now the plaintiff can raise your argument.

2. Plaintiff: (abridged)

3. Judge: The defendant's argument.

4. Defendant: (abridged)

5. Judge: Now proceed to the second-round debate. Has the plaintiff got any new point to add?

6. Plaintiff: (abridged)

7. Judge: Has the defendant got any new point to add?

8. Defendant: (abridged)

9. Judge: The last round debate. Has the plaintiff still got any new point to add?

10. Plaintiff: The defendant, do you think that the plaintiff's claim is legitimate and reasonable?

11. Defendant: The plaintiff's claim is not legally justified.

12. Plaintiff: Our claim is based on Term 11 of Supreme People's Court Interpretation on the Matters of Law Application Trial of Personal Injury Compensation Cases.

13. Defendant: You should have presented any evidence that could prove the existence of employment relationship between Mr. Wang * * and our party.

14. Plaintiff: We ARE grounded on facts. -

15. Judge: = Does the plaintiff have any new argument?

16. Plaintiff: No.

17. Judge: Does the defendant have any new argument?

18. Defendant: No.

19. Judge: The Debate is over. ...

During the debate, the turns of party A and Party B should have formed an adjacency pair. However, it turned out in the above extract that the judge intervened as the turn selector and the debaters had to respond to the judges' initiation in their debate. When the debate finally fell into a confrontation (from turn 10 to turn 14), the judge interrupted them (turn 15) and brought it to a halt. Turn 15 was significant as an action of turn control in this juncture, for it served as an interactional rather than informational question and cut short the plaintiff's turn in 14. By asking whether he had any new argument to make here, the judge implied that the previous free debate was not to the point or it was not appropriate to carry it on. This was acknowledged by both parties and they stopped the debate.

In our research, we noted that the self-initiated turn selection by the litigants was often subject to the judges' approval or sanction. That is, for the litigants, the participation in the interactional process was appropriate only when permitted by the judge. Lets' take the following excerpt as one example:

Extract 10 (C. O. 1)

(1: 00)

1. PL: Judge? °I have one more point to add°.

2. Judge: Now you can only ask questions. If you do not have any, you may make your comments later.

3. PL: =Sure, >I want to ask< Mrs Zhang * * , er, --

By asking for permission in turn 1, PL explicitly oriented to the frame of judges' turn control. In the response, the judge set a condition for PL's subsequent turn. This indicates that the turn control could also shape the interactional contribution from the selected participant.

Another indication of judges' turn control was the frequent occurrences of interruption by the judges. Judges enjoyed a great freedom or power to give or take the interactional turns. If the recipients did not follow their direction, the judge might contravene to interrupt or stop it. This is possibly the reason why trial discourses are not counted as conversation by Levinson (1983) .

4. 3. 1. 3 Topic Management

During the trial, the judges could also manage the subject matters or steer the information flow in the courtroom interaction. Such coordinative actions were usually performed through two speech acts:

a) Directive

The judges often coordinated the courtroom interaction by giving directions to inform litigants of what was proper or desirable.

Extract 11 (Case 1)

Judge: Does the plaintiff have any question to ask the witness? Witness shall answer questions related to the case but can refuse to answer irrelevant questions.

Here the judge advised what the witness "should" and "may" do in the proceeding. Like rule instruction, this action had much to do with the legal requirements. In other words, Extract 11 was a legally based coordinative, for what it addressed was the legal rights and obligations of the witness. However, it differed from the rule instruction in that it addressed specific matters. In the above extract, the intended purpose of the coordinative action was to extract needed answer from the witness. This can be illustrated with a further extract:

Extract 12 (Case 1)

Judge: According to Article 64 of the Civil Procedure Law, a party shall have the responsibility to provide evidence in support of his own claims. When providing evidence, you shall indicate its source, identification, content and the argument to make. The counterpart shall focus on its facticity, relevance, legitimacy and the potential capacity to prove when you challenge, elaborate or refute the evidence. Are you clear?

This was a direction on raising evidence and making argument. It informed the litigants how to participate in the said discursive activity. Different from rule instruction, what was involved in this discursive action was not the constitutive rule (Searle, 1969) of the activity. That is, if the litigants did not follow the direction, their actions would still be regarded as raising evidence and making argument. The point of making this directive action was intended for the categorization-(Amsterdam & Bruner, 2000) or rule-(Conley & O'Bar, 1990) oriented nature of law. To put it simply, the judge was acting to ensure that the litigants' discourse could meet the paradigmatic requirement of the law. This pragmatic intention was corroborated by the observed fact that directive coordinatives were mostly used when the plaintiffs or defendants were less educated or non-legal professionals.

Efficiency is another major concern when judges evoked directive coordinatives:

Extract 13 (Case 1)

Judge: The focus of court investigation is the issues over which both parties are disputing.

Extract 14 (Case 1)

Judge: Ok. (0. 2) The court investigation is over. (0. 5) Now proceed to the court debate. Both parties, uh (0. 2), shall raise your arguments over the disputed issues. Special emphasis shall be laid onwhether there was a causal relationbetween the defendant and the death of the victim, *** or focus on what kind of causal relation. Let's start with the plaintiff.

In both extracts, the judges requested the litigants to concentrate the debate on the disputed issues. Moreover, the judge in the second extract also specified what was important. That is, the judge was calling the litigants' attention to what was relevant or significant to the judicial decision. By doing so, the judge forestalled unnecessary prolongation of the proceeding. This action was by nature a revelation of judges' evaluative stances on case facts. Given the high stake of judges' attitudes on case facts, this directive act had a direct bearing on the litigants' behavior. That is, the litigants more often than not observed this directive. Directives served as an important tool for judges to ensure an efficient and smooth judicial process.

b) Persuasive

To facilitate the operation of the judicial process, judges also needed to elicit the cooperation from the litigants. This normally occurred when an interactional issue arose due to the attitude or position of the litigants. One juncture of particular interest was the judges' different approaches in conducting conciliation session. Our observation shows some judges would omit or mention the conciliation in passing while others would get out of their way to persuade litigants into conciliation. The following is one typical example:

Extract 15 (Case 8)

Judge: The case has gone through court investigation, (0.2) court debate. (0.3) In the civil cases, the people's court shall conduct conciliation on the voluntary and lawful basis. We hope that two parties can understand and forgive for the sake of harmony and the long term interest and reach an agreement under the court's auspice based on the facts and the realist principle. Do the plaintiff and the defendant agree to enter the conciliation?

In this extract, before asking for the litigants' positions on the invocation of the reconciliation procedure, the judge first explained the legal principle on it and then made a moral reasoning over the case. Thus, the persuasive orientation of the judge was evident. The judges made an ostensible effort to urge the plaintiff and the defendant to reach a conciliatory agreement.

The coordinative discursive actions could be taken as the metadiscourse (Hyland, 2005) of the courtroom interaction, which regulated the court interaction. Through coordinative actions, judges maintained the interaction order of the court. However, articulating coordinative actions *per se* involved series of decision making. By examining the coordinative discursive actions, we reveal the diversity of judges' concerns in their judicial behavior.

4.3.2 Inquisitive

By inquisitive, we refer to the discursive actions which were intended to elicit information. One basic judicial principle is that judges shall "base their decision making on facts". Although the law stipulates that the responsibility of fact finding lies in the claimant in the civil courts, it is actually a common practice for judges to inquire into the cases in order to arrive at more informed judicial judgments. Judges' judicial inquiry could take place at any judicial phase. Legal fact inquiry can be interruptions during (cross-) examination or debate, clarification after presentation, or sometimes independent.

Our exploration of judges' inquisitive draws on current studies of lawyers' examination. So far, we have already had extensive literature on the lawyers' inquisitive techniques in bringing out the intended answers from the witness (Danet & Kermish, 1978; Harris, 1984; Philips, 1984; Woodbury, 1984; Drew, 1985; Walker, 1987; Drew, 1992; Matoesian, 1993; Conley and O'Barr, 1998; Berk-Seligson, 1999; Rigney, 1999; Ehrlich, 2001; Cotterill, 2003; Gniscia & Pontecorvo, 2004; Matoesian, 2005; Aldridge & Luchjenbroers, 2007). Although the different roles between judges and lawyers may lead to different styles in their inquisitive actions, the theoretical approach and analytical methods in approaching lawyers' inquisitives are illuminative to the study of judges' inquiry. Gibbons (2003) characterizes inquisitive acts along two dimensions in terms of coerciveness: modality parameter and information parameter. The former is related to the interpersonal imposition while the latter concerns the freedom in the choice of subject matter. It is found that the varying degrees of coercion are related to the lexico-grammatical forms used in inquisitive actions.

Following Gibbons (2003), a general survey of judges' inquisitive actions was made in this research (see Table 4-1). The arrangement of the table is made along an increasing order in terms of coercion. As we can see, judges' inquiry acts mostly fell within the less coercive range. Obviously, this finding is different from the situation about lawyers who use mostly the highly coercive leading questions (Matoesian, 1993). We also notice that judges used more imperatives than any other grammatical forms in their inquisitive actions. Imperative is typically used as a directive in terms of its illocutionary force and implies a higher level of interpersonal imposition than that of interrogative. This suggests that judges preferred interactional dominance to informational control. According to the degree of nature of coercion, we group those inquisitive actions into three categories, each of which will be elaborated in the following sections.

Table 4-1 **Judges' Inquisitive Actions①**

	Linguistic variety of inquisitive actions	Tokens in the data
1	Broad request for narrative	94
2	Limited request for narrative	90
3	"what" question without embedded information	1
4	"why" or "how" questions	16
5	Statement with rising intonation	18
6	Polar (yes/no) questions	62
7	Wh-questions with embedded information	66
8	Either/or questions with a vacant slot	0
9	Either/or questions	6
10	Statements with tags	7
11	Statement	2
12	Projected statement (questioner)	0
13	Projected statement (witness)	0
14	Agreement statements	0
15	Memory statements	0
Total		352

4.3.2.1 Requestion

Requestion is defined by Gibbons (2003) as a command which has a verbal response as its demanded action. The fabricated form of this word suggests that it can be in the form of either request or question. It is borrowed here to refer to the

① In this statistical analysis, we counted only the head actions in macro-actions.

discursive actions (types 1-3 in Table 4-1) which judges used to pursue information without specific informational presupposition. When the inquiry was enacted in the form of request, there were three discursive features:

a) Verbs of saying

Judges used expressions such as "express opinions" (as in 1.), "state opinions" (as in 2.), "specify" (as in 3.), etc. when asking for information. These "verbs of saying" (Levinson, 1983) were formal, demanding a solemn confession:

Extract 16 (Case 3)

1. Judge: Bailiff, please pass on to the plaintiff the evidence produced by the defendant. (5) The plaintiff, examine the evidence. (0. 2) The plaintiff, express your opinions on the evidence.

2. Judge: As to the definition of directly responsible persons, the defendant can state your opinion.

3. Judge: How was it transferred? Which document? Please specify.

By using the verbs of saying, the judges requested a verbal response rather than the specific substantial information.

b) YOU-structure

When judges inquired the cases, they often did not directly address the targeted persons. Instead, they used a YOU-structure which enabled the judge to appear neutral:

Extract 17 (Case 6)

1. Judge: Now the court proceeds to investigation session. (0. 2) Firstly, (0. 1) let the plaintiff Mr. Zhao... state the reason of suing and his claims. Case 8

2. Judge: As to the first disputed issue, i. e. whether the disputed properties are Mr. Li's heritage after his death, firstly let the plaintiff make his statement and produce evidence

3. Judge: Next, let the plaintiff specify his claims and briefly remark on the reasons for the litigation.

YOU-structure consists of "YOU+agent+verb". It is semantically equal to "have something done by somebody", expressing a passive voice (Zhang, 2004). Such a structure implies a less personal involvement in the inquiring interaction on the part of judge.

c) Embedded questions

The third feature associated with the inquisitive action was that questions were often embedded as the objects of imperative predicates:

Extract 18 (Case 6)

1. Judge: The defendant, state the ground on which you claim that the plaintiff is the other directly responsible person.

2. Judge: The defendant, please state the ground to make the sued decision.

As these two extracts show, the judges' questions were embedded as the complements to their coordinative actions. Such a discursive structure integrated the imperative mood into the interrogative one. In this way, the discursive action transformed the question into a request. This indicates that judges' inquisitive relied more on interpersonal imposition than informational control.

Besides the imperative requests, judges' inquiry also made use of "real" questions (Stokoe & Edwards, 2008).

Extract 19

1. Judge: Does the defendant have any evidence or not? Case 1

2. Judge: Plaintiff, what evidence do you have to present to the court? Case 2

3. Judge: Does the defendant have any question to ask on the witness? Case 1

3. Judge: Both litigant parties can ask the witness if you have any question. Does the plaintiff have any question to ask? Case 9

4. Judge: Do both litigant parties have any factual information to add? Any new evidence to present? Case 5

5. Judge: Do both parties have any new argument? Case 9

In the above extract, we can find that the judges also used the forms of questions as we normally do in everyday life. However, compared with the questions by the lawyers (Danet & Kermish, 1978; Harris, 1984; Philips, 1984; Woodbury, 1984; Berk-Seligson, 1999; Rigney, 1999; Gniscia & Pontecorvo, 2004; Matoesian, 2005; Aldridge & Luchjenbroers, 2007), we found that judges' questions were overwhelmingly broad-ended. The typical syntactic structure was whether or wh-questions. Sometimes they were preceded by a declaratory statement as the starter and constituted the boundary moves in the trial exchange.

But the "real" questions were not purely used to elicit factual information. Among the 6 questions in Extract 19, 1 and 2 were used to elicit evidential presentation; 3 and 4 were articulated to invite litigants to examine evidence; and 5 and 6 were the closing remarks to end a session. This suggests that these utterances perform two discursive actions simultaneously, both as coordinative and as inquisitive. One that deserves attention is that a lot of personal opinion-seeking questions were also found in judges' discourse, even in the evidential phase when personal opinions were legally prohibited:

Extract 20 (Case 2)

Judge: The court will present a divorce agreement.

(the court reporter passed it to both parties in turn) (4)

Do both parties have any disagreement?

In this case, the material evidence was already in front of the judges. Thus, the judges' question was intended not for factual information but for the attitudes of the litigants towards the given evidence.

Even the information-seeking question could also differ in function. As Gibbons (2003) points out, a question can be used either to elicit unknown information or to confirm particular unverified information①.

① A similar distinction of police interviewing questions is made in Baldwin (1993). He refers to them respectively as pursuit of truth and pursuit of proof.

Extract 21 (Case 1)

Judge: Now the court will ask the litigants some questions. Both litigant parties shall give an honestanswer. (2) As to the fact that Wang ...was assigned to carry the wood by the village committee on February 28, 2007, do you have any objections?

Extract 22 (Case 5)

Judge: Now the court will ask both litigant parties some questions. Both litigant parties shall give an honest answer. (0.5) First, some questions for the plaintiff. Plaintiff, what is the size of the building land you applied for?

Plaintiff: 17 meters in length and 12 meters in width. Three *fen* in area.

In Extract 21, the judge's question had already contained the factual information. It was formulated to be challenged or confirmed by the litigant parties. The question in Extract 22 was, however, involved one specific item of unknown information.

All these data pointed to the fact that judges varied greatly in their orientation to inquiry. Although our data were not enough for a quantitative conclusion, the qualitative analysis does show that some judges abstained themselves from being involved in the disputes over case facts while others took advantage of almost every chance to lead in inquiry. It is shown that different judges in different trials might be interested in different information and elicited it with different discursive strategies. As further evidence of this kind will be revealed throughout this research, the analysis of judges' discursive actions presents a new perspective of the disparity in judicial behavior. Particularly, the discursive diversity helps to reveal how the judicial disparity is anchored in the judicial process.

4.3.2.2 Challenging

In the courtroom interaction, information provided by the confrontational parties of litigants can be authentic, partial or deceptive. Thus, judges needed to inquire for the purpose of authentification. One important strategy for this was to challenge the given information. In the study of lawyers' use of challenging or controlling questions, it is found that challenging questions mostly occurred in the cross-examination (Susan & Jack, 2006). It was usually linguistically realized in closed questions to undermine or disclose the assumptions or logic behind a version of events. Our research of JJB reveals that this type of discursive actions was also exploited by judges, although much lower in frequency. Some basic discursive strategies of lawyers were also applied to judges' discourse.

Extract 23 (Case 5)

1. Judge: The defendant, (0. 2) why did you build your house <u>on the land applied for by the plaintiff</u>?

2. Defendant: <I did it> for I had an agreement with the plaintiff.

3. Judge: Why didn't you apply for it on your own?

4. Defendant: My wife and I lived together with my sons in the rural area. (0. 2) I was qualified for application. But the village committee did not grant it. That was why I built my house on the agreement with the plaintiff.

This extract was taken from a case about a property dispute. The plaintiff sued to claim a building land that was applied for by him but used by the defendant. The defendant argued that the building land was applied for by him in the name of the plaintiff. Thus, the case was evolved around the ownership of the land. Obviously the defendant's argument appeared absurd at the first glance, for it was unusual to buy a property in the name of others. It was this abnormality that educed the challenging questions in turns 1 and 3. The challenging questions are "disaffiliative moves" (Halonen & Sorjonen, 2008; Heinemann, 2008; Monzoni, 2008) which aim to undermine the rationality of claimed arguments and convey a strong epistemic or evaluative stance (Koshik, 2003).

Different from lawyers, judges used much less the high control questions (Rigney, 1999). The judges' challenging questions were most frequently wh-questions with embedded information (66 tokens) and polar (yes/no) questions (62 tokens) (see Table 5-2). The other forms included "why" or "how" questions (16 tokens) and statement with rising intonation (18 tokens). This sort of questions was more useful to clarify rather than to undermine a given account of the case story. Judges seldom went out of the way to discredit witness's testimony. Instead, judges would choose to resort to their discretionary power when encountered with competing information. One illustration was the frequent acts to delay decision making over disputed issues in the judicial process.

4.3.2.3 Nailing down

To make a justified decision, it was sometimes necessary for judges to pin down a specific answer from the witness, normally by manipulating the witness's testimony. The discursive actions used for the purpose of manipulation are called "nailing down the answer" (ND) (Philips, 1998). They are collaboratively and interactively negotiated over sequential exchanges. Although this strategy is masterfully practiced in cross-examination by the lawyers (Matoesian, 2005), it was also found in judges' discourse of our data corpus.

Extract 24 (C.O.1)

1. Judge: The second question is concerned with the testament. Then, uh (0.2), when the will was drawn, were you on the scene?

2. Witness: (Signaling her inability to understand standard Chinese)

3. Judge: When the will was drawn, were you at the scene?

4. PL: (Translating it into Cantonese)

5. Witness: Yes

6. Judge: You were? >Who else?<

In this transaction of witness-examination, the judge first asked whether the witness was on the scene. When a positive answer was elicited, he followed up with another question to check who else was also there. The speeding up of the question made by the judge indicated that the judge was in a position to pin down an authentic answer. The design of the three consecutive questions showed that the judge was intentionally challenging the witness to ensure an honest answer.

Our findings resonate with Matoesian's (2005) argument that ND as a discursive action contextualizes identity, signals the participation framework and embodies the legal ideologies. For example, the judge in extract 24 built up his ND on the basis of the legal ideology that a will needs the signature of the testator and two witnesses. Besides this, we also noticed that judges' ND differed from that of the lawyers in other ways:

Extract 25 (Case 4)

1. Judge: On 21 when the plaintiff came to you, why didn't you refund him?

2. DL: Because the heel was worn out.

3. Judge: What does "worn out" mean?

4. DL: There are stripes on the heel.

5. Judge: How could the heel be worn out?

6. DL: Walking on the cement or uneven ground.

(turning to the plaintiff)

7. Judge: After buying the shoes, when did the plaintiff come for refunding?

8. Plaintiff: On the afternoon of the next day.

9. Judge: Did you try it on after you bought it?

10. Plaintiff: Walking a few steps for a try.

11. Judge: How did you discuss about the worn-out then?

12. Plaintiff: He said the heel was worn out. I asked on what criterion. He gave no answer.

13. Judge: Is it worn out or not on earth?

14. Plaintiff: It is hard to say. I do not know how we determine the worn-out.

The issue that this case involved was that the defendant bought a pair of shoes from the defendant and wanted to get refunded afterwards on the ground that the shoes were too large in size. The defendant refused this claim on the ground that the shoes were already worn out on the heel. The judge first asked

DL as to the condition of the shoes (turn 3) and how shoes could be worn out (turn 5). He then asked the plaintiff some factual questions (turns 7, 9, 11 and 13) to explore further the case facts. This alternation of the ND targets shows that the judge was sensitive to his role of justice. He tried to maintain a balanced interactional structure even in the ND process so that his position could be impartial.

4.3.3 Representative

The proceedings of courtroom trial are deliberately designed to enable the judges to discover "what really happened" (Philips, 1993) of the case in issue. However, the facts do not speak for themselves. Due to the adversary nature of judicial process, what the litigants and witnesses present to judges are often competing or contradictory versions of stories or arguments. Again, due to spatiotemporal limitations, much of the case facts cannot be recollected. Thus, what judges often have is fragmented and contradictory accounts. However, the final judicial opinions must be based on reasonable case stories. Therefore, judges need to transform those often messy fragments into coherent narratives. This implies that judges have to choose between opposing accounts, bridge informational gaps and find storylines to ground their final representation of the case.

In this section, we will refer to judges' actions that cope with the issue of facticity as representatives. Representatives are mainly found in the judgment. However, occasional instances also emerge throughout the courtroom interactions. Our analysis will center on three "rhetorical devices" (Edwards et al., 1995) that judges used to package their representations:

4.3.3.1 Voicing

Voicing was the most elemental component of case fact representation in judgment. The judicial process involved the interaction of different voices. Judges' representation of a case was to choose among those voices. Thus, the manifestation of a particular voice in judges' representative actions was an inherent feature of judges' judicial process. This suggests it is necessary for judicial behavior research to examine how different voices were registered within judges' case accounts. The following table gives a summary of voicing① in our corpus dataset.

Table 4-2 Voices Incorporated in Judgments *

Case no.	Plaintiff	Defendant	Court	Witness	Expert witness	Others
1	+	+	+	+	+	+
2	+	+	+	-	-	-
3	+	+	+	-	+	-
4	+	+	+	-	-	+
5	+	+	+	-	-	-
6	+	+	+	-	-	-
7	+	+	+	-	+	-
8	+	+	+	-	-	-
9	+	+	+	-	+	-
10	+	+	+	-	-	-

Note: * "+" means "found" while "-" "not found".

As we can see, among the ten cases, it was the voices of the three protagonists in the court that was articulated in judges' representative actions. The fact representation section of judgments normally fell into a pattern which began with "the plaintiff charges", followed up with "the defendant argues" and ended up with "the court finds". Other voices such as witnesses were also included. But they served only as either a consonance or dissonance of the three principal tones. That is, judges' representative actions were fundamentally concerned with the rearticulation of the three major voices.

The analysis of voicing had at least three significant implications on our

① Since the case account in the judgment is a report of what the litigants have said, we can not trace who actually said it. The criterion for our counting is the principal (Goffman, 1981) of each information chunk that the judgment attributes to.

understanding of judges' representative actions. Firstly, judges' representative actions were by nature the dialogic constructions produced in the judicial process. Judges did not simply map the reality in which the involved case took place. In fact, that reality was inaccessible to the judges. The one that judges had direct experience of was the judicial setting. Judges' perception of the original case facts was indirect, often with mediation by the litigant parties. In this sense, a proper way to look into judges' representative actions is to examine both the nature of other voices and judges' own way of perception. The focus shall be on the junctures where particular voices were articulated, suppressed or challenged. Our study has found that the dialogic nature of judges' representative actions was particularly illuminative of judges' policy in representing case facts. One simple case can illustrate it:

Extract 26 (C. F. L. 7)

During the retrial process, the plaintiff and the defendant agreed on the following facts. The court will confirm the following facts:

This discursive action was a preparatory for judges' representation. It specified how the upcoming representation was made. It clearly stated that the case facts were confirmed based on consensus between the plaintiff and the defendant. As we know, trial by consensus is a basic principle for JJB. The specification of this principle in judges' representative action reflects how the facticity of judges' case account is achieved by discursive appropriation—a strategy to seek external supporting discourse.

Secondly, judges did not just take in the different voices but also tuned their own voice in. When representing the case, the judges were not only seeing, feeling, hearing or perceiving what was presented to him but deciding on how to relate those different voices. Given the competing nature of information provided, judges must resolve this indeterminacy through deletion, transformation or addition. It was in these junctures of judicial process where judges took an active part:

Extract 27 (C. F. L. 2)

The Tecent Company charges that Mr. Chen entered into unfair competition by extraposing some programs on Coral Workshop. Due to the lack of evidence, the court will not accept this charge.

This was a rejection of the factual claim made by the plaintiff. It concerned the issue whether the defendant participated in an unfair play. This factual claim was by nature the judge' attributive decision in terms of the given fact that the defendant extraposed some programs on Coral Workshop. We find that the judge's representative action approached this issue from the legal category "unfair play", rejecting the facts based on "lack of evidence". This shows that the judges' voice could give shape to the version of case facts.

Thirdly, the representation of case facts was instrumental by nature. Our analysis of voicing in the fact representation suggests that case facts identified in the judgment were not objective, faceless and impersonal. As Baldwin (2005) has pointed out, judges often privileged certain narrators and smoothed over contradictory evidence in representing case facts. Following this, two central issues emerge: the first one is how a voice is included and the second is how different voices are related. The answer discursive psychology offers is that the judges' discursive actions are fundamentally purpose-oriented. For example, in Extract 26, the introduction of the consensus between the two litigant parties was to justify the confirmation of relevant case facts. Such an instrumental orientation was more obvious in Extract 27 in which the judge only cared about whether the fact conformed to the legal categories rather than the fact itself.

4. 3. 3. 2 Thematic Approach

Representing the case facts involves not only the voices of participants but also their content. That is, what and how to represent has much to do with the nature of its object. Some may be included or highlighted while others may be ignored or downplayed. Henning (1999) called the ways to make disparate choices concerning evidence through deliberation and evaluation "thematic approaches". They can be observed in the comments and summaries made after litigants' evidence presentations. Generally, there were two discourse junctures where judges' summation was often applied. One was the end of an investigation session and the other was the fact account in the judgment. These two had different foci. The former was normally concerned with the issues in dispute and often served as the orientation for the continuous debate session. The latter was more comprehensive and emblematic of judges' overall representation of the case.

Extract 28 (C. O. 2)

Judge: OK. Your argument focuses on two issues. That is, —]

DL: [the first one

Judge: = Firstly, the amount claimed by the plaintiff is not correct. Secondly, you remarked on (0. 5) the reasons for back payment.

DL: = right, right.

Judge: The first is, (0. 5) , delayed delivery. There is still the other () .

The judge in the above extract interrupted the DL who had been making a lengthy presentation (lasting about 3 minutes) . The DL had mentioned the difficulty his company had and the business malpractice of the plaintiff such as delayed delivery of product. However, in the summary by the judge, we only found two undecided issues, leaving behind all the factual information. That is, the case account by the DL was transformed by the judge. In doing so, the judge "decides precisely what the relevant facts are by separating the wheat from the chaff" (Heffer, 2002: 229) . Since this was at the very beginning of the trial, the judge was more interested in what the disputes were than what evidential information there was.

In the case of summary as found in the judgments, the thematic approach was more relevant. One illustration was that judges often grouped their narratives into topics according to their themes. But this did not mean that judges only listed facts. Instead, all the representatives were functional by nature. Our analysis shows that the judges' judicial representation of the case facts was normally developed after a problem-solution paradigm:

Extract 29 (C. F. L. 1)

①After the accident, Chengzhong Traffic Police Station, a local branch of the municipal Bureau of Public Security in Nan Jing, investigated the accident and made an investigatory record on receiving the accident report. ②When the case was brought to the court, the police who had investigated the case came to the court, made his statement on the accident and left with the interview record. ③The content of the interview was that the plaintiff and the defendant ran into each other. ④The plaintiff had no objection. ⑤The defendant argued that since the interview record was a report of the investigatory record the police made when he interviewed the plaintiff and the defendant on the day of accident and the day after it and it was not checked against the investigatory record, its authenticity could not be determined and thereby it could not be accepted as the evidence.

This paragraph of fact representation could be divided into two parts. The first three sentences were a narrative of the accident investigation by the police while the last two sentences were about the dispute over the police investigation record between the plaintiff and the defendant. As we can see, the representation was developed in such a way that the issue whether the plaintiff and the defendant ran into each other could be highlighted. In other words, the representative action was to identify and resolve the problematic part rather than the details of information. This was different from judicial summations to juries in common law system (Henning, 1999). The latter were found to employ various rhetorical devices to project particular case facts through clarification or obfuscation.

These two approaches to case fact representation could be regarded as issue-oriented and fact-oriented respectively. There were distinct differences in terms of their discursive features. When the representative actions focused on the fact, the summation of the case normally utilized narrative techniques such as temporal sequence, vivid description, listing, first person pronoun, and authoritative sources. However, in the issue-oriented summations, the incorporated case facts were often fragmented. Instead, they focused on the causal or consequential analysis. For example, in Extract 29, the representation did not provide the detailed information on how the police investigated the case and made the record. Instead, it directed our attention to the dispute between the litigant parties, an issue which judges needed to address in the judgment.

These two thematic approaches reflected the two styles of trying facts: narrative and categorization (Heffer, 2002). However, different from Heffer who emphasizes personal variation, we find that the two thematic approaches were also related to the nature of the cases involved and the purposes of representing. They depended on whether the dispute was related to the case facts or the law. It was often the case that the two approaches were juxtaposed in judges' representation of case facts. Both the fact-oriented and issue-oriented thematic approaches were adopted to serve specific discursive purposes. This suggests that the choice of a thematic approach was evaluative or ideological by nature. The tension of these two approaches gave shape to the particular form of representative actions.

4. 3. 3. 3 Anchoring

Anchoring is a concept in psychology referring to the cognitive bias that gives rise to a tendency to rely on specific information or a specific value when a person makes decisions. Anchoring is a general sociopsychological phenomenon underlying all activities including judges' judicial behavior. However, DP argues that anchoring effects are the resources for rather than the cognitive constraints of discursive actions. Our analysis of judges' representation of case facts shows that different anchors could be employed to constitute the boiled down versions of case fact. These anchors served a function similar to the premises in logic which were the prerequisite for a discursive action. Therefore, anchoring in our usage was not a bias but a discursive strategy.

In representing case facts, as we indicated in analyzing judges' two thematic approaches, the central issue was to decide whether certain information provided by the litigants was factual and, if so, what weights could be assigned to it. For the noncontested facts, judges could anchor their decision on consensus and corroboration (Edwards & Potter, 1992) between litigants. However, among the ten sampled judgments, six cases involved altogether 12 instances of factual disputes (see Table 4-3). Some were due to insufficient information while others were rooted in the different interpretations of the given information. Given the complexity of judicial cases, judges' judicial behavior could not simply rely on one anchor, for example, the legal rules. In fact, as is shown in our analysis of judges' representative actions, legal rules could only make a very limited contribution to judges' factual decision (2 out of 12).

Table 4-3 Anchors for Factual Representation in Judgment

Case	Contested factual issues	Anchors
C. F. L. 1	1	Social cognition Police interview record
	2	Social cognition
	3	Social cognition
	4	Material evidence
C. F. L. 2	1	Material evidence
C. F. M 3	1	Personal judgment
	2	Legal rule
C. F. L. 4	1	Social cognition
C. F. L. 5	1	Legal rule
	2	Social cognition
C. F. L. 6	0	
C. S. L. 7	1	Material evidence
C. F. L. 8	1	Expert testimony
C. F. L. 9	0	
C. F. L. 10	0	

Within the 15 instances of which the factual status was subject to the discretion of the judge, we found that there were two ways of representation in terms of its anchoring.

1) Substantially anchored

Substantially anchored representations were those which were established on given material evidence, supportive information from authoritative sources, deduction from legal principles, etc. For example, one factual issue that was often encountered with was the cost or damage incurred. Although some laws or regulations specify the items to be covered, the specific amount could not be determined with reference to the material evidence such as bills or receipts.

The most reliable anchors were those of authoritative sources. For example, the patent right was decided on the register certificate (C. F. L. 2); accidents were confirmed on the police records (C. F. L. 1 and C. F. L. 8); and physical injuries were authenticated with medical records (C. F. L. 8). However, the issue was often complicated by factors that might undermine the effect of available anchors. C. F. M 3 was one of such examples, in which the plaintiff charged the defendant of infringing the right of a design patent held by the plaintiff. In this case, two evidential issues were involved: The first one was whether the commodity sold by the defendant infringed the patent right. For this, a comparison between the sued product and the patented design was included in the factual representation:

Extract 30 (C. F. M 3)

The appearance design patent protects the products as illustrated in the published picture in the patent grant. Comparing the charged "Dream Paris Perfume Bottle" and the picture of "Perfume Bottle (Dreamy Paris)" as illustrated in the published patent grant, both of them consist of a body and a cap. The body of the bottle is cylinder-shaped and the cap cone-shaped. The lower part of the body is surrounded with a circle of isomorphic hollowed triangles. The defendant argues that they are different in color. But the patent of "Perfume Bottle (Dreamy Paris)" does not protect the color alone. The defendant claims that they are different due to the different degrees of delicacy in terms of workmanship. But no evidence is provided. Therefore, the charged "Dream Paris Perfume Bottle" and patented "Perfume Bottle (Dreamy Paris)" are the same in the appearance design.

As we can see, the representative action was complicated by the fact that the two products were similar in shape while differing in color. Although either the shape or the color or their combination could be patent-protected according to the Patent Law (2002), it was not specified in this patent certificate what exactly was. So, to confirm the claim of patent infringement, the judges' representation of the case fact included not only the similarities of the two products in appearance but also the legal ground to exclude the dissimilarity in color. However, both the factual and legal anchors did not naturally bridge the logical gap between the given evidence and the conclusive factual claim. Neither did the shape similarity lead to identity of two objects nor did the patent law or patent certificate stipulates that the shape alone constitutes the patented design. In this case, the factual representation was anchored on the judges' own perception. Of course, prioritizing shape in identity perception was consistent with the psychological finding that shape takes precedence over other perceptional factors (Huppert, 2003).

The second factual issue involved in the same case was the claim made by the defendant that the sued products were supplied by another company. This claim was rejected, as the judgment ruled, on the ground of insufficient evidence. Although the rejection on the ground of insufficient evidence was simply in line with the judicial principle, the anchoring for this representative action was more complex than it appeared if we explore into the way insufficiency was determined:

Extract 31 (C. F. M 3)

The defendant claims that they did not know "Dream Paris Perfume Bottle" was a product infringing a patent and it was purchased from Kehong

Industrial Co. Ltd. . They legally obtained it and should not be held responsible for the infringement. For this the defendant presents an invoice regarding a perfume sale. The invoice is stamped with a seal of Kehong Industrial Co. Ltd., Shenzhen. The court notices that the total amount of transaction is only RMB 260. It is not necessary to sign contracts when purchasing perfume. However, the court also takes into account the fact that the receipt is written by Kehong Industrial Co. Ltd. and it is not rare to buy and sell blank invoices or even forge invoices. The court holds that, to prove that the products were legally purchased, the defendant shall at least provide the information of Kehong Industrial Co. Ltd. registered in Administration for Industry and Commerce. In addition, although the invoice says the product "Dream Baris Perfume Bottle", which is similar to "Dream Paris Perfume Bottle", we do not know if they are identical. This also affects its power of proof. With all the above, the court rejects the defendant's claim on the ground of insufficient proof.

This extract aimed to develop an argument against the claim that it was not the defendant but some third party (Kehong Industrial Co. Ltd.) that infringed the patent. To build up such a representation, the judge resorted to four anchoring points:

- the small amount of transaction-only RMB 260;

This implied that it was not likely for a business transaction between companies;

- the invoice was written by Kehong Industrial Co. Ltd. ;

Since there was no official information about the organization, the authenticity of the invoice was susceptible;

- guard against possible forged invoice;
- a little difference in the brand name between the said products in the invoice and the sued product.

These four anchors were all relevant aspects of the case facts. However, none of them could definitely overrule the claim that the product was not purchased from other suppliers. The discursive strategy used in this representative action was to orchestrate all the relevant anchors. By doing so, the represented facts could be mutually corroborated. This was shown to be a main discursive strategy in cases where strong proof was not available.

2) Circumstantially anchored

Some judges' representations of case facts were anchored not on laws or hard evidence but on the folk beliefs or rationalizations (collectively listed as social cognition in Table 4-3) about the "normal patterns of human behavior" (Abrams, 1981). That is, those represented facts were inferred constructions based on our social cognition about our lifeworld. Since what was derived in this way is called the circumstantial evidence, we will refer to the representative actions based on this cognitive strategy as circumstantially anchored.

There were three cases in our data that contained altogether five instances of circumstantial anchoring. They appeared when evidence could not be obtained or decided on according to the legal criteria of facticity and due process. Previous research (e. g. Baldwin, 2005) has observed that the representative actions could rely on narrative techniques to establish the facticity such as "a narrative trajectory, the presentation of consensus, drawing on supportive discourses, the privileging of certain narrators and the smoothing over of contradictory evidence". In our research, we found two rhetoric strategies were widely used by Chinese judges.

a) Presupposition

In arguing for what could have possibly happened, judges could rely on some extralegal presuppositions. This constituted the major rhetoric for case representation in C. F. L. 1. In this case, the plaintiff accused the defendant of knocking her down while getting off the bus. The defendant denied the accusation. Thus, the central issue was whether they knocked into each other and who held the responsibility. The case information available to judges was only the competing statements made by the two litigant parties. The following extract was part of the inference made about the case fact in the judgment:

Extract 32 (C. F. L. 1)

When people were knocked down, they would normally make sure the sources of the external force and identify who they ran into. If the person who knocked ran away, the first response of the one being knocked would shout for help. This accident happened in a public place, a bus station where there were a lot of people and in the morning when the viewing was in good light. Moreover, the occurrence of accident was immediate. Therefore, the person who knocked the plaintiff was not unlikely to run away. The defendant confessed that he was the first one to get off the bus. According to common sense, it was most probable that he ran into the plaintiff.

This argument was a deduction based on two hypothetic premises: the reaction of a person being knocked down and the probable setting of the accident. As we know, a deductive argument is valid if and only if the truth of the conclusion actually does follow necessarily (or is indeed a logical consequence of) the premises and its corresponding premises and conditionals are true. Obviously, the argument in the above extract could meet neither condition. It was only a kind of subjective guessing about what was likely. Its validity was built not on the perfection of the logic structure but on the satisfactoriness of the presumption.

b) Dispositional formulation

Disposition is the mental state that prepares/restrains people for/from enacting specific behaviors. It is associated with the epistemological orientation of people and, therefore, generally employed as a resource to accounts for social actions. It is a common practice to relate to the actant's disposition (including interest or stake) when describing or explaining an individual action (Potter, 1996). This is actually a special type of presupposition we discussed above. Our analysis of judgments reveals that formulation of disposition was a significant discursive resource employed to anchor representative actions, especially those concerning human agentive behaviors:

Extract 33 (C. F. L. 1)

In light of evidence available, the defendant did not mention the act of kindness in the pretrial examination nor in the first session of the courtroom trial. He mentioned it only in the second session of the trial. If there was an act of kindness, it was unlikely that he would not have used it as the first point of plea. It was doubtful that he raised the plea in such an occasion. Therefore, his plea that he acted out of kindness was not accepted.

This extract (immediately following Extract 32) was the judicial ruling on a dispute over the intention of the defendant's offering money to the plaintiff after the accident. In this case, the defendant sent the plaintiff to the hospital and gave her 300 *yuan* after the accident. The plaintiff stated that the defendant offered it as the compensation for the injury he caused. This accusation was refuted by the defendant who argued that he did it purely out of kindness. So the disposition of the defendant was a critical element to define the intentionality of his action. However, this could not be observed or testified on any direct evidence. The judge's tactic in this case was to formulate the possible disposition by referring to the manner of the defendant in raising the argument-in the second not the first session of the trial. Based on this, the defendant's factual claim was rendered as inauthentic.

What was noticeable of the case representation in the above extract was that the defendant's disposition claim was compared with our normal socio-cognition. Consequently, the breach of script or the inconsistency (Edwards & Potter, 1992) was introduced as the anchor for the representative action. Thus, this action was built upon the assumed schematic knowledge. The use of litotes formulation ("impossible not to" and "unconvincing") (Bergmann, 1992) and modality ("as the first choice") (Maley, 1994) displayed the subjective nature of the dispositional formulation. This indicates that one significant nature of judicial representation of case facts was to embed the given case accounts within the lifeworld and understand what they most likely mean.

The examination of judges' representative actions is to construe how judges discursively reconstructed the world. Voice, thematic approach and anchoring were the three discursive devices which made the reconstruction possible. By analyzing how these discursive devices were served by the judges, we have shown the dynamism inherent in the representative actions. Underlying this dynamism was the various social ideologies that were brought into play by the judges.

4. 3. 4 Attributive

Every case which goes through the judicial system must be provided with a judicial answer. The discursive actions which provide the final legal answer to the judicial case are hereafter called attributives. The term "verdictive" is also used to refer to this action in Austin (1962). A judicial opinion involves not only delivering a verdict but also attributing the legal values to case facts on the one hand and the social impacts to legal decisions on the other. The analysis of the judgment texts shows that attributives were argumentative by nature. It follows the Toulmin model (Toulmin, 2003):

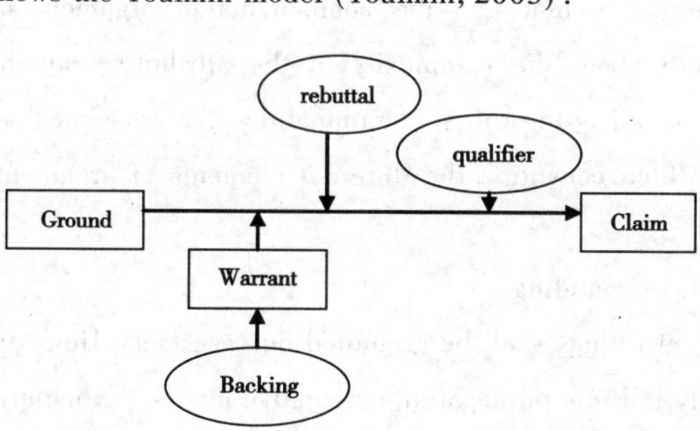

Figure 4-3 The Toulmin Model of Argumentation

This model consists of three major parts (those in squares) supported by another three optional elements (those in ovals): The claim is the decisional position being argued for or the conclusion of an argument. The ground is the facts or evidence that the claim is built on. The claim and ground are linked with warrant, i. e. the principle, provision or chain of reasoning. The warrant can be justified or supported with backing; counter-arguments may be included as rebuttal and limits to claim, warrant and backing are sometime specified with qualifier.

Extract 34 (C. F. L. 1)

Although this accident has caused great mental pains to the plaintiff, the court will not, considering the fact that no party was at fault, accept the plaintiff's claim for a sum of RMB 15, 000 compensation due to the lack of legal support.

Following Toulmin's model of argumentation, we could easily identify how this judicial ruling was constructed on different discursive elements: the claim was a rejection of the plaintiff's appeal; the ground was that the accident was not the defendant's fault and the warrant was that the claim for compensation for an innocent person was not legally endorsed.

Rationality is considered integral to argument (Wu, 2004) .However, the rationality for judges' attributive actions means more than following a model of argument. Our exploration into the components of argument has revealed something more about the complexity of the attributive actions. From the discursive perspective, the different rationalities are associated with different discourses①, which constitute the different elements of argument in judicial attributive.

4. 3. 4. 1 Grounding

All judicial rulings shall be grounded on case facts. However, case facts can notdirectly fall into the legal argumentative model, particularly when they are material objects. They need to be attributed legally. In the 10 judgments, 23 tokens of judicial ruling on case facts were found. Among them, 12 were attributed to some legal categories, 7 were categorized into some non-legal

① Discourse, as a countable noun, is used in its social-theoretical sense referring to the way of structuring knowledge and social practice.

concepts and the rest 4 were rejected for lack of evidence.

1) Legal categorization

Legal categorization was to map case facts to a legal conceptual domain. Judges need to specify the denotation of relevant legal categories. The following extract shows how a business act was established as a legal one:

Extract 35 (C. F. L. 5)

The plaintiff and the defendant have been contracted. The laundry bill offered by the defendant to the plaintiff is the proof. Thus, both parties are bound by the contractual rights and obligations. The fact that the plaintiff sent his clothes to the laundry shop without collecting them in the due time has breached the contract. Therefore, the plaintiff shall hold all responsibility for the loss. The defendant has fulfilled their due responsibility of care. They hold no responsibility of care for the clothes which have been overdue for half a year and have rights to dispose those which are overdue.

This case was about a customer who had his clothes washed in a laundry. He did not go to collect them until one year later. When he finally did, he was told that they were gone. The above extract described the case in such terms as "contract", "obligations", and "rights". Thus, the case was recapped from the contractual relation and reformulated in legal categories. Comparing the judge's categorization with the plaintiff's claim, we will find that there was a fundamental difference in their conception of the same case fact. For the plaintiff, the focus of the case was the defendant's failure to take care of the property in issue while the judge highlighted the delayed collection by the plaintiff. Their different perspectives resulted in different categorization. According to the tort law, there are two basic conditions to determine a tort: occurrence of a damage and liability for the damage. The plaintiff obviously emphasized the damage while the judge accentuated the liability.

From this simple case, we are able to see that alternative categorization is always possible in dealing with a given case facts. In such a circumstance, the judges often have to make strategic decisions to rationalize their attributive actions.

The legal categorization was not only contingent on the rules of law but also on the values that the judges uphold. For example, in our data there was a case about a victim who died for a medical accident. The plaintiff argued that it should be a case of personal injury while the hospital as the defendant deemed it as a medical accident. The former made relevant the General Principle of Civil Law while the latter sought support in the Regulations for Disposing Medical Accidents. What was striking was that the judge did not approach from the legal categorizations disputed by the litigant parties. Instead, he appealed to a human rights discourse by arguing that "the patient's rights of health prioritizes the operation of the hospital".

This case suggests that legal categorization for judicial attributive actions is a heuristic understanding of the case facts and laws. It is not grounded on the legal system alone.

2) Folk knowledge

In our research, we find that some attributive actions were grounded on facts which could not be legally categorized. That is, legal decisions could bemade without legal grounding:

Extract36 (C. F. L 6)

During the conciliation session convened by the court, the defendant, Zhang..., agreed to pay Huang... moderate compensation. The issue was that the agreed amount fell far behind what the plaintiff demanded. This could be seen as a sign of apology that the defendant made to the plaintiff. Considering the brotherhood between the plaintiff and the defendant, making apologies in public for their common mother does not conform to the conventional custom of family in the country. Therefore, the court rejects the plaintiff's claim for an open apology after ruling for the mental damage compensation by the defendant.

In this ruling, the plaintiff's claim for a public apology was rejected on the basis that the plaintiff had already expressed his apologetic stance. However, such a basis had no support from any direct evidence in the case. The defendant's agreement to pay does not mean expressing regret for his own fault. Neither was there legal or cultural ground to claim that making apology for the sake of common mother breached the custom. This practice of legal attribution is to incorporate judges' personal opinions or evoke their folk knowledge. Emotional and socio-cultural appeals were often found to scaffold the legitimacy of judicial rulings.

4. 3. 4. 2 Warranting

Warrants are chains of reasoning that connect the claim and evidence/reason. They are the underlying rationalities that justify an argument. They operate at a higher level of generality than a claim or grounding, and they are not normally explicit. Warranting can be achieved in various ways such as generalization, analogy, sign, causality, authority, and principle. In our analysis of judgment, we find judges mainly appealed to three sources.

1) Legal rules and principles

Under China's judicial system, judicial ruling are required to be warranted by law. Let's take Extract 35 above for example again. Since the contractual relation and a breach of it on the part of the plaintiff were established, the judgment ruled straightforward against the plaintiff's claim on the basis of the tort law.

However, when the case facts were not legally categorical, mundane reasoning would be evoked as the warranting. For example, in the case we have already mentioned in Extract 32, the plaintiff was hurt as she and the defendant ran into each other. The defendant was deemed as at no fault but the court held that the defendant should pay some damages for the plaintiff. In such a ruling, the principle of equity was introduced as the warrant.

2) Judicial discretion

There were also more complex cases which no single legal rules or principles were able to address. To solve such cases, the judges typically need resort to their own discretion:

Extract 37 (C. F. M 3)

Since the plaintiff, Heruixiang Industrial Development Co. Ltd. and the defendant could not ascertain the amount of profit from the infringement, the court will decide in accordance with the kind of patent and the nature of infringement.

In this case, since the loss due to the patent infringement could not be determined, the judge could only rule according to his own discretion. As this extract shows, judges' discretion was mostly necessary in the decisions over rewarding and punishing, for the law makers intentionally left some discretionary space for judges. In short, the indeterminacy of case facts and the ambiguity of law made it necessary for judges to exercise their discretion.

3) Extralegal justifications

For issues which were not specified in the law, judges could also seek extralegal justifications. For example, in one case related to the custom of co-burial, the plaintiff, the adopted son of a couple who had died, sued his brother (the son of the first marriage of the female party of the couple) for stealing their mother's corpse and reburied it with the defendant's biological father. In current law system there was no law governing such an action. To decide on this case, the judge resorted to the social value:

Extract 38 (C. F. L 6)

The fact that Zhang... privately moved the corpse of his mother flouted the good social custom of "bringing peace to the deceased by burying it". It was also socially regarded as irreverent to the deceased. It caused hurt and pains to the plaintiff, Huang..., and his family. Thus, it infringed the right of the defendant.

This ruling consisted of only moral reasoning. The accused action was not covered within current legal rules. But it was considered as an infringement by the judge on ground that it "flouted the good social custom of 'bringing peace to the deceased by burying it'". Such a warrant was by nature non-legal. But most attributive actions were found to make allowances for such considerations.

4.4 Summary

This chapter has addressed the construction and function (Edwards & Potter, 1992) of judges' decision constituting discourse. What is revealed through discourse analysis is the dynamics between structure and contingency of judges' judicial behavior. We specified both the general frame of courtroom trial and its constituting discursive actions. Although all judicial behavior could be categorized into four discursive actions, the realization of each of them was varied. The coordinatives could be interactional directives as in rule instruction and turn control or substantial manipulative as in topic management. To inquire case facts, judges could remain personally disinterested through requestion or interactionally involved by challenging or nailing down an answer from the litigants. The versions of case facts were often constructed out of the subjective selection of voice, theme and anchor. The non-legal values and considerations were found in grounding and warranting attributive actions. Although our characterization is not conclusive, the discourse diversity has fully revealed the tension between structure and contingency in judges' discourse activities.

The nature of the discourse tension was explicable by embedding the discursive actions within the sequential and categorical nature of the judicial discourse practice. Our discourse approach has construed the judges' discourse within their interactional context to show how judges negotiated and constructed their discursive actions in response to discourses of others. The findings indicate that judges' discursive actions often went beyond the legal register. That is, the force of their discursive actions was not defined by the rule-bound nature of law alone. The multi-function nature of discursive actions was determined by the order of discourse (Atkinson & Drew, 1979) in which different voices were articulated. The discourse approach in this research has been proved valuable to capture the nature of the particular order that constituted and was reenacted by the discursive actions. What we need is a "unifying theme" (Conley & O'Barr, 2005) to organize the discursive features which varied across discursive actions and judicial cases.

Chapter 5

Judges' Identity Performance in Discursive Actions

5.1 Introduction

This chapter will address the"identity-work" (Tracy, 2002) that judges undertook as part of their judicial discursive actions. As Antaki & Widdicombe (1998) put it, identity is both an achievement and a tool. The objective of this chapter is to show how variant identities were negotiated in the courtroom interaction and mobilized as the interpretive frames to justify judges' judicial behavior. In Chapter 4, this book has shown how the discursive actions have been enacted in judicial practice. In this chapter, a psycho-discursive analysis (Edwards & Potter, 1992; Harre & Stearns, 1995) will be made to reveal what particular identities were performed by the judges to maintain the order of judicial discourse (Goffman, 1983). In other words, we aim to elucidate JJB in terms of identities that were performed in their discourse.

In line with DP, identity is considered as a discursive construction which emerges in interaction (Bucholtz & Hall, 2005). This chapter aims to show "how identity is something that is used" (Antaki & Widdicombe, 1998: 1) in judges' discourse practice. We will examine how particular identities are assumed by the judge as a way to hold accountability for their own judicial behavior. Our focus will be on the dynamism that was displayed in judges' judicial discursive actions.

To capture identity work, DP relies on the analysis of the discursive details. DP holds that identity is indexed symbolically and occasioned locally. The relationship between identities and discourse has been extensively documented in existing scholarship (Sacks, 1992; Drew & Sorjonen, 1997; Heritage, 2004; Housley, 2006). The linguistic resources which are identity-implicative include lexico-grammatical, discoursal as well as pragmatic devices. Our approach to identity is synthetic as is advocated by scholars such as Wetherell (1998) and Chouliaraki & Fairclough (1999). It combines CA-inspired attention to conversational details with socially-involved analytic concepts such as the "stake and interest", "interpretive repertoire" (Potter & Wetherell, 1987; Edwards & Potter, 1992; Potter, 1996). In this chapter we will first briefly show how identity was made relevant in judges' discourse practice and then elaborate how the three kinds of identities formulated by Zimmerman (1998) were oriented to by judges and became consequential on their judicial judicial behavior.

5.2 Self-identifying

Any discourse practice involves a "self-identifying" element, i. e. a projection of self. Hadden & Lester (1978) argue that "in any event, rendering identity in a variety of ways and under a variety of circumstances is a recalcitrant feature of social life and is available for analysis as such." Proffering and patterning documents of who they are is also a prominent undertaking in judges' discourse practice. Such assumed identities package implied commonsense knowledge that is foundational to the smooth progress of judicial process and the presentation of the judicial opinions. For the relevance of self-identifying, we can examine the identity checking procedure which nearly precedes every trial:

Extract 39 (C. O. 2)

Judge: 1) Through examination, (0. 2) both parties are eligible to participate in the trial.

2) The Civil Court of ...City now publicly starts the trial, er (0. 2), of the case on a product processing contract filed by the plaintiff ... Trade Co. Ltd. against the defendant ... Textile Co. Ltd.

3) In this case, assistant judge Li, oh, no. For this case, the court has assembled acollegial panel. Li Zhang ... acts as the chief judge. Tang ... and Li ... are the members. The courtroom trial will be presided over by me, Li....

(Clear throat)

4) Since the other two panel members are on another meeting, they will not, er (0. 2), attend the hearing. They will join the panel discussion.

5) Will you appeal for a dismissal of any member?

This is an extract of opening remarks by a judge from which at least two junctures of self-identifying could be discerned. One was the pronouncement that"the Civil Court of...City now starts the public trial of the case of...Trade Co. Ltd vs. ... Textile Co. Ltd". "The court" was used as an abstract membership category along with which the judge identified herself in the announcing act. The other juncture of self-identifying was explicitly realized by two categories, "deputy judge"and"presiding judge".

Hadden & Lester (1978) point out that self-identifying is achieved through"contexting"①and"differentiating"②. In the above extract, the formal announcement to commence the trial procedure could be seen as a way of contexting which ascribed identities to all participants including the judge

① Contexting means that one locates as a member, coparticipant, or in some way related to a network of"others" (Hadden & Lester, 1978).

② Differentiating means that one distinguishes self by either depicting"unique"features that have no articulated social referent, or by distinguishing self with an explicit reference to others (Hadden & Lester, 1978).

herself. Meanwhile, the introduction of the panel members was the attempt to self-identify by differentiating in relation to the collegial panel. The repair in 3) (oh, no) signaled the significance of this self-identifying. The three membership categories (the court, the presiding judge and the collegial panel) were evoked as the different identities that were all the incumbents of "judge". It is important to note that only the presiding judge was physically present in the trial process. That means the presiding judge was the animator of different voices. Consequentially, this made it possible for the judge to oscillate between different identities. The consequence of this self-identifying can be seen in some parts of the sequential development of the trial procedure:

Extract 40 (Case 8)

1. Judge: Do the plaintiff and the defendant have objection to the investigation record?

2. Plaintiff: I do not know whether it is factual.

3. DL: No objection.

4. Judge: As to this investigated issue, the ruling will be made after a review by the collegial panel.

One category that was explicitly evoked here was "the collegial panel" mentioned in turn 4. Here the presiding judge seemed to recede into a role of mediator who passed the words for the collegial panel. This identification consequentially suspended the ruling on the given evidence and brought a closure to the possible dispute over the issue. If the judge had identified himself with the decision maker, the subsequent development of interaction might have been different.

Our research found that, possibly due to the flexibility of identity orientation, there seemed to be no consistent association between the identity categories and category-bound incumbencies. For example, who was the actual decision maker on certain legal issues seemed to vary from case to case. A comparison of the following two extracts can show this:

Extract 41 (Case 8)

Judge: This written record was made through investigation by the court ex officio. The validity of the record would be decided by the collegial panel according to the case facts.

Extract 42 (Case 8)

Judge: As to the notorial testament raised by the defendant, the court will confirm its legitimacy and validity since the plaintiff can not raise counterevidence. The plaintiff objected to the holographic testament by Li...but did not offer counterevidence.

In Extract 41, "the court" was the investigator of case evidence but its finding was subject to the review by the collegial panel. In Extract 42 "the court" instead acted as the decision maker. Since the decision was made on the spot, we can see that it was the judge that actually decided what identity category of the "court" they would orient to. This was again contradictory to the mediating identity of the presiding judge in Extract 40.

The abovementioned preliminary observation shows that identity orientation was a rhetorical device that judges could flexibly exploit to accomplish various international or practical purposes. Judges did not merely perform a pregiven identity, but interactionally constructed and reconstructed who they were. This finding resonates with Zimmerman & Pollner's view (1970) of identity as an assembled corpus which derives its sense from the particular creative work of the moment. The orientation to a specific identity brings into play a certain contextual element, either proximal or distal, for the social activity (Zimmerman, 1998). According to the contextual relevance, identities can be classified into discourse, situated and transportable.

5.3 Discourse Identities

Discourse identities are "the emergent feature of the sequential organization of talk-in-interaction, orienting participants to the type of activity underway and their respective roles within it" (Zimmerman, 1998: 92). They are the discourse status of participants (Goffman, 1979; Goffman, 1981) that are negotiated in the interaction. They are the emergent property of discourse and, therefore, can be captured by elaborating the details of discursive actions. Considering the highly institutionalized nature of judges' judicial discourse, this research will draw on the exchange structure theory to characterize how judges' discourse positions were distributed in relation to the IRF structure (Sinclair & Coulthard, 1975). The three discourse slots inscribe correspondingly three discourse identities for participants. We find that the first and third discourse slots were dominantly occupied by judges although there were some minor variations across different stages of judicial trial.

5. 3. 1 Initiator

Our data analysis shows that the exchanges in the judicial process were exclusively initiated by the judges except the examination of the witness by the lawyers or side talks (see further discussion in 5. 3. 2). In the study of civil courtroom interaction, Liao (2003) reports that 65. 08% of the adjacency pairs were initiated by judges among all question-answer sequences in the courtroom interaction. But question-answer sequences account for less than half of judges' discursive actions. According to our data, judges also initiated exchanges through declaratives and imperatives. This suggests that there is a more complex array of judges' identity. By assuming different identity categories, judges could realize varying interactional stakes or interest. The following two were dominantly prevalent in our data:

1) Monitoring the courtroom interaction

Judicial trial is a discoursing practice. Since it involves two or more competing parties, it is always critical to decide who shall say what and when. In our observation, judges were found to rely mainly on their initiator identity to manage the interactional issues. For example, they maintained a strict turn-taking system by allocating the rights to talk and the agenda to follow. The coordinative actions such as rule instruction, symmetrical turn transition system and topic management are found to be particularly helpful in this regard. The initiator discourse identity enabled judges to frame, focus and direct the discursive actions of other participants.

The initiator discourse identity could have either manipulative or facilitative consequence on the courtroom interaction. It depends on the way that the litigants were involved in the judicial process. In some cases, judges initiated agenda, concentrated the litigants on specific issues and licensed the rights to talk. The following extract was one such example:

Extract 43 (Case 5)

Judge: ①the court investigation session is over. (0. 2) ②Now the court will make a summary. (0. 2) ③After theinvestigation by the court, the main issue of dispute is whether the plaintiff still holds the rights to use the land that was certified as the homestead in 2002 and whether the defendant has obtained the rights to the homestead through transference. ④We will proceed to court debate. ⑤In the debate, both parties shall focus on the issue of dispute and state the reasons for your claims raised during the court investigation. ⑥ Let the plaintiff express your opinions first.

This extract took place in a boundary between the transactions of case investigation and court debate. The initiation of a transaction or exchange was achieved by the metastatements (including ①, ② and ④ in the above extract) which declared the end of a previous transaction and started a new one. To ensure that the upcoming interaction could be concentrated, the judge drew attention to the subject matter through summation and prompted the litigants to focus on it (③ and ⑤ respectively) . To maintain the proper order, the judge assigned the turn through nomination (⑥). All these three discursive actions were all contingent on the identity of discourse initiator. By orienting to it, the judge managed to steer the course of the courtroom interaction.

The most authoritative profile of judges' identity as the initiator is perhaps best manifested in their interruption (Liao, 2009) into litigants' discourse. However, judges' initiated actions can also be less manipulative and more facilitative.

Extract 44 (Case 6)

Judge: ① The plaintiff can raise counterevidence on the particular administrative actions that were performed by the defendant. (0. 5) ② Does the plaintiff have any evidence to show to the court?

Plaintiff: No.

In this exchange, the judge offered to remind the plaintiff of his rights (in ①). This was an invitation to the defendant to raise evidence for his own case. This initiative could be taken as an act to ensure the legal interest of the defendant. These facilitative actions distinguished judges from others in the judicial process.

2) Eliciting response

Besides maintaining the order of courtroom interaction, judges also oriented to the identity of discourse initiator to elicit specific responses from litigants. This discourse identity was normally associated with inquisitive actions. That is, the discourse initiator identity was often evoked to facilitate judges' case inquiry:

Extract 45 (Case 9)

1. Judge: Plaintiff, besides the apartment, did Yu ... leave any other property?

2. Plaintiff: We provided two lists of his heritage items to the court. The first list includes his furnished apartment, a 29" made-in-Japan TV set, a DCD player, a split-type air-conditioner, a printer, a computer, a sofa and so on. Before engaged with

Sun... they bought a notebook PC, a digital camera and a Sharp audio. On the second list are the possessions that were bought before Yu... were engaged with Sun.

3. Judge: Where are all these properties?

4. Plaintiff: They are all in the apartment.

5. Judge: The defendant, do you have any objection towards the two lists of properties?

6. Defendant: The PC and printer are not there. The car has been driven away by the plaintiff.

7. Judge: When was the car bought that has been driven away by the plaintiff?

8. Defendant: It was bought on Dec 18, 2005.

9. Judge: Defendant, do you have any to add?

10. Defendant: Except the PC, the printer and the car that has been driven away by the plaintiff, all the properties are in the apartment.

11. Judge: You must not dispose these properties in any way now. You shall take care of them. Do you see it?

12. Defendant: Yes, I see.

This extract consisted of six exchanges: four (turns 1, 3, 7, and 9) were concerned with factual information, one (turn 5) opinion and the other (turn 11) an adjudicative action. As Liao (2003) points out, when, how and what questions are asked is constrained by the participants' roles, judicial procedure and relevance of the content. We find that judges adjusted flexibly his discourse identity to these contextual constraints. The judge in the above case started with questions to seek factual information. When he did obtain some from the plaintiff, he shifted to ask the defendant's opinion. This was an invitation for verification or argument. When he noticed a point of legal interest, he undertook an adjudicative action-prohibiting the defendant from taking any possible actions to dispose the disputed property. A series of different discursive actions were evoked here. But from the discursive perspective, they were all underpinned with the judges' initiator identity. It was this initiative power in the judicial discourse practice that enabled the judges to perform various actions to address the complexity of judicial activities.

5. 3. 2 Evaluator

When occupying the third place of an exchange structure, judges were found to play typically the role of evaluator. That is, judges did not just acknowledge but also evaluate the previous discourse turns. The way this role was oriented to by the judges was best reflected in the rhetoric structure developed in the judgments. It consisted of three parts:

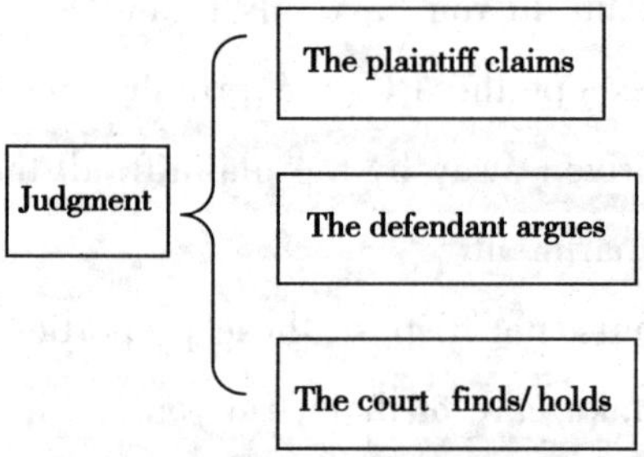

Figure 5-1 The Constituents of Chinese Judgment

As we can see, the sequence of the three voices as reported in the judgment clearly indicates that only the judges had the authority to give the final say. The judgment was formulated as an evaluative response to the discourses of the litigants. This discourse structure established the judges' identity as the evaluator. The performance of such a discourse identity was often associated with judges' representative and attributive actions.

However, the identity of evaluator was not only made relevant in the final adjudicative stage of the trial. It was also found to be part of the coordinative and inquisitive actions. For example, in the mediated turn-taking system as we suggested in 4. 3. 1. 2 (see Figure 4-2), the litigants did not address each other directly but had judges as their direct recipients or addressees. In this way, all the contributions made by the litigants were subject to the evaluation and verification of the judges. Judges' did not simply alternate the turns between the litigant parties. When they initiated or terminated a session, they had already made an evaluation of the ongoing activities.

How the initiator and evaluator identities were simultaneously articulated can be illustrated in the following extract which consisted of three exchanges between the judge and the litigants:

Extract 46 (Case 2)

1. **Judge:** Does the plaintiff have any more to add to the fact?

2. **Plaintiff:** There is another issue concerning the child support. The child is attending the junior middle school which charges a high tuition fee. The yearly tuition is 5000 *yuan*. If we count it as 500 each month, I agree to pay half.

3. **Judge:** Defendant, do you have any to add to the fact?

4. **Defendant:** She should pay me for the child support. She paid not only insufficiently but also in an inappropriate way.

5. **Judge:** Do both parties agree to solve it through negotiation?

6. **Plaintiff:** I insist on the four claims.

In this extract, the three discursive actions by the judge were coordinative. But if we read through the sequential development, the judge's evaluative orientation was conspicuous. As we can see, the plaintiff in turn 2 and the defendant in turn 4 offered their positions on a disputed issue without regard to the judge's fact-oriented initiatives. Although this was in the middle of investigation session, the judge appeared to follow closely the position statement and argument by the litigants. This led to turn 5 in which the judge shifted to make an attempt on conciliation. To understand this action initiated by the judge, we need to see the fact that turn 2 by the plaintiff and turn 4 by the defendant had just established a common position concerning the child support issue. From the judicial perspective, this discourse juncture offered the judge a good stand to bring off a possible solution to the dispute. The judges' attempt of conciliation was performing a "sequence-closing third" (SCT) (Schegloff, 2007) with a view to taking advantage of the interactional opportunity to resolve a dispute. Thus, it was the reification of the evaluator identity that grounded the performance of judges' initiator identity.

Based on our dataset, two characterizing features were evident in judges' performance of discourse identity:

a) Contingency

Although judges' discourse identities could be categorized and their discoursal actions could be characterized, their occurrence was not predictable based on the general frame of judicial interaction. The contingent nature of judges' identity was evident in the discursive actions in which their discourse identity was enacted. The following two extracts were both concerned with the determination of controversial cases facts. However, the two judges adopted quite different discourse strategies:

Extract 47 (Case 5)

Judge: The court will affirm the evidence over which both parties have no objections. The court will suspend temporarily its affirmation on the disputed evidence for which counterevidence shall be raised.

Extract 48 (Case 8)

Judge: As to the notorial testament raised by the defendant, the court will confirm its legitimacy and validity since the plaintiff can not raise counterevidence. The plaintiff objected to the holographic testament by Li...but did not offer counterevidence.

In the first extract, the clearly stated policy in performing the attributive action was to affirm what was agreed on while suspending what was in dispute. The judge in the second extract, however, ruled directly based on the given evidence. From this comparison, we can notice that judges differed in their orientation to the discourse identities when they were engaged in similar discourse junctures. Both extracts were the closing sequence of a case investigation session which involved evidence without affirmative corroboration. However, the judge in extract 47 did not end the session by making a judicative conclusion as the judge in extract 48 did. That is, the two judges differed in performing the identity of evaluator through the closing sequence. This difference could be due to their dispositional variation. It might also have something to do with the nature of the case facts involved. Our sequential analysis alone was not able to give a full account of it. Nevertheless, what the difference in performance implied was that the judges' discourse identity was contingent on the courtroom interaction.

b) Intersubjectivity

Another finding about judges' discourse identity was that it was intersubjectively constructed in the judicial process. That is, judges' discourse identity was interactionally negotiated, challenged and confirmed with other litigants. This finding echoes Zimmerman's (1998) perception of discourse identity in general. He points out that "who is doing what varies over the interaction, and the procession of discourse identities is interactionally contingent rather than determined ..." (Zimmerman, 1998: 91). This could be illustrated with the following extract:

Extract 49 (O. C. 1)

1. PL: Next, er, (0. 5) can the argument be raised about the part of evidence identification?

2. Judge: Which one?

3. PL: The one on page 4. Several items of evidence identified by the court.

4. Judge: Page 4? (0. 5) Any content in the section "the court finds" can be raised for examination. The section "the court holds" in page 5 is excluded.

This sequence of exchanges was first initiated by the plaintiff lawyer. The action in turn 1 was a consultative question which served as the presequence or a permission request for his argument raising. The fact that the plaintiff lawyer subjected his initiative to the judge for approval displayed his recognition of judges' discourse identity as the initiator. This in turn led to the judge's coordinative action to set the following agenda.

Different from traditional sociolinguistic approaches to judges' discourse which focus on the correlation between the judges' discourse practice and given identities, this study found that the trial participants made different discourse identities interactionally relevant to perform specific judicial activities. Judges needed to shift their discourse identities turn by turn to accommodate their interaction with the litigant parties. They might also project layered identities as they addressed the complexity of the interactional, institutional and social concerns. Judges were constantly found to position and reposition themselves in the judicial process when presiding, persuading, enticing, requesting, ordering, suggesting, asserting, insisting, doubting, and so on. This play of discourse identity was tied to the situations as well as the standing social arrangements and institutions which judges had knowledge about.

Discourse identities are integral to the structuring of interaction in that they "furnish the focus for the type of discourse activity projected and recognized by participants, what they are doing interactionally in a particular spate of talk" (Zimmerman, 1998: 92). With an analysis of judges' discourse identities, we are able to see how the different discursive actions figured in maintaining the sequential ordering and the intersubjective relations. The analysis so far shows that the two discourse identities were flexibly drawn on by judges to pursue various judicial purposes. However, judges' discourse identities were only one discursive resource that was available for their judicial behavior. The diversity of judges' discursive action, which has already been shown in Chapter 4, could not be addressed by judges' discourse identity alone. What characterized those discursive actions as doing justice was also associated with other aspects of judges' identity.

5.4 Situated Identities

Before the courtroom trial begins, there is usually a ritual practice-all attendants in the courtroom rise when the judges enter the court. This practice does not only mark the beginning of the courtroom trial but more importantly serves as a way of showing respect or deference to the judges. The fact that both competing parties show the same respect to the judge implies that a common identity of the judge is oriented to by both parties. In fact, the commencement of a legal suit is premised on the conviction that judges can do justice to it. From this very moment on, this identity of the judges is situated and sustained throughout the whole judicial process. The situated identities are consequential on judges' discursive actions by "delivering pertinent agendas, skills and relevant knowledge" (Zimmerman, 1998: 88). To deal with the different interactional businesses, judges would vary in their situated identities. In our research, we found that the set of judges' situated identities generally fell into three categories.

5.4.1 Procedure Organizer

One basic condition for judicial justice is fair procedure (Rawls, 1971) or due process. The whole underlying philosophy is that all concerned parities in the judicial parties be afforded equal opportunities to affect the judicial outcomes. In other words, the litigants shall be given the proper rights to be represented at the trial, to put forward arguments and evidence, to cross-examine witnesses, and so forth (Sanders & Hamilton, 2000). Someone shall be authorized to decide who could do what and when in the trial process. The large proportion of coordinatives in JJB indicates that the responsibility of the procedure organizer was on the judges' side. For example, judges often upheld control over the turn selecting by implementing the mediated turn-taking system (see Figure 5-2) .The dos and don'ts for litigants were also instructed by the judges. There were two main discourse junctures where judge's identity as the procedure organizer was most often made interactionally relevant. The first one was the transaction boundaries where decisions should be made as to whether a session should be ended and a new one started. They normally articulated declaratives and directives to guide and control the procedure. The following extract was one example of this transitional action undertaken by the judge:

Extract 50 (Case 1)

Judge: ① The court investigation is over. ② Now we proceed to court debate. (0. 3)

③ In the session, both parties shall concentrate your comments on the controversial issues on the base of evidence and law. ④ No personal or insulting remarks are allowed. Now the defendant can express your opinions.

In this move, the judge articulated three discursive actions to transit the judicial procedure from the court investigation to court debate:

- declaring an opening or end of a session (① and ②)
- instructing on other litigants the way of discoursing (③)
- assigning turns (④)

In the above case, the judge employed all the three types of coordinative actions to set an interactional frame for the ongoing judicial activities. However, the orientation to the identity of procedure organizer was not always defined by this routine turn-taking. The significance of this identity performance was more obviously seen in junctures where the interactional issues became contested and the interference of judges as the procedure organizer was called for. For example, in the following case the appellant appealed to the court for a call of a witness and it became a critical issue to decide whether this motion should be allowed:

Extract 51 (C. O. 1)

1. Judge: Before the courtroom trial, the appellant appealed to the court for a call of a witness. Is the witness Zhang...?

2. PL: Right.

3. Judge: What opinion does the appellee hold on their appeal for a call of a witness?

4. DL: We object because it has exceeded the time limit for appeal.

5. Judge: Exceeded the time limit for appeal? (turning to the appellant) Why did the appellant not call the witness until the second instance?

6. PL: Omitted (introduction of the case)

7. Judge: All right. Is the witness here?

8. PL: Yes

9. Judge: Since the witness is here. Let's hear what the witness will say and leave it () to be decided by the collegial panel.

In this case, the procedure issue was in dispute. When the appellee argued against the procedure motion by the appellant (in turn 4), the judge did not comment or conclude this dispute. Instead, he chose to suspend the dispute temporarily and allow the witness to testify, leaving the decision making to the collegial panel. In doing so, the judge separated the identity of adjudicator from that of the procedure organizer. As a result, the latter identity was projected. We also notice that although the motion to call a witness was originally made by the appellant, it was the judge who raised it in the judicial process (turn 1). This suggests that judges' procedure organization was also achieved through agenda setting.

In the civil courts, judges differed in terms of their alignment with the identity as procedure organizer. Judges could be proceduralists by following closely the trial scheme as specified in the procedure law and using mostly the turn selection. They could also align themselves more with the pragmatists by prioritizing their own interest in the judicial process. For example, they might cut short the session for efficiency. They might per-or dis-suade the litigants into or from particular judicial actions. Although our research did not have enough examples to conclude on all the patterns of judges' such coordinative actions, we did make some interesting observations about the relation of situated identity orientation to the sociopsychological nature of both the judges and the litigants. For example, in the last chapter we pointed out that the use of rule instruction or topic control was often associated with cases in which the litigants were considered as less competent in the legal literacy. This implies that the orientation to the procedure organizer was related to the degree to which the litigants were accommodated to the judicial culture.

5.4.2 Fact Investigator

In China the judge is also called "judging officer" which connotes a dual sense of investigator and adjudicator. That is, judges are entitled to conduct both pre-trial discovery process and the court investigation. However, the introduction of the adversary system makes the institutional role for judges controversial. There is no agreement over the extent to which judges shall be involved in the case discovery process. Judges are shown to have gone in two opposite directions based on our ethnographic observation and discourse analysis of their behavior:

1) Complementing the adversary investigation

For some judges, the judicial principle that whoever makes the claim shall hold the responsibility to prove it was strictly observed. They shifted the responsibility of fact finding to the litigants. Consequently, the trial typically proceeded with the fact presentations and examinations by the litigants while judges' questions served only to clarify ambiguous information. That is, judges' investigation was simply considered as complementary to the (cross-) examination between the litigants. Judges of this type tended to use a lot more coordinatives than inquisitives in discourse practice. In our study we found one extraordinary case (case 10) in which the judge did not ask any inquisitive questions. In cases where judges did investigate, the requestions which conveyed a sense of coordination were more often used. So these judges were mostly proceduralists since they were more concerned with the due process than the substantial issues in the trial proceedings.

However, the reason why judges adopted such an approach was more complicated than what appeared. It could be the judges' personal judicial style or associated with the nature of the cases. Since our research was not diachronic, no information about the personal variation was provided. However, some external factors could be identified through a rough comparison of different cases. For example, the low occurrence of fact investigator identity by the judge could be accounted for by the clarity of case facts in Case 10: it involved a business contract between a customer and a laundry and the central issue was who breached the contract. Since the case facts were directly retrievable, the judge could have formed a full idea about the case before the courtroom trial. So the case could be adjudicated with no need of further investigation. This was much in contrast to cases which, as we will see in the next section, were extensively explored by the judges.

2) Tracing every possible clue

This was the other extreme of judges' identity orientation in terms of their inquisitive actions. For these judges, the trial proceedings were centered on specific issues which the judges considered relevant. In other words, it was the judges' own exploratory agenda that guided the courtroom interaction. This orientation of identity was also manifested in judges' discursive actions. Firstly, there was a different turn taking system in investigation compared with trials presided by judges of the first type we discussed above. For those who considered their identity of fact investigator as complementary, they did not ask inquisitive questions until both litigant parties had made their cases. But for the investigation enthusiastic judges, they would build the version of a case based on their own exploration:

Extract 52 (Case 5)

1. Judge: Next, the defendant can raise the evidence.

2. Defendant: I have the receipt of the charge for using the building land. (0. 4) It can prove that the application fee was paid by me for the building land.

3. Judge: Why was the receipt signed by Yang..."? Who gave it to you?

4. Defendant: It was mediated by the plaintiff. I gave it to him before the new year and he gave it to me after the new year.

5. Judge: What will the plaintiff contend about the receipt of the charge for using the building land?

This extract was a segment of case investigation. We note that when the defendant presented one item of evidence (turn 2), the judge immediately took the floor to raise a doubt (turn 3). The plaintiff was not allowed to participate until the judge had already finished his questions. For judges of this type, they were more inclined to challenge the witness or nail down specific information (as in turn 3) to actively build his own story of the case.

Another feature related to the turn taking controlled by the judges who were more oriented to self-investigation was the more frequent use of reformulation. In our data, we found some judges tended to add a reformulative turn after the litigants discourse turn. That is, the questions or answers by the litigants were reformulated by the judge. For these judges, summation was also a device used to facilitate their investigation.

In sum, these two tendencies of identity performance were found to form a cline along which judges' discursive actions were distributed. There were both cross-individual and cross-case differences.

5. 4. 3 Order Maker

A court order is obligatory for any judicial proceeding. Issuing court orders is the core task of judges as the justice doer. Depending on the type of proceeding, the judges can issue restraining order, temporary protective order, emergency protective order, search warrant, child custody, child support, or lawsuit rulings. Our research focused mainly on the lawsuit rulings by the judges. It shows that varying orders were issued by the judges. Our discourse approach has construed the judges' identity as order maker by examining their representative and attributive actions. It is found that such an identity could be characterized along two canons that were integral to judges' discursive actions.

1) Rationality

The emphasis of the hard evidence and legal rules or principles available could be seen as the projection of this canon. Specifically, this canon was realized in the judicial orders as striving for facticity and justifiability. Rationality can be either external or internal. Of the external sources, judicial orders rely on the extensive narration of the primary reality which brought the case to the court or the secondary reality of the courtroom (Hale & Gibbons, 1999), i. e. the articulation of different voices in the court. But judges' own voicing is often lowered. Of the internal sources, rationality is associated with the categorization of case facts in terms of law and the rule-bound deduction.

2) Consequentiality

Consequentiality is related to the evaluative considerations of judicial decisions. If we examine the relation between the judicial decisions and the law that was applied, we will find few conformed to the arithmetic property dictated by the logic. In the jurisprudential scholarship, it is now generally recognized that judicial disparity is normal (Thomas, 2003).Judges are endowed with discretionary power in judicial practice. However, there is no consensus over the nature of this phenomenon or an agreed theory to account for it. Various attributions have been related to both the legal and extralegal factors (Bushway & Piehl, 2001). From the discursive psychological perspective, we argue that judges' judicial behavior is consequence-oriented. That is, as the order maker, judges are led with their awareness of the consequence that their decisions may have on the litigants as well as the general audience. Take Case C. F. L 1 as an example. The case fact was that the plaintiff got hurt when running into each other with the defendant who was getting off a bus. In the final judicial ruling, partial liability for compensating the plaintiff was imposed on the defendant although the judge held that the defendant was at no fault. The following was the extracted argument for this decision:

Extract 53 (C. F. L. 1)

According to the principle of equity, the court orders that the injuring party shall compensate the injured party for the property loss. The loss shall be divided fairly between the two parties based on the injury that was incurred, the economic conditions of both parties and other relevant circumstances. According to the case facts, the court decides that it is appropriate for the defendant to pay the plaintiff 40% of the loss.

The judgment claimed that the decision to order the defendant to hold 40% liability for the loss was warranted on the principle of equity. However, as we can see, the principle itself did not automatically lead to the conclusion. What was more informative about the ruling was the statement that this decision took into consideration the factors such as the suffering of the plaintiff and the economic conditions of both litigant parties. The introduction of the principle of equity and other considerations was served as the discursive resources for the justificatory purpose. Put it in another way, judges had variant cares in making their orders. What deserves our attention is that these cares were often found not to be about the orthodox case facts or legal rules. It was often the case that the judges sought justification on their own values. This implies that the judge's order making was a function of the judge's subjective evaluation of the case.

Rationality and consequentiality were not always compatible with each other. Sometimes, it was the competition and interaction of these two orientations that gave shape to the attributive actions and reified the identity of order maker. Fundamental to this process were the senses that judges made of the activities they were involved in. It is this discursive nature of judges' order making that the disparity of judges' judicial behaviors could be pinned down. For example, in the two cases (C. F. L. 2 and C. F. L. 3) which were both concerned with the infringement of intellectual property, the two judges were found to rule differently on the plaintiff's demand for the defendant's public apology. The first judge granted it without any justificatory reasoning while the second judge rejected by arguing that it was not legally based:

Extract 54 (C. F. L. 2)

Within ten days as from the effective day of the judgment, the defendant Chen... shall publicize his apology to the plaintiff Tencent Sci-tech Co. Ltd. (Shenzhen) on the website of"Tencent Workshop".

Extract 55 (C. F. L. 3)

The two plaintiffs demanded that the defendant publicize his apology on Southern Metropolis Daily and eliminate the effect of the infringement. The court will not grant this demand because what the defendant infringed was the property right of the plaintiff and therefore such a demand was not legally grounded.

The contrast of these two cases lies not only in the types of consequentiality that the two judges attributed to the act of apology but also in the kinds of rationality-the legal categorization of the infringement of intellectual property. In the first case, the apology was recognized as a remedy for intellectual property infringement. But the second judge held that it was not legally supported. Since both attributive actions were legally binding, they were both doing justice. The variant discursive reifications of justice suggest that judicial order was contingently produced as situated choices made by the judges.

Judges' situated identitiesare their participant roles in the judicial activities. The analysis of the three situated identities shows that they could be performed in a range of possible forms and the different forms bore on their specific discursive actions and the judicial outcomes.

5.5 Transportable Identities

As Goodwin (1987) points out, the way in which the relevance of a particular discourse identity is invoked may also in turn occasion the relevance of wider social identity. These social or cultural identities are "latent" and "transportable" (Zimmerman, 1998) in that they "'tag along' with individuals as they move through their daily routines". As for judges, their institutional identities are not only defined by their contingent discourse or specific situational roles. Instead, there are aspects of their identity which surface across situations and are potentially relevant in and for any spate of interaction. These identities are assignable or claimable on the basis of physical or culturally based insignia. The following three are found to be, among others, the distinct sets of identities judges oriented to.

5.5.1 Justice Doer

Within modern judicial system, judge is the justice administrator. Judges' judicial behavior is to a great extent contingent on such an identity. To explore such a relation, we found it was fruitful to consider how judges actualized the principle that underscored judicial justice-*When trying civil cases, the People's Courts must base themselves on facts and take the law as the criteria* (Article 7 of the Civil Procedure Law). This principle suggests judicial justice is associated with two ideological concepts: respect for law and worship of objectivism. Following this, the fundamental requisite for judges to perform their identity as the justice doer is to adhere to the law and ground their decisions on the given case facts. In our research, we found that much of judges' discursive actions could be accounted for by their orientation to this identity, even in cases where no law or fact was immediately available.

The most ostensible effort to adhere to the law was marked in the declarative coordinatives and attributives. The following are the most frequent syntactic patterns we found in judges' discursive action:

a) The People's Court of...is to hear the case according to the law.

b) According to the law, this case will be tried through the summary procedure. It will be tried by the judge...alone.

c) According to relevant laws, the court could conciliate the litigant parties on the voluntary basis. Now the court wants your opinions. Do both agree to settle it through conciliation?

d) To protect the legal rights of the parties involved, the court orders in line with the rules (as specified in...Law) that:

Besides the explicit reference to the law, judges' adherence to the law was also palpable in other forms of their discursive actions. For example, the extensive use of requestions could be taken as an incumbency of the identity as the justice doer. To direct litigants' actions was inherent to the capacity of the justice doer. Most of the judicial argumentation was at least partly grounded on or warranted by legal rules or principles.

The fact-based requirement of justice was another incumbency associated with judges' identity as the justice doer. Efforts in this direction could be seen in all types of discursive actions. For example, the fact that judges' attention was alternatively paid to both litigant parties through the turn control revealed a conscious management of courtroom interaction for objective discovery of the case. Challenging and nailing down a version of the case was driven by judges' interest in specific case seeking facts. The balanced choice of voicing and thematic approach could be taken as their endeavor to construct a coherent and reasonably anchored representation of the case. All the attributive actions were necessarily grounded on certain case facts.

We could say that all judges' discursive actions served the interest of law. However, the nature of law was variously defined by different judges in terms of specific case circumstances. This open texture of law sometimes made judges' judicial behavior problematic. That is, there were other concerns associated with judges' orientation to the identity of justice doer.

5.5.2 Officialdom

"*Faguan*", the Chinese term to address the judge, literally means "law official". A *guan* (an incumbent of the officialdom) is the legitimate individual who has the power to rule or govern. There is one important built-in sense of *guan* in Chinese culture, that is, there is a hierarchy or strict power division in the officialdom (Gu & Zhu, 2002). The alignment with this politically shaped identity is also evident in judges' institutional practice. One manifestation of this is the differentiation of address forms for judges. There are the presiding judge, the chief judge and the panel members in a case. For some important cases, the judicial decisions have to be referred to the trial committee of the court. The whole judicature is subordinated to the political leadership of the people's congress and in turn the CPC. Therefore, the operation of the judicature is in many ways the same as other administrative organs. Judges are not immune from the institutional hierarchy when making decisions. The following extract was one instance of performing this institutionalized identity:

Extract 56 (O. C. 1)

1. Judge: All right. Is the witness here?

2. PL: Yes.

3. Judge: Since the witness is here. Let's hear what the witness will say and leave it () to be decided by the collegial panel.

In this extract, the judge allowed the witness to testify while leaving the legitimacy of this testimony to the collegial panel. In making this decision, the judge identified himself as the mediator between the litigants and the collegial panel. This suggests that there were issues over which the judge could not decide on personally. Within the institution, there was the division of work. Judges acted as the representative of the judicial institution.

Officialdom is characterized by its hierarchical management. One category-bound predicate of judges' identity as officials is their accountability to their superiors. In our observation, judges were seen to display their particular sensitivity to this identity. That is, judges meticulously distinguished and aligned themselves with a particular participant role, either as the "animator", "author" or "principal" (Goffman, 1981) in their judicial discursive actions. Generally, the judges were the principals in the coordinative and inquisitive actions. Such a discourse authority was performed in discourse actions such as rule instruction and requestion. In the representative and attributive actions, judges were more likely to project themselves as the author or animator. This was illustrated by the fact that few judgments were passed directly after the trial. Instead, it was formulated in the name of the judge.

For judges, there was another incumbency associated with the identity of officialdom. That is, judges displayed a strong political concern in their discursive actions. For example, in one case which had been remanded by the appellant court for a new trial (Case C. S. L. 7), the judgment made after the *de novo* hearing was greatly expanded to include reasoning on both factive representation and legal reasoning. In order to decide on one legal rule to apply when there were two competing ones applicable, the judge drew on a socio-political discourse to justify it. The following was the outline of the argument made in the judgment:

Extract 57 (C. F. L. 7)

During the *de novo* hearing, the court meticulously weighed the pros and cons and oriented to the valued principle that judicial function lies in its possibility to strike a balance between the modest restraint and subjective agency and discovered a better resolution. The answer to the question is cautiously formulated as follows:

The value underscoring the judicial judgment: The rights to life and health take precedence over the operation and development of the hospital.

The conclusion based on theoretical analysis: It conforms to the legal principle to apply the General Principles of Civil Law and relevant judicial interpretation to cases concerning the damages caused in medical negligence, particularly to the compensation for death.

The way for the hospital to overcome difficulties: Participating in Medical Liability Insurance.

Besides showing respect to the superior (as the whole judgment seemed to be developed as a response to the court of the higher level), the argument made as in the above extract was not a reasoning on legal principles but sounded more like a political deliberation. Firstly, this judgment used some self-promotional remarks (e. g. "meticulously weighed", "cautiously formulated") which was unusual in judicial judgments and was put here, although implicitly, with an intention to gain recognition from the higher court. Secondly, the different discourses that were drawn on to form this argument were political by nature. For example, the first argument was a human rights discourse which was now politically accepted. The third argument was related to the hospital operation which was at present the business of government administrators in China. The especial mention of the administrative issue displayed the policy-oriented nature of judges' discursive actions. This projection of political interest in judicial behavior was explicitly recognized in law. For example, in Article 2 of the Civil Procedure Law, it is stipulated that:

> *The Civil Procedure Law of the People's Republic of China aims to..., educate citizens to voluntarily abide by the law, maintain the social and economic order, and guarantee the smooth progress of the socialist construction.*

With this predisposition of political interest, judges would naturally integrate the political cognition into their discursive actions (van Dijk, 2004). Political discourse was incorporated as a resource for judges in making decisions, particularly in cases of wider social interest.

5.5.3 Social Member

Our analysis of judges' discursive actions shows that they drew on, besides law and hard case facts, a wide variety of discourses which were associated with a broad scope of social knowledge. They took the form of presupposed concepts, vision of reality or lines of argument. These were the "soft facts" that were necessary to constitute and justify discursive actions. The incorporation of these soft facts had much to do with the fact that every case which was brought to the court was rooted in certain specific social context and judges'decisions would have consequential impacts not only on the parties involved but also on the general public. To resolve a dispute, judges must take into consideration the particularities of case on the one hand and, to gain the public recognition, identify with their values, attitudes, moralities, etc. on the other. This practice expanded the scope of case facts and law. It could be taken as the ideological nature of judicial behavior. The question is how specific social discourses or ideologies were incorporated into the judicial actions. Our discursive-psychological explanation is that judges aligned themselves with an identity as the social member which was based on the "forms of life" (Wittgenstein, 1997) that judges shared with their audience. Let's take a divorce petition case for example. This case had been brought to the court three times previously and the divorce petition was rejected by the court every time. In the fourth attempt, the court, however, granted the petition:

Extract 58 (C. F. L. 4)

The plaintiff filed the suit to the court for divorce three times, respectively in December 2005, June 2007 and January 2008. The defendant asked the court to reject the petition on the ground that he was receiving medicinal care. The court took into consideration all the arguments made by the defendant and rejected the plaintiff's petition in favor of the defendant's recovery. However, the marital relation between the plaintiff and defendant has not improved thereafter. According to Article 3 in *Suggestions on How The People's Courts Determine the Marital Rupture in Trying Divorce Cases* issued by the Supreme People's Court, the court can grant the divorce petition when one party of the spouse suffered from the mental illness during the marital life and could not be cured over a long period of time. In the said case, the defendant has suffered from mental illness caused by epilepsy. He has not been cured after receiving long-term medical cares. The spouses have been living separately for more than two years. It makes no sense to sustain the marriage. With this, the court rules that the marital relation between the plaintiff and the defendant has broken up. The court grants the petition made by the plaintiff Zhang...to divorce the defendant Gao....

Although the Marriage Law stipulates some general categories of situations in which the petition for divorce can be granted, it is not always legally categorical in deciding whether the divorce petition is legally allowable. In reality, there is more than one factor which judges need to consider and the different factors may contradict to each other. In the above case, the petition for divorce was firstly rejected three times on the factual ground that the defendant was ill and was granted in the fourth time based on a legal provision (i. e. the breakup of the relation). This contrast in decision making could not be satisfactorily explained by the legal provisions alone since there is no specification on exactly how long one party of the spouse must endure for the medical treatment of the other party. The delay of granting the divorce petition, however, was reasonable given our culture which appreciates the external invention to enhance rather than rupture the marital relation. The identification with this cultural or ethical values could be seen as an act of discourse appropriation (Fairclough, 1992) through which the social identities of judges were evoked in their judicial behavior.

By orienting to the social identity, the judge recognized himself as a social member and identified his rationality with that of the community membership. Such an orientation was also taken as the norms for judicial discursive actions by the judges to complement the legal rules. In our research, we found a most explicit projection of the social identities in judges' discursive actions was the moral teaching in some judgments. The following was one example:

Extract 59 (C. F. L. 6)

The court will especially point out that since the plaintiff and the defendant have been in brotherhood and lived together for many years, they shall understand that the deep mutual affection exits between brothers and the great kindness that the parents devoted to them. It will be the greatest filial piety you can show and the greatest comfort you can bring to your deceased parents if both can make allowances for each other, get along well and cherish the mutual affection in the daily life. It is a reverence shown to each other as well as the deceased parents if both of you can make good negotiations, show respect to each other and resolve quarrels in time based on law and social moral values over the issue of burying the deceased mother so that the deceased mother can get rested soon. If the deceased could know it in the heaven, what she disliked most was the fact that the two sons have become hostile to each other over the place to bury her and damage the brotherhood of years. Meanwhile she would not be willing to see her own remains to be transferred from place to place by her two sons. Therefore, both the plaintiff and defendant might harbor no ill-intention initially. But the plaintiff and the defendant shall realize that it is adverse to their real intention if the dispute is not settled, the brothers are at odds and the deceased can not get rested. Although conciliations have been tried several times, the two parties have reached no consensus. It is hoped that the plaintiff and the defendant shall be able to reflect and resolve disputes after receiving the judgment so that their parents' souls in heaven can be comforted.

This is extracted from the judgment of a case concerning a dispute between an adopted son (the plaintiff) of a deceased couple and a son of the female spouse with her ex-husband (the defendant) over the disposition of their mother's remains. The latter transferred his mother's remains from her tomb to his father's graveyard without notifying the former. The plaintiff filed a petition to the court for a reinstatement of the remains and claimed for mental stress compensation. In the judgment, the defendant's action was deemed as legally inappropriate. However, the court did not grant the petitions by the plaintiff. What made this judicial behavior remarkable was that it was not grounded on the law. Instead, the judge appealed to the emotional reasoning by mentioning the socially cherished values: the affections between brothers, filial piety and deference to the deceased. When incorporating these social discourses, the judges shifted from a stiff justice doer into an ordinary social member. The judgment was persuading the litigants to make allowances for each other in this case. By doing so, the form of family life was projected and consequently the "public opinions" (Sun & Xiong, 2007) was introduced as a resource for solving this case so that the limitations of judicial judgment could be curtailed.

5.6 Summary

This chapter shows how judges' multiple identities constitute a pervasive and complex grammar for "doing" justice. Judges' identity is the stake and interest that the judges oriented to in their judicial behavior. By drawing on the sociolinguistic theory on discourse and identity, we explicate the three levels of identity that underscored judges' discursive actions. Specifically, we spell out how the multiple identities of judges were oriented to in their judicial practices and how they impinged on the judicial outcomes. Discourse, situated and transportable identities were found to be assumed respectively as the linguistic, institutional and socio-cultural resources which shaped the judges' discursive actions. With this identity framework we identified of judges, the four discursive actions and their variation could be accounted for. A rationale we provide for judges' judicial behavior goes as follows: Judges in the judicial process are all occupied with the mission to resolve social conflicts and our judicial system has set up a procedure through which a judicial resolution normally undergoes. Under such a system, the judges are institutionally positioned as the procedure organizer, fact investigator and order maker. In performing these institutional identities, two discourse identities are relevant: To initiate and control the participation of the litigants, judges orient to the initiator identity and to bring off conflicts, judges rely on evaluative actions. We also note that each situated or discourse identity can be realized in various discourse forms. The specific forms and their distribution are related to the transportable identities that are made relevant in the context. For example, when a case arises for which no explicit law is applicable, some judges might attribute their decisions to an approximate law while others might deliver a policy-related argument (The rejection and grant of the divorce petition in C. F. L. 4 can serve as an illustration of this contrast). This disparity, we argue, is rooted in their different identity orientations.

The strength of our multi-layered analysis of judges' identity is that various epistemological elements are able to be flexibly integrated in a theoretical account of JJB. As noted by Bucholtz & Hall (2008), traditional conceptualization of identity as a set of enduring social categories such as gender, race, and class fails to address the dynamics of social interaction. None of the spectrum of identities will be made visible in all stages of judicial procedure. Nor is it possible to exhaust the spectrum of identities that judges assume in judicial process. Identity analysis in such a tradition can only take certain perspectives and account for data of particular types. Our approach enjoys much more flexibility in addressing the complexity of this social phenomenon.

Chapter 6

The Ontology of Judicial Behavior

6.1 Introduction

Our analysis of judges' discursive actions has shown that there was no unified way of "doing justice". No general rules of justificatory reasoning or epistemic and axiological premises (Wroblewski, 1988) could account for all JJB, nor could we reduce their behavior to the function of judges' personal dispositions. That is, the theoretical-model approach may fail to capture the contingency of JJB. Judicial decisions are now considered as the synergetic effects of variant factors such as the relevant laws, case facts, judges' attitudes, and so on. Although an integrated approach has been proposed, how the relevant factors shall be incorporated to derive a decision is still under-explored. In this research, we find that all the various factors did not automatically generate a fair and just judicial decision. Our analysis is based on judges' own account of their behavior, i. e. their identity performance. The findings suggest that the divergence of judges' discursive actions was associated with judges' varying identifications. By drawing on Bourdieu's sociological conception of praxis (Bourdieu & Wacquant, 1992), we argue that identity performance was judges' "capital" that was made available by the "habitus" and the locus that judges occupied in the filed of judicial practice. Thus, in this chapter, we will explore further into the "field" to see how judges were positioned within it. The objective is to capture how variant identities were mobilized, temporarily stabilized and turned into JJB.

Our account will differ from the traditional sociological approach in that we focus on the personal order (Wetherell, 2007) rather than on the abstract social context. In other words, our objective is to provide an ontological account for the dynamism between the agency and structure for JJB. To do so, we will begin with an account of judicial disparity as revealed in our analysis of judges' discursive actions and identity performance. Following this, our discursive-psychological approach to judicial behavior research will be revisited by drawing on Heideggerian philosophical insights.

6.2 Disparity in JJB

The analysis of judges' discourse practice in Chapter 4 reveals four general discursive actions judges undertook in the judicial process. The actualization of these actions, however, varied from case to case. For example, the inquisitive was normally fulfilled in the form of interrogatives. But imperatives were also commonly seen in judges' case investigation. Meanwhile, both the interrogatives and imperatives could be used as coordinatives. The variation in enacting discursive actions suggests that JJB was not law-bound in a strict sense. The form that a specific discursive action took turned out to be the emergent property of the courtroom dynamism. That is, we can not account for JJB simply based on their form of language use. For this, let's examine one discourse phenomenon, i. e. attitude checking questions (ACQ), and see how judges oriented to different identities and performed different discursive actions by using the same discursive form. An ACQ is semantically a question which elicits personal opinions:

e. g.

Does the defendant/plaintiff have different opinions or not?

(Translated literally)

In our sampled data, 27 tokens were located. Analysis shows that they were used to perform both coordinative and inquisitive acts.

Extract 60 (C. F. M. 6)

1. Judge: Next, we will proceed to examine the procedure through which the defendant made the sued decision.

2. Defendant: The Shenxin Taifeng case was placed on file for investigation on May 31, 2005. Our Letter of Administrative Penalty was sent to the parties involved on May 10, 2007. Then the plaintiff appealed for a hearing, which was held for the defendant on July 25, 2007.

3. Judge: Does the plaintiff have any objection?

4. Plaintiff: No objection over this point.

Extract 61 (C. F. L 9)

1. Judge: The plaintiff, you said you doubted about the signature by Yu ... on the will. Do you really have any objection over the signature by Yu...? Will you apply for an authentification?

2. Plaintiff: I have objections over the signature. But I will not apply for anauthentification.

In Extract 60, turn 3 by the judge was an ACQ which followed a factual account given by the defendant. This occurred in the sequence of evidential examination in which one party had just presented an account. The judge's ACQ was obviously a mediating act served to assign the turn and coordinate the interaction order. The judge's ACQ was articulated either to encourage or to give permission for the other party to participate. Within this discursive action, we can see that the judge did not display his personal uptake on the subject matters. What was addressed through such a discursive action was simply the turn control. That is, the judge was assuming the identity of procedure organizer. Different from this, the judge in Extract 61, although articulating the same ACQ, was inquiring into a specific substantial issue. This interest of the judge was further highlighted in his use of the emphatic ("on earth"). The judge appeared to be insisting on a definite answer from the plaintiff. What he performed was a fact finder. It was found that the frequent use of ACQ by different judges did not lead to the same nature of their judicial behaviors. The reason for this inconsistence is that judges assumed several identities at a time and the projected identities might vary across cases. In the above two cases, the articulation of an ACQ was common to both judges but what they actually performed was different.

The lack of correlation between the discursive actions and identities suggests that although judges could buy into the institutionalized discursive forms, what they actually did was more varied than they appeared. One significant implication by attending to this phenomena is that judicial behavior research shall go beyond most current theories which are basically deterministic or correlative as expressed in statistical terms and hence unable to specify how judges' biographical characteristics as well as the socio-cultural environment are related to judges' judicial behavior. Our analysis of judges' identity performance has focused on how judges fulfilled their interest and stake in their own behavior. In this section, we will further examine the distribution of judges' identities based on our discourse analytic findings and ethnographic observations to understand the epistemological basis for judges' judicial practice. It is found that judges' discursive actions can be roughly characterized along three instantiation clines, based on the identities that were framed.

6.2.1 Procedure-oriented vs. Substance-oriented

The first dimension along which judges' discursive actions varied was their stake or interest shown towards the topical issues. Our research suggests that judges could either be proceduralists who observe the judicial proceedings or fact investigators who actively participate in the judicial investigation. This contrast was manifested in the employment of coordinatives and inquisitives. As the statistical analysis of the ten sampled cases in our ethnographic dataset (Table 6-1) shows, the coordinatives accounted for 65.9 percent of all the discursive acts articulated by the judges. However, there was a great variation across different cases. Some cases had a surprisingly higher proportion. For example, in Case 10, among the 25 discursive actions, 23 were coordinatives. The remaining two were attributives: one was the ruling on an item of evidence and the other was the passing of judgment. No inquisitive was undertaken by the judge. On the contrary, there were some other cases in which the inquisitives were more prominent, such as Cases 3, 4 and 7. The difference shown through this simple statistics suggests that justice could be pursued in different ways. Some judges attached more importance to the procedure and involved the defendant more while the others allowed greater flexibility in procedure and concentrated more on the issues relevant to their decision making. These two types of judges are hereafter characterized respectively as "procedure-oriented" and "substance-oriented".

Table 6-1 Distribution of Discursive Actions

Case	Coordinatives		Inquisitives		Representatives	Attributives
	Tokens	Percentage	Tokens	Percentage		
Case 1	59	65.6	30	33.3	1	0
Case 2	31	77.5	9	22.5	0	1
Case 3	26	51.0	25	49.0	0	0
Case 4	16	47.1	18	52.9	0	0
Case 5	44	68.8	18	28.1	2	0
Case 6	31	75.6	9	22	1	0
Case 7	11	46.3	12	50	0	1
Case 8	37	68.5	9	16.7	7	1
Case 9	50	66.7	23	30.7	0	2
Case 10	23	92	0	0	0	2
Total	328	65.9	153	30.7	10	7

For the procedure-oriented judges, the mediated turn taking system was dominantly practiced. The details of relevant rules were instructed in *extenso*. The interactional order was monitored to ensure equal and balanced opportunity of all litigant parties. The judicial proceedings generally followed the procedure law. Judges' own inquisitive actions were enacted as complementary and consequently the litigants were often allowed more freedom to pursue specific subject matters. Fewer interruptions or interventions occurred in the course of courtroom interaction.

The situation was opposite when judges were substance-oriented. They tended to assume the identity of fact investigator in the judicial process. That is, the judicial agenda was set by the judges and the litigant parties were subordinated to the status of respondents in the courtroom interaction.

This variation of judges' interest in either procedure or substantial issues could be related to various factors. Through the analysis of our sampled data, we found that there were three contexts in which judges often explicitly oriented to the proceduralist identity: Firstly, it occurred when the case facts were rather evident. That is, it was not necessary for judges to investigate since there was no controversy over the cases facts or the applicable laws. This was already illustrated when we discussed Case 10 in 5. 4. 2. Secondly, when litigant parties were equal in terms of accessibility to the information about the case and the stake in interest, judges were more likely to remain restrained from getting involved in the investigatory tasks. The typical example we located was a case about a dispute over the visiting rights of their daughter between a divorced couple. The judge allowed both parties to state their positions and made little effort to explore the case by himself. Thirdly, judges were also concerned only with procedural matters when the litigant parties were well represented by legal professionals. For example, Case 6 was an administrative case in which a company and a government department were both represented by lawyers. Throughout the trial process, the judge only sparsely made some complementary requisitive actions.

Similarly, the substance-oriented approach could also be shed light on by considering the specific conditions of the cases. Our data suggest that when the case facts were in dispute, judges would regularly lend more efforts to investigation. In Extract 25 (see Chapter 4), for example, the judges asked the plaintiff a series of questions concerning the condition of the shoes and relevant information on the purchase of the shoes. These inquisitive actions were pertinent given the argument made by the defendant that the plaintiff's demand for refunding was rejected on the ground that the shoes were worn out and the fact that the plaintiff did not bring the shoes to the court.

Judges would also elaborate his inquisitive interest when the litigants were less competent in the legal literacy. In Case 1, the plaintiff was a woman whose husband died when carrying wood on a job with the villagers' community committee. She filed the case for death compensation and support for the surviving spouse. After the statement and evidence presentation, the judge asked several questions concerning his economic status and physical conditions. These questions were facilitative in that they contributed to legitimatizing the plaintiff's claim.

Substance oriented judges often pursued a specific plot of the story by their own. That is, they were particularly interested in the coherence of the whole case account. This was well illustrated in Case 3 in which after the opening statement and testification, the judge started to pursue the whole story by asking some comprehensive questions. The following was the initial one:

Extract 62 (Case 3)

1. Judge: The court will interrogate both litigant parties in terms of the case facts. Both parties shall give honest factual statements on the execution of the entrusted resettlement agreement, including the house transfer and payment. The agreement was signed in 1995. State the deals you have made so far.

In this case, both litigant parties were represented by lawyers. Their presentations and arguments were well adapted to the legal categorizations. That is, they were logically sufficient for the formation of judicial opinions. However, the judge in this case displayed an interest in the storytelling and made a case to elicit factual information.

6. 2. 2 Authority vs. Solidarity

Besides the different interests in topical issues (procedure vs. substance), judges might also vary in their interpersonal styles when they enacted their trial discursive actions. One interesting judicial juncture we found was the conciliation motion. The civil procedure stipulates that "In trying civil cases, the people's courts shall conduct conciliation for the parties on a voluntary and lawful basis" (Article 9). However, among the 10 cases in our corpus data, two judges did not try the conciliation procedure (Case 4 and Case 6). For Case 7, the conciliation procedure was not necessary or impossible, since only one party of the litigants appeared in the court. The other 7 conciliatory acts were initiated as follows:

Extract 63

1. Judge: The court debate is over. According to the stipulations in relevant laws, the court can conduct conciliation for the parties on a voluntary and lawful basis. Now I would like to ask both parties. Do you agree to enter conciliation? Case 1

2. Judge: According to the stipulations of relevant laws, before passing the judgment, the litigant parties can enter conciliation with the court's mediation on the voluntary and lawful basis. Now the court is seeking the plaintiff's opinion. Do you want to enter court conciliation? Case 5

3. Judge: The court proceeding continues. According to the evidence found in the court investigation and presented by the plaintiff, the plaintiff has displayed her care and love for the child. Do both parties agree to enter the conciliation?

Case 2

4. Judge: The case has gone through court investigation, (0. 2) court debate. (0. 3) In the civil cases, the people's court shall conduct conciliation on the voluntary and lawful basis. We hope that two parties can reach an agreement under the court's auspice based on the facts and the realist principle; two parties can understand and forgive each other for the sake of harmony and the long term interest. Do the plaintiff and the defendant agree to enter the conciliation? Case 8

5. Judge: The court debate is over. Now the court proceeds to conciliation. Do both parties agree to enter the conciliation? Case 3

6. Judge: Do both parties agree to enter the conciliation? Case 9

7. Judge: The court debate is over. Can both parties enter the conciliation? Case 10

Among the seven judges, we can identify three approaches they adopted to initiate the conciliation procedure. The first two judges were record-oriented (Philips, 1998), for they only stated the relevant legal regulations as the warrant for their initiation of the conciliation procedure. The third and fourth instead adopted a more humanistic approach. The judge in the third case pointed out the common interest between the two parties-the love for their child. In doing so, the judges displayed his intention to persuade the litigants to reach conciliation. The fourth judge also encouraged the litigants to enter the conciliation by expressing his advice that the two parities should be realistic and consider their long-term interest. Both judges identified themselves with the litigants and adopted an affect-oriented approach in initiating coordination. The last three judges appeared to be ego-centric in that the conciliation-initiation action was treated as routine. No justificatory grounding was provided for it either.

The three approaches to perform the conciliation initiation task shed light on three types of transportable identities of judges and three approaches to judicialbehavior. The record-oriented judges oriented to the identity of justice doers, for whom judicial decisions were reached by strictly applying the rules and principles that constitute the law. The affect-oriented judges would consider themselves as the policy makers and resolving conflicts as the objective of their judicial practice. For them, the law was the resource rather than the sole criterion in decision making. They recognized and explicitly emphasized the particularities of each case. So politics, economics, and personal and social values could all possibly shape their judicial behavior. Judges identified themselves with the social members in general. For the routine-oriented judges, decisions were also built on the rules of law but relied more on their own discretion than the record-oriented judges. Their role was much like the administrative officials who acted to the law but also allowed leeway to their own creativity in decision making. These different identities form a continuum of judges' power in relation to the litigants, with the authority and solidarity located at the two ends. The three types of judges we identified above were respectively occupying three loci from the upper end to the lower end:

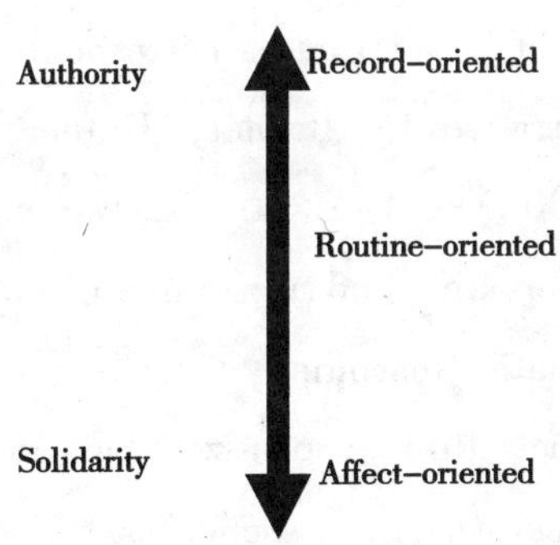

Figure 6-1 Judges'Power Orientation

The three types of judges can be shown to subscribe to different configurations of their discursive actions and identities. For example, in inquiry, some judges adopted the strategy of solidarity by allowing the litigants more freedom to construct a version of the case. Some others might tend to care more about the application of rules rather than the substance in issue. Again still some others could exercise their authority through challenging or nailing down specific information they wanted. The nature of this variation was related to the trial styles of different judges and the specific conditions of the judicial process. It was too complex to provide a systematic characterization since it involved many factors (for relevant studies in other legal systems see Conley & O'Bar (1990) and Philips (1998)). Our research does, however, indicate that judges' judicial behavior had much to do with the interaction of the three major transportable identities. When evaluating a judge's judicial behavior, it is important to see what he or she values in terms of their identity orientation.

6. 2. 3 Paradigmatic vs. Narrative

The third dimension concerning variation in judges' judicial behavior was related to their modes of thinking, i. e. how judges dealt with the substantial content in their judicial behavior. In 5. 4. 3, we mentioned that judges could focus either on rationality or on consequentiality in making judicial order. These two theories of judicial cases correspond with the differentiation of paradigmatic and narrative by Bruner (Bruner, 1986; Amsterdam & Bruner, 2000; Heffer, 2002) ①. They are the two modes of reasoning that underscore judges' representative and attributive discursive actions.

6. 2. 3. 1 Paradigmatic Reasoning

Paradigmatic reasoning (PR) emphasizes the truth or rationality of an argument based on logical consistency or soundness. It transcends particularities to achieve systematic, categorical cognition. Fundamental to this mode of thought is categorization (Heffer, 2002). In judicial practice, the information available to the

① A similar finding of American small claim court judges is made by Conley & O'Bar (1990) who use the term of rule-oriented and relationship-oriented.

court is often fragmented or circumstantial. It should be categorized before fitting into the judicial logic constructions. As Bruner (1986) argues, "to make decisions is to categorize." Judges' judicial behavior involves categorization by reformulating various case accounts into a legal argumentation. The following extract can illustrate how paradigmatic reasoning was utilized to establish a legal fact:

Extract 64 (C. F. L. 8)

As to the plaintiff's claim for mental damages compensation, the court takes into account the special cause of the disease the plaintiff suffered and the fact that it was not diagnosed until the plaintiff had visited several hospitals. After the diagnosis was confirmed, the plaintiff was hospitalized for medical treatment for a long time, which inflicted both physical and mental pains on the plaintiff. The court decides that the defendant pay the plaintiff 5000 *yuan* for the mental damages.

This extract was concerned with the arrival of the decision whether the plaintiff suffered mental damage and what amount of compensation should be granted. This judicial process involved a discursive recontextualization (Bernstein, 1990) which related the lifeworld discourse to that of law. That is, the cause of the disease the plaintiff suffered and the long period of medical treatment (lifeworld discourse) were relocated into the attributive discourse as the justificatory ground for the affirmation of mental damage (a legal category). As we can see, the affirmation of mental damages was not contingent on the existence of mental suffering in the individual involved. There was no direct evidence to affirm the psychological reality of mental damages. The two quoted reasons were by nature circumstantial. Moreover, it was never certain how the compensation for mental damage could be measured by the amount of money. So what is interesting to judicial behavior researchers is the nature of the warrant for judge's categorization. It was more than an issue of rule application. An analysis of the two decisions involved in the above extract could illustrate its complexity:

Firstly, the mental damage was affirmed. This affirmation was legally warranted, for claim for mental damage compensation was accorded in *The*

Supreme People's Court's Explanations on Issues Concerning Law Application When Trying Cases on Physical Injuries on the condition that there was the damage to the health (Article 1) .

Secondly, the mental damage compensation was granted. This decision making was much more complex than the first one. According to the legal rules, the judge needs to make allowance for variant case facts including the liability of the injuring party, the cause and consequence of the injury, the economic conditions of the concerned parties, etc. However, there are no principled rules to measure all these facts. The actual decision making is to a great extent subject to judges' discretion. As Extract 64 indicates, the decision on mental damage compensation was up to the judge's personal opinion. The mundane reasoning is often applied by the decision makers. This suggests that the warrants for judges' paradigmatic reasoning are not exclusively legal. Instead, social, political, moral and ethical principles can all serve as the warranting for paradigmatic reasoning. The following extract is another example in which the paradigmatic reasoning was warranted by the extralegal principles:

Extract 65(C. F. L. 6)

Although the joint burial of a couple is not specified in the law, it signifies the potential rights of the person, an inherent rights enjoyed by a couple. It conforms to the good social custom and normal ethical and moral criteria. It shall be confirmed in the law.

This case involved a cultural practice—the joint burial of a couple. Since it is a social phenomenon not addressed in the current codes of law, how to classify it into a legal category is totally up to the discretionary decision by the judge. In the judgment, two justifying principles were provided: one was that the joint burial of a couple conformed to the good social custom and normal ethical and moral criteria, the other was that the socio-culturally justified practice was legally confirmed. This suggests that judges could go on free excursions from the domain of law to the domain of broad social context.

Paradigmatic reasoning was mainly found in the part of judgment which began with "the court holds" part. It was an inherent component of every judicial judgment. However, the proportion it took up in the judgment varied from case to case. Table 6-2 was a simple statistical analysis of the 10 sampled judgments in our dataset. It was calculated by dividing the total number of Chinese characters in the PR part① by that of each judgment:

Table 6-2 Proportions of Paradigmatic Reasoning in the Judgments

Cases	Length of PR *	Length of judgment	Proportion (%)
C. J. L. 1	2416	4769	50. 7
C. J. L. 2	238	2899	8. 2
C. J. M. 3	1062	4509	23. 6
C. J. M. 4	250	1790	14
C. J. L. 5	327	1500	21. 8
C. J. L. 6	3114	4648	67
C. J. L. 7	4836	9051	53. 4
C. J. L. 8	647	3488	18. 5
C. J. M. 9	1415	4630	30. 6
C. J. L. 10	174	1080	16. 1

Note: * The length is calculated on the number of Chinese characters in the texts.

This table shows that PR was unevenly distributed. According to our data, PR was prominent in performing two judicial functions:

a) Resolving controversy

According to Table 6-2, C. F. L. 6 contained the longest part of paradigmatic reasoning in terms of proportaion (67%). This case involved a theft of a woman's corpse by his son (with her ex-husband) from the grave where she was buried with her second susband. Her son transferred it to his father's grave. The case was brought to the court by the adopted son of the

① We only included the-court-argues part. There was also paradigmatic reasoning in the fact report part which was mainly a reproduction of the litigants' argumentation.

woman and her second husband. The controversy of the case was that no existent law regulates the disposal of the deceased bodies. The judgment developed a lengthy paradigmatic reasoning, containing four sections:

a) the judicature over the case

b) the legal status of the woman's adopted son in the suit

c) the ownership of the corpse

d) the legal attribute of relocating the corpse

Except b), the remaining three issues were not explicitly treated in current laws. So the judges had to seek extralegal support in the paradigmatic reasoning (see Extract 65 discussed above). To do so, moral reasoning was extended as part of the judicial decision:

Extract 66 (C. F. L. 6)

It was not an appropriate act for the defendant Zhang... to move his mother's corpse on his own. But it was ethically acceptable considering the fact that Zhang...has buried his father and mother together. Since it did not exceed the moral tolerance, if we moved the corpse by force again, it also went against the custom of "bringing peace to the deceased by burying it" and was disrespectful to the deceased. Thus the court will not award the demand by the plaintiff that the corpse of Zhang...be buried together with his step father Huang.

In this paradigmatic reasoning, the defendant's act of moving his mother's corpse was considered legally inappropriate but ethically acceptable. This suggests that competing princinples were operating here. The defendant's act was inappropriate from the plaintiff's perspective in that it infringed the plaintiff's interest but it was ethically acceptable from the defendant's perpective, for it was a way of showing love to his deceased parents. The first argument was based on the legal regulative rules while the second was purely moral. Following this, the judge rejected the plaintiff's demand of restoring the corpse by introducing a moral principle again. We can see the whole argument appropriated both legal and extralegal regulative rules. This appropriation was associated with the two identities of judges: a law administrator and a member of the social community. The former was oriented in formulating the judicial decision while the latter was reflected in the morally implicated attributive terms such as "inappropriate" and "tolerance". The assumption of different identities made it possible for judges to resolve controversial issues which were not well addressed in law.

b) Aiming for accountability

C. F. L. 7, another case containing a large proportion of PR, was a retrial of a case of which a previous judicial opinion had been overruled by the court of appeal. In 5. 5. 2, we have already shown how judges oriented to both an identity of law interpreter and one of policy maker in arguing for the legal rule applied. We argue that it was their institutional identity as officials that made it necessary to incorporate the policy analysis of public hospital admininstation into their paradigmatic reasoning. Judges made extensive use of some self-promotional remarks in the judgement. This had much to do with their intention to gain recognition from their institutional superior in the higher court. Besides this, the paradigmatic reasoning in this judgment was also characterized by its insertion of endnotes which made reference to some authoritative sources such as academic articles, government documents, and public speeches by the officials. This could be taken as efforts to draw on other institutional discourses for support. By doing so, the judge established his warrant for his judicial decisions. This seemed to violate the independent status of judges in the trial. But if we consider the judges' hierarchical institutional identity, this action was reasonable. Within our judicial system, the judges were subject to the supervision from their superiors. Since the case discussed here was one that was ordered to conduct a *de novo* hearing, it was necessary to make the second judgment as a response to the superior court. It was this political concern that made those paradigmatic rules reasonable.

6. 2. 3. 2 Narrative construction

Besides paradigmatic reasoning, judges also relied on their story-telling or narration in developing theories of cases. Narration of the case fact is an integral requirement of fact-based judicial principle and a way of structuring our sense of reality (Bruner, 1991). Narrative is characteristic of its own logic of plausibility. That is, there is an internal coherence in which information is structured. Bruner points out that there are two dimensions of narrative thinking: the "landscape of action" (the plot) and the "landscape of consciousness" (the motivations). The former outlines the actions and the actors and the latter their mental states (goals, beliefs, emotions). He also argues that a narrative can be characterized in terms of five features: ordinariness and legitimacy, narrative time, the narrative teleology of human striving, the nature of the trouble, the fate of protagonists, and delineating plights (Amsterdam & Bruner, 2000). For the judicial narrative, our research reveals that judges differed mainly along two distinct dimensions:

a) Structured vs. fragmented

This dichotomy was related to the organization of the content in narrative. The drafting of judicial judgment seemed to follow a template in which a case narrative consists of the following sections:

- General case information
- The plaintiff's statement and claim
- The defendant's argument
- The court's discovery

Under this formulaic composition, we could, however, still discover great variety among the narrative structures. In the part of "the court discovers through investigation", for example, judges' narrative of the case facts could be either fully structured into a story or selectively fragmented into a summative outline. The following extract was one example of the more structured story. It reported the testimony by a witness:

Extract 67 (C. F. L. 1)

On November 20, 2006, he (the witness) was waiting for Bus 21 on Shuiximen Bus Station. The plaintiff was also waiting for the bus then. Two buses came in a while. The plaintiff wanted to take the bus in the second place and ran towards it passing by the defendant. The plaintiff was holding a bag and a thermos bottle then. Later, he saw the plaintiff lying on the ground. The defendant helped the plaintiff to rise. He also went over to help. But he was not noticing the moment the plaintiff fell nor did he see how the plaintiff fell. The plaintiff was already lying on the ground and the defendant was helping the plaintiff when he saw it. On that afternoon, he went to the police station on call for making a written record. A Mr. Shen police interviewed him. As to this testimony, the plaintiff objected and stated that there was a third person on the spot but not the one who was called by the defendant. The defendant affirmed the testimony and argued that this testimony should be admitted as the legal facts.

The above story followed "the landscape of actions" by showing the sequential development of the case. Besides information on what happened, this narrative also contained both a summary of the witness's testimony and the response to it from the plaintiff and the defendant. That is, the narrative attended to two realities of the case (Hale & Gibbons, 1999). One was the primary reality that referred to ' the here and now of the courtroom itself'. The other was the secondary reality, or "the particular context and events that were the subject of the court's deliberations". This was a distinctive feature of narrative in the judicial judgments. It involved not only the description of the case but also the variant voices within the judicial process.

However, judges did not always make such full-fledged stories. Case accounts were sometimes more attributive than representative. As the below extract shows, judges' representations of case facts sometimes did not follow a narrative time or a structured plot. Instead, discrete items of facts were enunciated through listing, often preceded with a topic-focusing phrase:

Extract 68 (C. S. L 7)

Ⅵ The alteration in the Letter of Consent on Anaesthetization for The Hospital of... County, it was stated that " intraperitoneal hemorrhage was diagnosed before operation. It is scheduled to perform exploratory laparotomy at 20: 30 on May 25, 2004". According to the Authentification Report (2005) No. 28 issued by the provincial High Court, it was confirmed that "20: 30 was an alternation of 10: 30". (It was annotated that 10: 30 here shall be 10: 30 pm.)

Different from structured stories, the fragmented narratives included only factive assertions. That is, what was presented was (dis) affirmed facts. The details and controversial information were avoided. The narration was developed along some focused themes. Consequently, there was no obvious storyline for the whole narrative. Instead, the thematised enunciation constituted the arguments for the attributive actions.

These two types of narrative indicate that judges could either represent the case facts in a balanced and objective manner or only take up patches through careful sifting. However, both discursive strategies accomplished the same judicial purpose-doing justice. The variation of the narrative styles was related to the variant discursive purposes in JJB. For example, in Extract 67, the dispute was about whether the defendant knocked the witness down. Since no witness or evidence was available to reproduce the scene. What the judge had access to was only circumstantial evidence. In this case, a structured narrative was able to enhance the objectivity of the case by developing "a narrative trajectory that limited what could and could not be said" (Baldwin, 2005). The example above shows that the narrative could be rendered in such a way to discredit the witness. During the judicial proceeding, the witness had been called by the defendant to appear in the court obviously. He testified that the defendant did not run into the plaintiff. The narrative in the judgment, however, distorted the witness's testimony by projecting partially the fact that the defendant helped the plaintiff up after the accident. Such a structured narrative held the defendant culpable.

The fragmented narrative was instead emphasizing the legitimacy in affirming case facts. For example, in Extract 68 the evidence involved was an authentification report by the provincial High Court. The fact in point was thus affirmed by means of the legal evidence rule.

Our research of the ten sampled judgments shows that the two narrative styles were correlated with the central disputes of the case. When the case facts were insufficiently ambiguous, a structured narrative was often made. It could enhance the circumstantial evidence which judicial decision making had to rely on. When the case facts were informatively clear, the fragmented narrative could be used to project the legitimacy and relevance in terms of the values of involved case facts.

b) Constitutive vs. representational

Another dimension along which narratives vary is what they do to fix on reality. Narrative can be either constitutive or representational (Anton, 1999). In constitutive narrative, the facts are materially, rhetorically, and discursively crafted by the narrator while the representational narrative is a construal of "what really happened" (Baldwin, 2005). One key differentiating feature in judicial narratives between these two styles is the degree of judges' involvement in shaping the legal facts. Constitutive narratives tend to highlight judges' personal conception of the cases in their accounts while the representational approach can be used to project the objectivity of case representation. A comparison of the following two extracts will elucidate the use of the two narrative strategies:

Extract 69 (C. F. L 4)

The defendant Gao ... suffers from epilepsy which has caused psychonosema. It is organic psychosis and can not be cured. In 2007, the defendant was classified as the seriously handicapped and unemployed in the rural area. Since April, 2008, he has started to receive subsistence allowances of 347 *yuan* each month. He also enjoys free medicine (exclusive to home-made brands). If hospitalized, he can get reimbursed from the department of cooperative medical service administration according to the policy or obtain financial subsidy from the department of civil affairs.

Extract 70 (C. F. L. 1)

The investigation found that on the morning of November 20, 2006, the defendant was waiting for Bus 83 at the Bus Staion of Shuiximen. At about 9: 30, two No. 83 buses pulled in simultaneously. The plaintiff wanted to take the bus in the second place. When she passed the back door of the first bus, the defendant was the first person to get off the bus. The plaintiff fell and got hurt. The defendant noticed it and helped the plaintiff to the roadside. When the plaintiff's family came, the defendant and the plaintiff's family sent her to the hospital. The plaintiff was diagnosed to have fractured thighbone and cervical vertebra.

Both extracts were taken from the section of"The court discovers through investigation". They were the recapitulation of case facts from the perspective of the judge. A comparison of the two extracts will give a snap-shot of the difference between the constitutive and representational approaches to case narrative:

Firstly, the narrated content in the first extract was thematized while that in the second was somewhat isolated. The first extract could be found to evolve around a focused topic, i. e. the defendant's incapability to maintain his subsistence. Through the juxtaposition and structuration of relevant facts (e. g. the social pensions the defendant has received), the evidence was established or constituted in the narrative. However, the narrative in the second extract only enumerated relevant case information among which no logical connectors were provided. For example, it was mentioned that the defendant got off the bus and the plaintiff fell. But the causal relation between the two events was only presupposed. What was narrated in the representational approach was only informational patches, leaving an informational gap in the case account.

Secondly, the two extracts differed in the nature of"the narrative teleology of human striving" (Amsterdam & Bruner, 2000). The constitutional narrative had a clear end. This was shown in the rejection of the plaintiff's claim for alimony and child support made right after the first extract. The representational narrative instead remained vague in terms of its telos. In the second extract, we can hardly read off the purposes of the judges except a representation of relevant case information.

Thirdly, these two narratives displayed different ways of judges to exercise their jurisdiction. The constitutional narrative was often projected as the judge's own cognitive representation of the case. That is, judges' evaluative stance was ostensibly marked. In representational narrative, judges, however, assumed a more neutral stance. What they incorporated in the narrative was restricted to the case facts rather than their legal significance. The absence of key narrative elements① and the lack of coherence (due to the fragmented nature) could be often found. However, this narrative pattern is not judicially flawed. Instead, it provides the juncture for judges to insinuate their judgment which they could not pass otherwise.

In this section, we have shown how judges' behavior varied in three dimensions by relating to their discursive actions and identities. Our findings suggest that judicial disparity can not be simply reduced to the institutional or cognitive constraints. By relating judges' discursive actions to their identity performance, we have shown how judicial behaviors are contingent on the judges' orientation in terms of their discourse, situational and socio-cultural identities. What deserves our particular attention is that the judicial disparity does not necessarily lead to injustice. Different discursive actions serve particular judicial purposes, all of which can be enveloped within the semantic field of "judicial justice". In this sense, one key agenda of JJB research is to explore the semantic potentials of "judicial justice".

---

① According to Kenneth Burke, agent, act, purpose, agency and scene are the five minimally required constituents of narrative (cited in Amsterdam & Bruner, 2000). However, we found in Extract 70 that some elements were missing. For example, it mentioned that the plaintiff fell. But the agent, agency and scene were not provided.

6.3 The Ontological Structure for JJB

Rejecting the reductionism in traditional approaches to judicial behavior, our discursive-psychological approach has revealed how JJB is epistemologically contingent on judges' identity orientation in the judicial process. Our analysis of judges' discourse practice shows that the type and form of a particular discursive action that judges enact can be accounted for by relating to the specific discursive frame in which judges orient to a specific identity. Although discourse theories enable us to see what identities are articulated in judges' discursive actions, no systematic account is provided for why a specific identity is oriented to by judges. That is, the question still remains as to how JJB is ontologically grounded. To answer this question, we will take our lead from Heidegger (1985) in relation to his work of *Dasein* Analytic. The main theoretical insight we draw from it is that the care of judge is the preconditions for judges' knowing. We will establish the ontogeny of JJB on the care structure of judges.

6.3.1 Heideggerian Theory of Being

The question of Being was the central issue that runs throughout the Heideggerian philosophy. Heidegger (1985) begins with the distinction of Being and beings. He argues that in the course of over two thousand years of history, philosophy has attended to all the beings that exist in the world (the entities including the "world" itself), but has not dealt seriously with what "Being" (*Sein*) itself is. Western philosophy has treated "Being" as something transparent. Such a tradition has consequently failed to address the important philosophical questions by confining philosophical investigations solely to beings (*Seiende*). Against this philosophical tradition, Heidegger seeks to interpret the meaning of Being as such by focusing on a particular

Being viz., Human Being (*Dasein*). He conducts the *Dasein* Analytic to uncover the fundamental structures of Human existence. Two observations about *Dasein* are:

(1) *Dasein* is in each case mine

(2) The "essence" of *Dasein* lies in its *Existenz.*

Heidegger identifies two modes of Existenz: authentically (free to choose their life style) or inauthenticially (imposed with a pre-designed role in their society, family, peer group etc). Heidegger argues that the most general structure in which human beings exist is the "empirical", ontic level of average everydayness or *Being-in-the-world*. This average everydayness thus forms the starting point for the interpretation of *Dasein*. Although *Being-in-the-world* is a unitary structure which must be seen as a whole, it is methodologically "divided" into different parts and levels. Being-in-the-world denotes *Dasein*'s concernful being alongside entities and tarrying with others (being-with-others). That is, Heidegger's analysis discloses two fundamental moments that are always present in *Dasein* and, for the most part, are also involved in a third moment.

(1) *Befindlichkeit* ("How one finds oneself")

This moment reflects the "fact" that *Dasein* always embeds itself or dwells in a situation. Heidegger describes it as throwness (*Geworfenheit*). That is, *Dasein* is "thrown" in a world (most radically at birth) and is always already in a world.

(2) *Verstehen* ("Understanding")

Dasein is characterized for its active comportment towards possibilities. Heidegger says that understanding is altogether permeated with possibilities. It can be directed towards both the world (the referential totality of involvements) and *Dasein* itself (a self-understanding).

Since understanding can be directed towards the for-the-sake-of-which, i. e., *Dasein* itself, it is possible for *Dasein* to be transparent to itself. Heidegger's Dasein Analytic is particularly after this kind of understanding.

(3) *Verfallen* ("Fallenness")

This moment expresses *Dasein*'s average everydayness—*Dasein*'s immersion in the world of its everyday concerns and projects. This is the level at which the moments of *Befindlichkeit* and *Verstehen* usually operate.

The aforementioned three moments constitute the essential unity of *Dasein*'s basic state. But they are never wholly separate from one another. Heidegger calls the unity of this unitary "structure Care" (*Sorge*). That is, "Care" is the Being of *Dasein* or the Nature of Human Being. Moreover, Heidegger also notes that the care-structure is grounded in Temporality (*Zeitlichkeit*). Each of the structural moments manifests what Heidegger calls a temporal ecstasy: *ahead-of-itself*, *being-already-in-(the world)* and *being-alongside-entities (and caring-for-others)*. In other words, the care which underscores *Dasein* is associated respectively with three temporal directions: *futural*, *past* and *present*.

Heidegger also investigates the sense of the self manifested for the most part in everyday existence. His conclusion is that proximately and for the most part, everyday Dasein has no "self" of its own. One's sense of self is instead given from the outside. Heidegger characterizes this as "the they-world", or simply as "the they" (*Das Man*).

6. 3. 2 Judges' Caring and Knowing

In line with Heidegger, the fundamental issue of any philosophical exploration shall be the Being of beings. According to Heidegger's distinction of Being and being, judges' discursive actions and their identities are the ramifications or beings of judges' Being. In this sense, judicial behavior research is to uncover the Being of judges. For human beings, Being takes the form of their concernful activities or care. Therefore, the analysis of judges' Being is to describe judges' care structure.

6. 3. 2. 1 Judges' Care Structure

Heidegger argues that care is the condition of possibility for the being. It has a unitary structure which can be delineated into three moments. For JJB, they are: 1) judges' relation to the judicial setting. It involves the litigation process, the litigants, the legal rules, the institutional arrangement and so on; 2) judges' understanding of the Being of those relevant entities in the judicial setting (including the judicial activities to undertake and the legal consequence and significance to expect) and of the Being of their own (e. g. the sense of honor as a judge, self-respect, etc.). This is concerned with the reflexivity of JJB; and 3) judges' everyday practical comportments through which the first two moments operate. This moment constitutes the JJB proper. The Being of judge is manifested in their participation in the judicial activities.

Based on this conception, judges' identity is a function of their care structure. Our characterization of judges' identity into discourse, situated and transportable is comparable to the three moments of care structure. The discourse identity reflects judges' caring about their comportments or discursive actions in everydayness (or *Verfallen* in Heidegger's terminology). The situated identity is rooted in the world in which judges are thrown in (*Befindlicheit*). The transportable identity is the judges' sense of the possibility toward which actions are directed (*Verstehen*).

6. 3. 2. 2 Caring and Justice

Within the legal scholarship, one dispute concerning JJB is what rules or knowledge is essential for judges to do justice. Attempts have been made to chart the cognitive ground for the judges. However, the chance of this endeavor to succeed is slim, for JJB is not simply an issue of knowledge. Our discursive analysis shows that judicial behaviors are often made without sufficient legal reasoning. Judges may also reach different judicial decisions when the circumstances of cases are similar. In this case, it is not likely to pinpoint the exact knowledge that judges exploit. Neither are judges always conscious of the way they behave.

Compared with the given theories of JJB, the view which takes JJB as a function of judges' care structure has two theoretical strengths. Firstly, it can address both the structural and contingent nature of judicial justice. The CPA generally treats JJB as a rational choice. However, the discourse analysis of JJB indicates that not all JJB meets the standard of rationality. Judges do not always rely on their propositional knowledge about law. Neither do they have consistent policy preference or fixed set of intentional goals. In other words, there is a contingent nature of doing judicial justice that is not well addressed in the traditional theories of JJB. By attending to the care structure of judges, we are, however, able to reveal the dynamism between structure and agency that underscore JJB. The three moments of care embrace the personal, situational and socio-cultural dimensions of JJB. Understanding JJB in this way suggests that "judicial justice" shall be transformed from an ethical or moral concept to a discursive construct. In this light, we shall reject the pursuit of a transcendental entity of "justice" in JJB research. Instead, our focus is on how justice is lived out as an emerging social phenomenon. This will enable us to account not only for the rational behavior or act of justice but also for the deviant behavior or "act of injustice".

Secondly, the analysis of the care structure can shed new light on the nature of knowledge for JJB, particularly on the implicit knowledge which is often neglected. Heidegger argues that there are two modes of human being: authentic and inauthentic. They provide two types of knowing for social behavior. The former is the most fundamental mode of being for human beings. That is, human beings exist in their Being-in-the-world or everydayness. This ontonic level of knowing is fundamentally characterized by contingency. Based on this ontological ground for human beings, judicial behavior shall have for its foundation a way of being which is not cognized representationally. Judges shall interpret the cases holistically rather than analytically. It is the phenomenological understanding that forms the background against which judicial deliberation occurs. However, it is noticeable that the operational focus of current judicial practice is almost invariably on the inauthentic mode of judges' knowing, which is externally imposed. Our judicial system relies on the formulated legal rules. For judges, the procedure laws and judicial guidelines are stipulated to manipulate judicial behavior. Judges' discretion is circumscribed. But judges' authentic knowing is largely ignored or illegitimated.

In practice, judges need to reconcile these two types of knowing. They constitute two theories that are juxtaposed in JJB. The narrative and paradigmatic distinction is a manifestation of the two types of knowledge. The ignorance of judges' authentic knowledge will limit our understanding of JJB. Although it is intuition-based and lacking prima facie justification, it is an essential component of judges' practical knowledge. In judicial practice, judges' deliberation and reasoning are precipitated mostly by essentially problematic situations, where established rules and propositional knowledge break down. In this sense judges' knowledge based on their authentic caring will be more significant in resolving legal issues.

In short, the authentic and inauthentic knowing reflect two basic modes of judges' Being. By attending to the two types of caring displayed in judges' behavior, we are able to reveal a fuller picture of the epistemological ground for JJB.

6. 3. 2. 3 On the Way to Discourse

The discussion of caring and justice suggests that an appropriate way to construe JJB is to look into their care structure rather than the transcendental concept of "justice". In other words, judicial behavior research involves a description of judges' experience in their everydayness. Heidegger argues that to be able to describe experience properly means finding the being for whom such a description might matter. For Heidegger, the description of human experience shall be conducted with reference to "Dasein", the being for whom being is a question. This implies that research into JJB shall be made with reference to the being of judges.

For Heidegger, what characterizes human being, or *Dasein*, is its self-comportment (relating itself to its Being). Or put most simply, *Dasein* cares about its life, its existence. There is reflexivity in *Dasein*. Heidegger characterizes this feature as *Existenz* and argues that the "essence" of *Dasein* lies in its *Existenz*. There are two modes of Existenz which unify *Existenz*: A) *Eigentlichkeit* (authenticity or that which is my own) *and Uneigentlichkeit* (inauthenticity or that which is not my own). The manifestation of Existenz is realized in everyday actions. Heidegger (1947: 1) remarks on the dependence of being on action as follows:

> *The essence of action is perfecting <something>. Perfecting means to unfold something in the fullness of its essence, <and in so doing> to bring it forth, producere. Therefore, <the> perfectible is actually only that which already is. Yet that which above all "is" is be[-ing].*

This suggests that actions offer the channel to gain access to the Being. Continuing with this argument, Heidegger states that it is thinking that relates Being (*Dassein*) to the everyday coping of man. That is, thinking is considered as the most important action of all. However, thinking does not make or cause the relation between them. Thinking just brings forth or manifest beings solely as something handed over to them from Being. When discussing the mediating role of thinking between beings and Being, Heidegger (1977) introduces a most significant being involved in *Dasein*—language:

> *...in thinking Being comes to language. Language is the house of Being. In its home man dwells. Those who think and those who create with words are the guardians of this home. Their guardianship accomplishes the manifestation of Being insofar as they bring the manifestation to language and maintain it in language through their speech.* (*p.* 217)

By regarding language as the house of Being, Heidegger sets out his *Dasein Analytic on the way to language*. As the above quotation indicates, Being is manifested through thinking in the form of language. Our thinking is not separatable from the language we use. The ontological status of things is not given apriori. It arises from naming and using them in concernful activity. It is language that makes this process possible. Thus, language is not only one element of the Worldhood that *Dasein* is embedded in and cares about but also constitutes the beings of *Dasein*. In other words, language occupies a central position in Heideggerian theory of Being. Language is the focus for *Dasein* Analytic.

In short, the central theme of Heideggerian theory is to approach the Being of *Dasein* by focusing on actions and language. In this sense, we find that our approach to JJB by focusing on the discursive actions and identity is consistent with Heideggerian theory of Being. Our research can be seen as a project to explore the Being of judges. The identities that judges oriented to are the focused manifestations or moments of judges' care structure or Being. Judges' Being is construable from their actions which are performed in language (They are called discursive actions or discourse in our theoretical framework).

In light of these philosophical insights and our research work, two arguments can be made in terms of research into JJB:

1) It shall be better off starting from the phenomenal point, i. e. judges' beings in everydayness or their forms of life (Wittgenstein, 1997). The traditional view of judges' behavior is mainly concentrated on the abstract conception of justice and the propositional knowledge that is necessary for the performance of justice. This neglects the phenomenological nature of judges' Being. One consequence of this is that judges' authentic knowledge is often deprived of and discretion which is necessary given the contingent nature of legal case will be hopelessly twisted. Following the civil law system, only the statutes and laws are recognized as effective in China. Judge-made law is prohibited. Even the rights to judicial interpretation are

confined only to the Supreme People's Court. The judicial experience, however, indicates that judges' judicial behavior involves, besides legal rules, various other sources of knowledge such as social values, political interests, psychological dispositions, etc. (Fu, 2001). Most of these are not the propositional knowledge but knowing that is based on judges' authentic mode of Being. Although they are fundamental or more essential than propositional knowledge to JJB, they are scarcely acknowledged on the table. That is to say, we are ignoring aspects of JJB which are practically more fundamental.

To balance this situation, attention shall be devoted to judges' lived experience. Research is required to explore the configurations of the specific moments of judges' care structure or Being. To do so, an ethnographical sketch of judges' everyday professional life shall be made first of all, for Being always implies a holistic view of the past, present and future of the Worldhood in which being is made possible.

2) A discourse approach shall be called for to relate the ontic level of judges' behavior to the ontological level of judges' Being. The purpose of judicial behavior research is to uncover the care structure that underscores judges' actions. However, the Being is not a being that are observable. What is accessible to the outsiders is the actions that are mainly performed by means of language. We cannot directly reach judges' Being through their discursive actions. It is necessary to incorporate some discourse theories so that the relationship between care and discourse or actions can be illuminated.

In this research, we have attempted to bridge this gap by drawing on pragmatics, DP, interactional linguistics and anthropological linguistics. We propose a theoretical framework which consists of two key concepts: discursive actions and identity. This framework enables us to address the possibility of understanding judges' Being. Firstly, by focusing on judges' discursive actions, we are able to capture judges' concernful activities. These activities are the beings of judges' Being. By examining how the beings were made possible, we are able to reveal the nature of judges' Being. Our functional taxonomy of judges' discursive actions is proposed as one strategy for this purpose. Secondly, the analysis of judges' identity performance can reveal how judges' discursive actions are underscored with their care structure. Our study of judges' identity is based on systematic linguistics theories (CA and sociolinguistics specifically). By doing so, we are able to relate judges' discourse practice, identity and the discourse order they are positioned in.

6.3.3 Summary

This chapter starts off with judicial disparity, a central issue in legal practice as well as legal scholarship. Based on our characterization of judges' discursive actions and identity performance in the last two chapters, we are able to show that judges in trial differ not only in their decisions regarding certain legal issues but also more fundamentally in their ways of engaging in the judicial process. Three dimensions along which judicial behavior can vary are evident in our data. From the perspective of subject matters that interest judges, the focus of judicial behavior can be on either law in its limited sense or the issue in its broad social sense. The judicial process is an interactional process involving more than contemplative activities. When engaging the relevant litigants, judges can act either as the authority or in a more facilitative role. This difference can lead to different participation framework in the judicial process and consequently result in variation of judges' perception of the cases. In processing the case information, judges can adopt either a paradigmatic or narrative approach. This difference directly bears on their conceptions of legitimacy and justice. According to our data and findings, there is no patterned variation in terms of these three dimensions. However, when we come to a specific performance, we are able to discover how each discourse strategy is employed to do justice that is situated.

To address the nature of the variation in judges' discursive actions and identity performance, we find theoretical support from Heideggerian theory of Being. In line with Heidegger's philosophy, we can say that judges' judicial behaviors (i. e. discursive actions) are the manifestation of judges' Being or care structure and these two are related with judges' identity, the psychological instantiation of care. Since identity can be discursively construed by means of current discourse theories, the phenomenal understanding of judges' Being is made possible. With this, a methodological implication for further research in JJB is that a combination of ethnography with discourse analysis is necessary to explore into the Being of judges.

Chapter 7

Conclusion

7.1 Introduction

This chapter first presents a brief summary of the reported research. Next, the major findings will be reviewed. Then, the theoretical and practical implications are discussed. Concerns are addressed in relation to the bearings that this discursive-psychological study may have on JJB and the judicial behavior research for academic interest. Finally I take up the limitations of this research, along with possibilities of further studies suggested by the current project.

7.2 Summary of the Research

This research is initially stimulated by the legal anthropology which focuses on the actual judicial process rather than the universal legal principles, and on conflict rather than accord (Conley & O'Bar, 1990). Our objective is to gain a heuristic understanding of JJB. Our foray into discourse is guided by the discursive turn in social sciences. This transdisciplinary effort turns out to be a fruitful perspective into judicial practice.

In this study, we begin with ethnographic observations of some judicial trials and look into the judicial judgments produced by judges. This study is based on an extended Discursive Action Model (DAM) which draws on some other linguistic and philosophical theories to enhance its applicability. Discursive action and identity form the two central analytical foci. Based on the findings of discourse analysis, an ontological account of JJB is proposed. To be specific, our research is done in three consecutive steps:

Firstly, the judges' judicial discourse is characterized by referring to linguistic theories such as CA, SAT, EST and LA. We develop an analytical framework for construing discursive actions. All judges' discourse is coded for the structural frames it falls into and the discursive categories it exploits. Based on this, we taxonomize judges' discursive actions and elaborate the discursive diversity in the realization of judges' discursive actions.

Secondly, we examine how judges' discursive actions are rhetorically constructed by evoking judges' particular identities. It is generally recognized that judges' discursive actions are designed in ways that anticipate their possible refutation or undermining as false, partial, or interested and that they are likely to be designed to undermine, in turn, alternative versions. In this light, a discursive psychology of JJB shall address a dilemma of judges' stake or interest. This dilemma is manifested in judges' identity performance, for identity provides the interpretative framework for judicial behavior. In our research, we code our data according to judges' Zimmerman's (1998) taxonomy of identity. We explore how different identities are exploited in judges' discursive actions.

Thirdly, we elucidate how judges deal with the issue of accountability in their judicial behavior. Judges' discursive action and their identity performance are underscored with their justificatory reasonings. For example, in presenting judicial opinions, judges need to justify the authenticity of the case facts they base on and confirm the legitimacy of their legal reasoning. In doing so, the agency and responsibility of judges are involved. In our research, we find that they can be manifested by relating to judges' identity performance, for judges' identity orientation is emblematic of the epistemological positions underscoring their judicial behavior. Based on the findings of judges' identity performance from our data, a discursive account of judges' judicial disparity is provided in this research.

To provide an ontological account of JJB, this research subscribes to Heidegger's theory of being and relates judges' knowing to their care structure.

7.3 Major Findings

This study shows how some heuristic understanding of JJB can be gained from a DP perspective. We do not only demonstrate how DP can be operationalized in judicial behavior research but also provide a new theorization of this institutional phenomenon. The major findings will be presented in the following three subsections, which constitute our answers to the three research questions proposed in Chapter 1:

7.3.1 Discursive Characterization of Judicial Behavior

In this research, the JJB is pinpointed in terms of their discursive actions. Based on our data, we find that a general frame of courtroom interaction was oriented to as the constituent phases of trial. We also identify four types of discursive actions that judges undertake: coordinative, inquisitive, representative and attributive. These four discursive actions can serve as the conceptual construct of JJB. Each discursive action serves particular judicial function. Besides this general characteristic of judges' judicial discourse, we also note the following features of judges' judicial discourse:

1) Their discursive actions are diversely enacted;

Judges' discursive actions one varied in terms of their linguistic realization. Each discursive action could be enacted in different ways. For example, the coordinatives could be performed in the form of a demand, request or direction. Moreover, each speech act in the linguistic sense could perform more than one discursive action.

2) Judges differ in their preference to particular discursive actions;

Although judges on the trial normally follow the general frame of trial, there is no fixed pattern of action. For example, we find that in some cases, no inquisitive was undertaken by the judge. On the contrary, there were some other cases in which judges dominate the proceeding with their inquisitive actions.

3) There is no neat correspondence between the trial phases and judges' discursive actions.

Judges have their own styles of trial. For example, in the phase of investigation, some judges just acted to coordinate the court interaction by maintaining the order while others tend to control the information flow by taking up the interrogating opportunity as much as possible.

In short, our findings suggest that there is a tension between structure and agency in judges' discourse practice. There is an institutionalized judicial proceeding but there is no fixed way of doing justice.

7. 3. 2 Judges' Epistemological Positioning

To account for the judicial discursive actions, we explore judges' "epistemological positioning" (Bednarek, 2006) by focusing on their self-identifying, an inherent feature of judges' discourse practice. Identities are the interpretive frames that constitute judges' knowing. By examining judges' identity performance, we are able to reveal the knowledge base of JJB.

To construe the identities that judges oriented to, we focus on such discourse analytical topics as speech acts, turn taking system, conversational exchange structure, and identity-implicative linguistic categories. Based on Zimmerman's three dimensions of identity, we have identified the repertoire of judges' identities in our data:

- Discourse: Initiator and evaluator

- Situated: Procedure organizer, factor investigator and order maker
- Transportable: Justice doer, officialdom and social member

Obviously, not all these identities accorded to the institutional roles of judges. This suggests that JJB relies on not only legal but also extra-legal knowledge. The discourse identity provided the linguistic resources that judges drew on. The situated identity gave shape to the interactional organization of the trial. The transportable identity offered the judges social ideologies.

Our study also shows that judges' identity orientation is contingent on the interactional process. The different identities judges oriented to realized different practical functions in the judicial process. By looking into the details of judges' discursive actions, we find that judges' identity was interactionally negotiated to accomplish various judicial activities.

These findings indicate that the study of discourse and identity can shed light on judges' epistemological positioning but no unified account could be provided based on discourse or identity theory alone.

7.3.3 An Ontological Account of JJB

According to the identity performance in judges' discursive actions, we find that JJB could deviate at least along three dimensions:

- procedure-oriented vs. substance-oriented
- authority vs. solidarity
- paradigmatic vs. narrative

This discursive reflection reveals the complexity of JJB that other approaches fail to. Although the three dimensions along which JJB differs have already been noted in some existent literature, the findings of our DP approach suggest a different theorization of it. In the traditional judicial behavior theories, the judicial behavior is generally treated as the constant function of judges' cognitive property or institutional constraints. The deviation is reduced to the malfunction of either the judge or the legal institution. In our discursive psychological view, we do not distinguish the normal from the deviant JJB. We hold that every instance of JJB is discursively accountable.

To propose a discursive account of JJB, we refer to Heidegger's theory of being. We relate the discursive dynamics to the various beings of judges. The being of judges is determined by judges' care structure or Being. In this light, the dichotomy of the three dimensions can be identified with two modes of being and caring as identified by Heidegger: authentic and inauthentic. These two types of caring nourish respectively phenomenological and propositional knowing for judges. We find that judges manifest both their authentic and inauthentic beings in their judicial behavior.

In the traditional legal scholarship, only the inauthentic being (i. e. institutional constraints) is emphasized. Judges authentic knowing (i. e. judges' emergent understanding) is instead neglected or considered as problematic. To address this gap, we argue that a theory of JJB shall attend to all the three elements of judges' care structure: judges' comportments or discursive actions in everydayness (or *Verfallen* in Heidegger's terminology), judges' sense of the possibility toward which actions are directed (*Verstehen*) and the world in which judges are thrown in (*Befindlicheit*).

In sum, this research begins with an ethnographic observation of current judicial practice and continues with heuristic understanding by drawing on a discursive action model. The findings of this research point to the ontological and epistemological nature of JJB. This can be conceived as a land clearing project, based on which further critical reassessment or institutional change can be made possible.

7.4 Implications

This study is an exploratory investigation of current institutional practice by Chinese civil judges. Although the cases we observed are limited in number and variety, the findings and the way we approach this topic do shed light on JJB in general. In this section, we will discuss how our findings can bear on law and judicial practice and what methodological implications we can draw from it for judicial behavior research.

7.4.1 Discursive Construction of Justice

By respecifying judicial behavior as discourse practice, our study reveals that there is a tension between structure and agency in JJB. There are on the one hand the general categories of judges' discursive actions and diverse ways of enactment on the other. This finding indicates that judicial behavior does not happen in practice in the ways suggested by the cognitive models. There is no fixed ways of doing justice in practice. There are two main points of interest resulting from this. One is that judicial justice is a concept whose nature needs to be negotiated from case to case. No specified rules can ensure the derivation of a justice decision. Justice is not automatically generated from law through deductive rules. The other is that the specific way of doing justice is associated with the stakes or interest that judges identify with. Justice is a discursive construction which is contingent on judges' identity orientation. This discursive perspective of justice challenges the foundation of modern judicial system in that law is premised on the discursive resources that are available to judges.

One important implication of this discursive view of justice is that the focus of jurisprudence shall be shifted from rule to people. As we know, the nature of law has always occupied the central place of modern jurisprudence. If law does not say all about judicial justice, we must explore how justice comes about. In our discursive perspective, the more immediate nexus is judicial behavior where judicial justice emerges as the discourse practice. By focusing on judges' discursive actions and identities, we have shown that JJB is ontologically rooted in their own care structure. The moments of this structure are interactionally constructed. This implies a heuristic approach is more appropriate than the dominant positivistic in addressing judicial behavior.

7.4.2 Possibility for Judicial Reform

According to the judicial principle laid down for judicial practice, judicial rulings shall be based solely on facts and law. That is, judges shall apply only legal rules and commit to facts as the premise for legal decision making. The practice of law is assumed as a univocal phenomenon. This is, however, found not to be the case in reality. According to our data, the diversity of judicial discursive actions and identity orientation is normal rather than exceptional. This finding echoes the conclusion from an anthropological study that judges' decision making is "an inconsistent collection of varying styles and approaches to law" (Conley & O'Bar, 1990). There is no unitary knowledge basis for judges. As Philips (1998) states, "law is richly and pluralistically ideological".

However, our judicial system ignores the varied influences that have been built on the seemingly common and unified discourse (Candlin & Maley, 1994). Our discursive study shows that law and fact are seldom fixed in terms of meaning and that judges can hardly be value-neutral in their institutional practice. The interpretation and application of law are inevitably affected by judges' personal perspectives of value. The problem with our current judicial system is that this contingent nature of justice is not adequately treated. For example, although judges' discretionary power is entertained in some laws and statutes, it is mainly treated as problematic and is subject to institutional intervention and regulation. The judicial judgments are often passed in the name of the court. The judges' personal voice is obscured. They hold no personal responsibility for their judicial behavior. Consequently, judges can either reduce their judicial behavior to the mandate of law or remain implicit over the epistemic sources of some discursive actions. In this way, judicial opinions are often not warranted by sufficient reasoning and the root of bias in judicial behavior is covered.

To avoid these deficiencies, it is necessary for judges to participate in the judicial interactional process as a personality. Only when judges are drawn attention to their own cares, particularly those authentic elements of care that are not officially recognized, can they be aware of the nature of their own behavior. To do so, we need first of all to be able to make evident the implicit knowledge, i. e., how discursive actions set in motion inferences about their identities or cares. This raises an interesting question of cause and effect. Critical legal scholars (e. g. Ungs & Baas, 1972; Kennedy, 1976) and feminists (e. g. West, 1988) have attended to this question. However, they have not provided a systematic means to document it.

> *In much of the literature, the reader hears only the voice of the scholar asserting the putative position of women, minorities, the working class, the poor, etc. Thus, critical scholarship has given us representations of a new set of voices, but the voices themselves remain muffled.*
>
> (Conley & O'Bar, 1990: 170)

Different from these scholaristic traditions, our study starts with discovering the authentic voices guided with a discursive action model. That is, we focus on judges' discourse practice and make systematic analysis by drawing on discourse theories that relate discourse to personal and social knowledge. By doing so, we are able to show the judges' actual epistemological positions. This in turn reveals the order of judicial discourse and the possibility of discourse transformation. For example, in our study, we notice that there is a lack of explicit caring for their colleagues in judges' discursive actions. Among the ten judgments we collected, we did not find any reference to other judicial opinions except the mention of the appellate opinions in the judgments of the second instance. Neither did we find the opinions of the different members of collegial panel in the judicial judgments. This indicates that current judicial practice does not respect peer authority. This obviously runs counter to the professionalization of judicature.

In short, our study has indicated how DP can shed light on the various cares judges display in their judicial practice. The judges' care structure will in turn enable us to see what to reform in current judicial system.

7.4.3 Critical Discourse Awareness

One main contribution of the DP approach to JJB is that judges' knowledge that is hidden, denied, unrecognized, and unacknowledged can be made manifest. For judicial behavior research, it can be problematic if we simply read off the cognitive process from what we can perceive of judges. There is no easy route to penetrate into judges' mind through their self-description or external observation. Our DP study of judicial behavior has demonstrated how this "black box" can be shed light on through an analysis of the pragmatics of their discursive actions. The distribution of discursive actions and the category of judges' identity are emblematic of judges' epistemologic positions. Since DP focuses not only on the general discursive patterns and constituents but also on the so-called noise, the variability, and the seemingly cognitive inconsistency or unreliability, both the specified or official knowledge and the implicit "ordinary practical reasoning" skills can be made explicit. Thus, one insight that flows from the contribution of this study is that it enables judges to realize their own epistemological positions. Our findings suggest that judges do not always act in line with the law. If judges' attention is attracted to their implicit knowledge, a critical reflection on JJB can be achieved and a "critical approach to expertise" (Myers, 1990: 252) can be generated. In this sense, DP can enhance judges' critical discourse awareness and promote their professional change.

7.5 Limitations and Suggestions for Further Research

This research has approached JJB from a DP perspective and produced a new theorization of JJB. Such a research, however, also has some inherent limitations which need to be taken into account in interpreting our findings:

Firstly, the ethnomethodology that DP relies on will restrict the generalizability of the research findings. The data that are collected are not representative in the statistical sense. Since DP bears a particular interest in the contingency of JJB, its findings shall be carefully taken when applied to other cases.

Secondly, the discourse analysis can only be partially made. We must acknowledge the possibility of alternative readings of the data. This is partly due to the dynamic and complex nature of judicial practice. We can hardly fix our perception on such a reality. This limitation is recognized as a general challenge to all linguists:

> *Linguists potentially expose their own in-house practices and beliefs to the scrutiny of a wide range of professionals in fields outside academia. They also make themselves accountable in some general sense to the general public. The question is: can linguistics as a whole meet this challenge?* (Hutton 1996: 205)

Although our research has approached judicial behavior from various linguistic perspectives, we do not assume that this analysis is exhaustive. We do not have all the necessary case information (e. g. ethnographic background of the judges) or the theories to cover all the discourse aspects. The DP accounts need to proceed only as far as is necessary to establish a working interpretation of the actions that constitute a social episode. Our interpretations of JJB are capable of further refinement.

Thirdly, our research does not grapple with an established proposal for the reform in the judicial practice. This research only presents a critical review of current judicial behavior. No argument is made on how judges shall behave on particular judicial context. One reason for this negligence is that examining judges' discursive actions and identity performance is not enough to conclude a constructive proposal for judges' judicial behavior change. JJB is a function of judges' care structure which is dictated by judges' relation to other participants in the judicial process. That is, to gain a comprehensive understanding of judges' care structure, we need to involve all the other beings. Such a project is out of the capacity of current research. The second reason to avoid proposing a version of judicial behavior change is that an ideological stance has to be taken in such an effort. But this is perverse to our heuristic purpose of research. Nevertheless, we do imply some possibilities of judicial behavior change in our discussion of the implications. One step that is necessary to go beyond critical to constructive is to realize "rational communication" (Habermas, 1986) in judicial process. That is, there must be first of all an agreement on a specific rationality. For this purpose, we propose that we could raise judges' critical discourse awareness.

As implied in the discussion of limitations, we can still further research into this topic along two directions: one is to go in-depth into specific judicial issues of practical concern. For example, our findings have indicated that some judges tended to assume the identity of law-maker when trying cases involving legal disputes. It is of great practical interest to find how such a law is made. Is it related to other identities of judges? How is it shaped through the courtroom interaction? How do other litigants reach to it?

We can also make comparative exploration into JJB to see the variation across cases or individual judges. This can be done through certain quasi-experiments by controlling the variables. For example, do the female and male judges differ in their orientation to the identity of law maker? Does the stake of possible judicial outcome shape the judges' orientation of identities?

Our research has taken a heuristic perspective on JJB. This perspective necessitates a relativist methodology. According to Potter (1998), the political interest of such a methodology "supports freeing up from established systems, change and openness" (p. 41). Our exploration into JJB allows for a reevaluation of the established practice of judicature. With more work along this line, we hope that new ways of doing justice will be opened up.

References

Abrams, R. (1981). The Nature of the Arbitral Process: Substantive Decision-Making in Labor Arbitration. *UC Davis Law Review*, 14 (3), 551-589.

Adeodato, J. M. (1999). The Rhetorical Syllogism (Enthymeme) in Judicial Argumentation. *International Journal for the Semiotics of Law*, 12 (2), 133-150.

Aldridge, M., & Luchjenbroers, J. (2007). Linguistic Manipulations in Legal Discourse: Framing Questions and "Smuggling" Information. *The International Journal of Speech, Language and the Law*, 14 (1), 85-107.

Amsterdam, A. G., & Bruner, J. S. (2000). *Minding the Law*. Cambridge, Mass. /London: Harvard University Press.

Annus, T., & Tavits, M. (2004). Judicial Behavior After a Change of Regime: The Effects of Judge and Defendant Characteristics. *Law & Society Review*, 38 (4), 711-736.

Antaki, C. (1994). *Explaining and Arguing: The Social Organization of Accounts*. London: Sage Publications Ltd.

Antaki, C., & Widdicombe, S. (1998a). *Identities in Talk*. London: Sage.

Antaki, C., & Widdicombe, S. (1998b). Identity as an Achievement and as a Tool. In C. Antaki & S. Widdicombe (Eds.), *Identities in Talk* (pp. 1-14). London: Sage Publications.

Anton, C. (1999). Beyond the Constitutive-Representational Dichotomy: The Phenomenological Notion of Intentionality. *Communication Theory*, 9 (1), 26-57.

Ashworth, A. (1982). *Judicial Independence and Sentencing Reform*. Cambridge: Cambridge University Press.

Atkinson, J. M., & Drew, P. (1979). *Order in Court: The Organisation of*

Verbal Interaction in Judicial Settings. London: Macmillan.

Austin, J. L. (1962). *How to Do Things With Words*. London: Oxford University Press.

Babbie, E. (2005). *The Basics of Social Research* (3rd ed.). Beijing: Peking University Press.

Back, K. W. (1961). Decisions Under Uncertainty Rational, Irrational, and Non-rational. *American Behavioral Scientist*, 4 (6), 14-19.

Baldwin, C. (2005). Who Needs Fact When You've Got Narrative? The Case of P, C & S vs. United Kingdom. *International Journal for the Semiotics of Law*, 18 (3), 217-241.

Baldwin, J. (1993). Police Interview Techniques: Establishing Truth or Proof. *British Journal of Criminology*, 33 (3), 325-352.

Ballou, M., Tabol, C., Liriano, D., Vazquez-Nuttall, K., Butler, C., & Boorstein, T. H., et al. (2007). Initial Development of a Psychological Model for Judicial Decision Making in Continuing Restraining Orders. *Family Court Review*, 45 (2), 274-286.

Baum, L. (1997). *The Puzzle of Judicial Behavior*. Ann Arbor: University of Michigan Press.

Baum, L. (2006). *Judges and their Audiences: A Perspective on Judicial Behavior*. Princeton, N. J: Princeton University Press.

Bavelas, J. B. (2005). The Two Solitudes: Reconciling Social Psychology and Language and Social Interaction. In K. L. Fitch & R. E. Sanders (Eds.), *Handbook of Language and Social Interaction* (pp. 179-200). New Jersey: Lawrence Erlbaum Associates.

Becker-Lindow, S. L. (2007). *Rape Shield Laws: The Effects of Admitting Prior Sexual History Evidence at Trial on Verdict and Sentencing Recommendations*. PhD Dissertation, Alliant International University, Fresno Campus.

Bednarek, M. (2006). Epistemological Positioning and Evidentiality in English News Discourse: A Text-driven Approach. *Text & Talk*, 26 (6), 635-660.

Benwell, B., & Stokoe, E. (2006). *Discourse and Identity*. Edinburgh: Edinburgh University Press.

Bergmann, J. R. (1992). Veiled Morality: Notes on Discretion in Psychiatry. In P. Drew & J. Heritage (Eds.), *Talk at Work: Interaction in Institutional Settings*. New Brunswick, NJ: Rutgers University Press.

Berk-Seligson, S. (1990). *The Bilingual Courtroom: Court Interpreters in the Judicial Process*. Chicago, IL: University of Chicago Press.

Berk-Seligson, S. (1999). The Impact of Court Interpreting on the Coerciveness of Leading Questions. *Forensic Linguistics*, 6 (1), 30-56.

Bernstein, B. (1990). *Structuring of Pedagogic Discourse, Volume IV: Class, Codes and Control*. London: Routledge.

Betsey, C. (2005). Income and Wealth Transfer Effects of Discrimination in Sentencing. *The Review of Black Political Economy*, 32 (3), 111-120.

Bhatia, V. K. (1983). *An Applied Discourse Analysis of English Legislative Writing*. Birmingham, England: University of Aston in Birmingham.

Black, J. (1997). New Institutionalism and Naturalism in Socio-Legal Analysis: Institutionalist Approaches to Regulatory Decision Making. *Law & Policy*, 19 (1), 51-93.

Bond, R. A., & Lemon, N. F. (1981). Training, Experience, and Magistrates' Sentencing Philosophies. *Law and Human Behavior*, 5 (2), 123-139.

Bourdieu, P. (1985). *Outline of a Theory of Practice. transl by R Nice*. Cambridge: Cambridge University Press.

Bourdieu, P., & Wacquant, L. J. D. (1992). *An Invitation to Reflexive Sociology*. Chicago: University of Chicago Press.

Bowers, F. (1989). *Linguistic Aspects of Legislative Expression*. Vancouver: University of British Columbia Press.

Brown, G., & Yule, G. (1983). *Discourse Analysis*. London: Cambridge University Press.

Bruner, J. (1986). *Actual Minds, Possible Worlds*. Massachusetts: Harvard University Press.

Bruner, J. (1991).The Narrative Construction of Reality. *Critical Inquiry,* 18 (1), 1-21.

Bucholtz, M., & Hall, K. (2005).Identity and Interaction: A Sociocultural Linguistic Approach. *Discourse Studies,* 7 (4-5), 585-614.

Bucholtz, M., & Hall, K. (2008). Finding Identity: Theory and Data. *Multilingua-Journal of Cross-Cultural and Interlanguage Communication,* 27 (1-2), 151-163.

Burton, S. J. (1985).*An Introduction to Law and Legal Reasoning.* Boston: Little, Brown.

Bushway, S. D., & Piehl, A. M. (2001).Judging Judicial Discretion: Legal Factors and Racial Discrimination in Sentencing. *Law & Society Review,* 35, 733.

Candlin, C. N., & Maley, Y. (1994). Framing the Dispute. *International Journal for the Semiotics of Law,* 7 (1), 75-98.

Carbaugh, D. (1995).Decision-making. In R. Harre & P. Stearns (Eds.), *Discursive Psychology in Practice* (pp. 137-163). London, UK: Sage Publications Ltd.

Case, D. O. (2007). *Looking for Information: A Survey of Research on Information Seeking, Needs, and Behavior* (2nd ed.).London: Academic Press.

Charnock, R. (2009). Overruling as a Speech Act: Performativity and Normative Discourse. *Journal of Pragmatics-Speech Acts in Legal Language,* 41 (3), 401-426.

Chouliaraki, L., & Fairclough, N. (1999). *Discourse in Late Modernity: Rethinking Critical Discourse Analysis.* Edinburh: Edinburgh University Press.

Cohen, F. S. (1935). Transcendental Nonsense and the Functional Approach. *Columbia Law Review.* 35 (6): 809-849.

Conley, H. M., & O'Bar, W. M. (1990). *Rules versus Relationships: The Ethnography of Legal Discourse.* Chicago: University of Chicago Press.

Conley, H. M., & O'Barr, W. M. (2005). *Just Words: Law, Language, and Power* (2nd ed.).Chicago: University Of Chicago Press.

Cotterill, J. (2002). *Language in the Legal Process.* New York: Palgrave

Macmillan.

Cotterill, J. (2003). *Language and Power in Court: A Linguistic Analysis of the O. J. Simpson Trial*. New York: Palgrave MacMillan.

Coulthard, M. (2005). The Linguist as Expert Witness. *Linguistics & the Human Sciences*, 1 (1), 39-58.

Coulthard, M., &Brazil, D. (1992). Exchange structure. In M. Coulthard (Ed.), *Advances in Spoken Discourse Analysis*. London and New York: Routledge.

Coulthard, M., & Cotterill, J. (2007). *An Introduction to Forensic Linguistics: Language in Evidence*. London: Routledge.

Danet, B., & Kermish, N. C. (1978). Courtroom Questioning: A Sociolinguistic Perspective. In L. N. Massery (Ed.), *Psychology and Persuasion in Advocacy* (pp. 413-441). Washington, DC: Association of Trial Lawyers of America, National College of Advocacy.

Delaney, A. E., McLay, H. A., & van, D. W. (2007). Influences of Discourse on Decision-making in EU Fisheries Management: The Case of North Sea Cod (Gadus morhua). *ICES Journal of Marine Science: Journal du Conseil*, m15.

Diamond, S. S. (1981). Exploring Sources of Sentence Disparity. In B. D. Sales (Ed.), *The Trial Process: Perspectives in Law and Psychology* (Vol. 2, pp. 387-411). New York: Plenum Press.

Drew, P. (1985). Analyzing the Use of Language in Courtroom Interaction. In T. van Djik (Ed.), *Handbook of Discourse Analysis* (Vol. 3, pp. 133-147). New York: Academic Press.

Drew, P. (1992). Contested Evidence in Courtroom Cross-Examination. In P. Drew & J. Heritage (Eds.), *Talk at Work* (pp. 470-520). New York: Cambridge University Press.

Drew, P., & Heritage, J. (1992). *Talk at Work: Interaction in Institutional Settings*. London: Cambridge University Press.

Drew, P., & Sorjonen, M. L. (1997). Institutional Dialogue. In T. van Dijk (Ed.), *Discourse Studies: A Multidisciplinary Introduction*. (Vol. 2, pp. 92-118).

London: Sage Publications.

Duranti, A. (1988). Ethnography of Speaking: Toward a Linguistics of the Praxis. In F. Newmeyer (Ed.), *Linguistics: The Cambridge Survey* (Vol. 4, pp. 210-228). Cambridge: Cambridge University Press.

Duranti, A. (1997). *Linguistic Anthropology*. London: Cambridge University Press.

Dworkin, R. (1977). *Taking Rights Seriously*. Cambridge: Harvard University Press.

Dworkin, R. (1999). *Law's Empire*. Harvard: Harvard University Press.

Ebbesen, E. B., & Kone, V. J. (1981). The Process of Sentencing Adult Felons: A Causal Analysis of Judicial Decisions. In B. D. Sales (Ed.), *The Trial Process* (pp. 413-458). New York: Plenum Press.

Edwards, D. (1994). Script Formulations: A Study of Event Descriptions In Conversation. *Journal of Language and Social Psychology*, 13 (3), 211-247.

Edwards, D. (1997a). *Discourse and Cognition*. Lonclon: Sage Publications Ltd.

Edwards, D. (1997b). Toward a Discursive Psychology of Classroom Education. In C. Coll & D. Edwards (Eds.), *Teaching, Learning and Classroom Discourse: Approaches to the Study of Educational Discourse* (pp. 33-48). Madrid: Fundacion Infacia y Aprendizaje.

Edwards, D. (1998). The Relevant Thing About Her: Social Identity Categories in Use. In C. Antaki, & S. Widdicombe (Eds), *Identities in Talk*, (pp. 15-33). London: Sage.

Edwards, D. (2004). Shared Knowledge as a Performative Category in Conversation. *Rivista di Psicololinguistica Applicata*, 4 (2-3), 41-53.

Edwards, D. (2005). Discursive Psychology. In K. L. Fitch & R. E. Sanders (Eds.), *Handbook of Language and Social Interaction* (pp. 257-273). New Tersey: Lawrence Erlbaum Associates.

Edwards, D. (2006). Facts, Norms and Dispositions: Practical Uses of the Modal Verb Would in Police Interrogations. *Discourse Studies*, 8 (4), 475-501.

Edwards, D. (2008). Intentionality and *Mens Rea* in Police Interrogations: The Production of Actions as Crimes. *Intercultural Pragmatics*, 5 (2), 177-199.

Edwards, D., Ashmore, M., & Potter, J. (1995). Death and Furniture: The Rhetoric, Politics and Theology of Bottom Line Arguments Against Relativism. *History of the Human Sciences*, 8 (2), 25-49.

Edwards, D., & Middleton, D. (1986). Joint Remembering: Constructing an Account of Shared Experience through Conversational Discourse. *Discourse Processes*, 9 (4), 423.

Edwards, D., & Potter, J. (1992). *Discursive Psychology*. London: Sage Publications.

Edwards, D., & Potter, J. (1993). Language and Causation: A Discursive Action Model of Description and Attribution. *Psychological Review*, 100 (1), 23-41.

Edwards, D., & Potter, J. (1999). Language and Causal Attribution: A Rejoinder to Schmid and Fiedler. *Theory & Psychology*, 9 (6), 823-836.

Edwards, D., & Potter, J. (2005). Discursive Psychology, Mental States And Descriptions. In Molder, H. and J. Potter [eds], *Conversation and Cognition*, (pp. 241-259). New York: Cambridge University Press.

Eggins, S., & Slade, D. (1997). *Analyzing Casual Conversation*. London: Cassell.

Ehrlich, S. (2001). *Representing Rape*. New York: Routledge.

Elwork, A., Sales, B. D., & Suggs, D. (1981). The Trial: A Research Review. In B. D. Sales (Ed.), *The Trial Process* (pp. 1-68). New York: Plenum Press.

Everett, R. S., & Wojtkiewicz, R. A. (2002). Difference, Disparity, and Race/Ethnic Bias in Federal Sentencing. *Journal of Quantitative Criminology*, 18 (2), 189-211.

Ewick, P., & Silbey, S. S. (1995). Subversive Stories and Hegemonic Tales: Toward a Sociology of Narrative. *Law & Society Review*, 29 (2), 197-226.

Fairclough, N. (1992). *Discourse and Social Change*. Camhrdge: Polity

Press.

Fairclough, N. (1995). *Critical Discourse Analysis: The Critical Study of Language*: London: Longman.

Fitzmaurice, C., & Pease, K. (1986). *The Psychology of Judicial Sentencing*. Manchester: Manchester University Press.

Fleury-Steiner, B. (2002). Narratives of the Death Sentence: Toward a Theory of Legal Narrativity. *Law & Society Review*, 36 (3), 549-576.

Foley, L. A. (1993). *A Psychological View of the Legal System*. IA: Wm. C. Brown Communications, Inc.

Fuchs, A. H., & Milar, K. S. (2003). Psychology as a Science. In D. K. Freedheim & I. B. Weiner (Eds.), *Handbook of Psychology: History of Psychology* (Volume 1, pp. 1-26).New Jersey: John Wiley & Sons, Inc.

Garfinkel, H. (1967). *Studies in Ethnomethodology*. New Jersey: Prentice-Hall, Inc.

Garfinkel, H., & Sacks, H. (1970). On Formal Structures of Practical Actions. *Theoretical Sociology*, 337-366.

Gibbons, J. (1994a). Introduction: Forensic Linguistics. In J. Gibbons (Ed.), *Language and the Law* (pp.).London and New York: Longman.

Gibbons, J. (1994b).*Language and the Law*. London: Longman.

Gibbons, J. (2003).*Forensic Linguistics: An Introduction to Language in the Justice System*. Malden, Mass. /Oxford: Blackwell.

Gibson, J. L. (1978). Judges' Role Orientations, Attitudes, and Decisions: An Interactive Model. *American Political Science Review*, 72 (3), 911-924.

Gibson, J. L. (1983). From Simplicity to Complexity: The Development of Theory in the Study of Judicial Behavior. *Political Behavior*, 5 (1), 7-49.

Gilzer-Katz, A. (2007). *Law, Religion and Domestic Violence: A Study of Judicial Decision-Making by Israeli Religious Courts in Cases of Domestic Violence*. Essex, University of Essex.

Gniscia, A., & Pontecorvo, C. (2004). The Organization of Questions and Answers in the Court Examination. *Journal of Pragmatics*, 36, 965-995.

Goffman, E. (1979). *Frame Analysis: An Essay on the Organization of Experience*. Cambridge, Mass.: Harvard University Press.

Goffman, E. (1981). *Forms of Talk*. Pennsylvania: University of Pennsylvania.

Goffman, E. (1983). The Interaction Order. *American Sociological Review*, 48 (1), 1-17.

GonzaLez, P. (2006). Interpreting Strategic Recontextualization Cues in the Courtroom: Corpus-Based Insights into the Pragmatic Force of Non-Restrictive Relative Clauses. *Journal of Pragmatics: Translation and Context*, 38 (3), 390-417.

Gottfredson, M. R. (1987). *Decision Making in Criminal Justice: Toward the Rational Exercise of Discretion*. New York/London: Plenum Pub Corp.

Gottfredson, M. R., & Gottfredson, D. M. (1988). *Decision Making in Criminal Justice: Toward the Rational Exercise of Discretion* (2nded.). New York/ London: Plenum.

Gu, Y., & Zhu, W. (2002). Chinese Officialdom (Guan) at Work in Discoruse. In C. Barron, N. Bruce & D. Nunan (Eds.), *Knowledge and Discourse: Towards an Ecology of Language* (pp. 97-115). Essex: Pearson Education Limited.

Habermas, J. (1986). Communicative Rationality and the Theories of Meaning and Action. In M. Cooke (Ed.), *On the Pragmatics of Communication* (pp. 183-214). Cambridge, Massachusetts: MIT.

Hadden, S. C., & Lester, M. (1978). Talking Identity: The Production of "Self" in Interaction. *Human Studies*, 1 (1), 331-356.

Hale, S., & Gibbons, J. (1999). Varying Realities: Patterned Changes in the Interpreter's Representation of Courtroom and External Realities. *Applied Linguistics*, 20 (2), 203-220.

Halliday, M. A. (1994). *An Introduction to Functional Grammar* (2nd ed.). London: Edward Arnold Limited.

Halonen, M., & Sorjonen, M. L. (2008). Using Niin-Interrogative to Treat the Prior Speaker's Action as an Exaggeration. *Discourse Studies,* 10 (1), 37-53.

Harre, R. (Ed.). (1986). *The Social Construction of Emotions*. Oxford: Blackwell.

Harre, R. (2001). The Discursive Turn in Social Psychology. In D. Schiffrin, D. Tannen & H. E. Hamilton (Eds.), *The Handbook of Discourse Analysis* (pp. 688-706) .Oxford: Blackwell Publishers.

Harre, R., & Stearns, P. N. (1995). *Discursive Psychology in Practice*. London: Sage.

Harris, R. C. (2008). *Black Robes, White Coats: The Puzzle of Judicial Policymaking and Scientific Evidence*. Piscataway, N. J.: Rutgers University Press.

Harris, S. (1984). Questions as a Mode of Control in a Magistrate's Court. *International Journal of the Sociology of Language,* 49, 5-27.

Hart, H. L. (1994) .*The Concept of Law* (2nd ed.) .Oxford: Clarendon.

Hedderman, C., Gelsthorpe, L., & Great, B. H. (1997). *Understanding the Sentencing of Women*. London: H. M. S. O.

Heffer, C. (2002a). "If You Were Standing in Marks and Spencers": Narrativisation and Comprehension in the English Summing-up. In J. Cotteril (Ed.) .*Language in the Legal Process*. New York: Palgrave Macmillan.

Heidegger, M. (1947/1977). Letter on Humanism. Frans. by M. Groth. In D.Krell(Ed.), *Basic Writings*(pp.213-266) .New York: Harper & Row.

Heidegger, M. (1985) .*Being and Time*. Oxford: Basil Blackwell Ltd.

Heinemann, T. (2008). Questions of Accountability: Yes-no Interrogatives that are Unanswerable. *Discourse Studies,* 10 (1), 55-71.

Henning, T. (1999) .Judicial Summation: The Trial Judge's Version of the Facts or the Chimera of Neutrality. *International Journal for the Semiotics of Law,* 12 (2), 169-210.

Heritage, J. (2004) .Conversation Analysis and Institutional Talk: Analysing Data. In D. Silverman (Ed.), *Qualitative Research: Theory, Method and Practice* (pp. 161-182) .London: Sage Publications.

Hettinger, V. A., Lindquist, S. A., & Martinek, W. L. (2006). *Judging on A Collegial Court: Influences on Federal Appellate Decision Making*. Charlottesville/London: University of Virginia Press.

Hirst, P. Q. (1979). *On Law and Ideology*. London: Humanities Press.

Holmes, O. W. (1880). Book Review of Langdell's Casebook. *American Law Review*, 233-235.

Housley, W. (2006). *Membership Categorisation Analysis, Sequences and Meeting Talk*. PhD Dissertation, School of Social Sciences. Cardiff University.

Huppert, L. A. (2003). *Shape vs. Color: Which Is the Primary Perception?* California: California State Science Fair.

Hutton, C. (1996). Law Lessons for Linguists? Accountability and Acts Of Professional Classification. *Language & Communication*, 16 (3), 205-214.

Hyland, K. (2005). *Metadiscourse: Exploring Interaction in Writing*. London: Continuum.

Jayyusi, L. (1993). Premeditation and Happenstance: The Social Construction of Intention, Action and Knowledge. *Human Studies*, 16 (4), 435-454.

Jefferson, G. (2004). Glossary of Transcript Symbols with an Introduction. In G. Lerner (Ed.), *Conversation Analysis: Studies from the First Generation*. Amsterdam/Philadelpia: John Benjamins Publishing Company.

Kasper, G. (2004). Speech Acts in (Inter) Action: Repeated questions. *Intercultural Pragmatics*, 1 (1), 125-133.

Kempf-Leonard, K., & Sample, L. L. (2001). Have Federal Sentencing Guidelines Reduced Severity? An Examination of One Circuit. *Journal of Quantitative Criminology*, 17 (2), 111-144.

Kennedy, D. (1976). Form and Substance in Private Law Adjudication. *Harvard Law Riew*, *89* (8), 1685-1778.

Kennedy, D. (1998). *A Critique of Adjudication*. London: Harvard University Press.

Klein, D. E., & Mitchell, G. (2010). *The Psychology of Judicial Decision*

Making. Oxford: Oxford University Press.

Komter, M. L. (1994). Accusations and Defences in Courtroom Interaction. *Discourse & Society*, 5 (2), 165-187.

Konecni, V. J., & Ebbesen, E. B. (1984). The Mythology of Legal Decision Making. *International Journal of Law and Psychiatry*, 7 (1), 5-18.

Koshik, I. (2003). Wh-questions Used as Challenges. *Discourse Studies*, 5 (1), 51-77.

Krell, D. F., & Heidegger, M. (1977). *Basic Writings: From Being and Time (*1927*) to the Task of Thinking (*1964*)* (Rev. and expanded ed.). San Francisco, Calif.: Harper.

Kryk-Kastovsky, B. (2009). Speech Acts in Early Modern English Court Trials. *Journal of Pragmatics-Speech Acts in Legal Language*, 41 (3), 440-457.

Kunselman, J., & Vito, G. (2002). Questioning Mandatory Sentencing Efficiency: A Case Study of Persistent Felony Offender Rapists inKentucky. *American Journal of Criminal Justice*, 27 (1), 53-68.

Kurzon, D. (1994). Linguistics and Legal Discourse: An Introduction. *International Journal for the Semiotics of Law*, 7 (1), 5-12.

Kurzon, D. (1997). "Legal Language": Varieties, Genres, Registers, Discourses. *International Journal of Applied Linguistics*, 7 (2), 119-139.

Levi, J. N., & Walker, A. G. (1990). *Language in the Judicial Process*. New York/London: Plenum Press.

Levinson, S. C. (1983). *Pragmatics* (1 ed.). London: Cambridge University Press.

Liao, M. (2009). A Study of Interruption in Chinese Criminal Courtroom Discourse. *Text & Talk*, 29 (2), 175-199.

Loeffler, R., & Lawson, T. (2002). Age and Occupational Status of Defendant in Relation to Mock Juror Sentencing Recommendations. *Current Psychology*, 21 (3), 289-292.

Lovegrove, A. (1989). *Judicial Decision Making, Sentencing Policy, and Numerical Guidance*. New York: Springer-Verlag.

Lovegrove, A. (1997). *The Framework of Judicial Sentencing: A Study in Legal Decision Making*. Cambridge: Cambridge University Press.

Luchjenbroers, J., & Aldridge, M. (2008). Language and Vulnerable Witnesses across Legal Contexts: Introduction to the Special Issue. *Journal of English Linguistics*, 36 (3), 191-194.

MacMartin, C. (1999). *Discursive Constructions of Child Sexual Abuse: Conduct, Credibility And Culpability In Trial Judgments*. PhD Dissertation, The University of Guelph.

MacMartin, C., & Wood, L. A. (2005a). Sexual Motives and Sentencing Judicial Discourse in Cases of Child Sexual Abuse. *Journal of Language and Social Psychology*, 24 (2), 139-159.

Maines, D. R. (1993). Narrative's Moment and Sociology's Phenomena: Toward a Narrative Sociology. *The Sociological Quarterly*, 34 (1), 17-38.

Maley, Y. (1994).The Language of the Law. In J. Gibbons (Ed.), *Langauge and the Law* (pp. 11-50).London and New York: Longman.

Manning, K. L., Carroll, B. A., & Carp, R. A. (2004). Does Age Matter? Judicial Decision Making in Age Discrimination Cases. *Social Science Quarterly*, 85 (1), 1-18.

Matoesian, G. M. (2001).*Law and the Language of Identity Discourse in the William Knnedy Smith Rape Trial*. New York: Oxford University Press.

Matoesian, G. (2005).Nailing Down an Answer: Participations of Power in Trial Talk. *Discourse Studies*, 7 (6), 733-759.

Matoesian, M. G. (1993). *Reproducing Rape: Domination Through Talk in the Courtroom*. Lordor: Polity Press.

Mauet, T. A. (2002). *Trial Techniques* (5th ed.). New York: Aspen Law & Business.

Maynard, D. W., & Perakyla, A. (2003). Language and Social Interaction. In J. Delamater (Ed.), *Handbook of Sociology* (pp. 233-257). New York: Kluwer Academic/Plenum Publishers.

McKnight, C. (1981). Subjectivity in Sentencing. *Law and Human*

Behavior, 5 (2), 141-147.

Mellinkoff, D. (1963). *The Language of the Law*. Boston: Little, Brown.

Merryman, J. (1985). *The Civil Law Tradition: An Introduction to the Legal Systems of Western Europe and Latin America* (2ed.). Stanford: Stanford University Press.

Miller, M., & Bornstein, B. (2006). The Use of Religion in Death Penalty Sentencing Trials. *Law and Human Behavior*, 30 (6), 675-684.

Mitchell, O. (2005). A Meta-Analysis of Race and Sentencing Research: Explaining the Inconsistencies. *Journal of Quantitative Criminology*, 21 (4), 439-466.

Monzoni, C. M. (2008). Introducing Direct Complaints Through Questions: The Interactional Achievement of "Pre-sequences"? *Discourse Studies*, 10 (1), 73-87.

Morcol, G. (Ed.). (2007). *Handbook of Decision Making*. Boca Raton: CRC Press.

Murphy, W. (1964). *Elements of Judicial Strategy*. Chicago: University of Chicago Press.

Murphy, J., & Coleman, J. (1990). *Philosophy of Law: An Introduction to Jurisprudence*. Colorado: Westview press.

Myers, G. (1990). *Writing Biology: Texts in the Social Construction of Scientific Knowledge*. Madison, Wisconsin: University of Wisconsin Press.

Nardulli, P. F., Flemming, R. B., & Eisenstein, J. (1984). Unraveling the Complexities of Decision Making in Face-to-Face Groups: A Contextual Analysis of Plea-Bargained Sentences. *American Political Science Review*, 78 (4), 912-928.

O'Barr, M. W. (1982). *Linguistic Evidence-Language, Power and Strategy in the courtroom*. New York: Academic Press.

Pennington, D. C., Lloyd-Bostock, S. M., Centre, S. L., & University, O. C. (1987). *The Psychology of Sentencing: Approaches to Consistency And Disparity*. Oxford: Centre for Socio-Legal Studies Wolfson College.

Philips, S. U. (1984) .The Social Organization of Questions and Answers in Courtroom Discourse: A Study of Changes of Plea in anArizona Court. *Text*, 4, 225-248.

Philips, S. U. (1993) . Evidentiary Standards for American Trials: Just the Facts. In J. H. Hill, & J. T. Irvine, *Responsibility and Evidence in Oral Discourse*, (pp. 248-259) .Cambridge, Cambridge University Press.

Philips, S. U. (1998) . *Ideology in the Language of Judges: How Judges Practice Law, Politics, and Courtroom Control (Oxford Studies in Anthropological Linguistics)*. New York: Oxford University Press.

Plessner, H., Betsch, C., & Betsch, T. (Eds.). (2007). *Intuition in Judgment and Decision Making*. New York: Lawrence Erlbaum Associates.

Potter, J. (1996). *Representing Reality: Discourse, Rhetoric and Social Construction*. London: SAGE.

Potter, J. (1998). Discursive Social Psychology: From Attitude to Evaluation. *European Review of Social Psychology*, 9, 233-266.

Potter, J. (1998) . Fragments in the Realization of Relativism. In I. Parker (Ed.), *Social Constructionism, Discourse and Realism* (pp. 27-45) .London: Sage.

Potter, J., Edwards, D., & Wetherell, M. (1993) . A Model of Discourse in Action. *American Behavioral Scientist*, 36 (3) , 383-401.

Potter, J., & Edwards, D. (1999) . Social Representations and Discursive Psychology: From Cognition to Action. *Culture & Psychology*, 5 (4) , 447.

Potter, J., & Edwards, D. (2001). Discursive Social Psychology. In P. Robinson & H. Giles (Eds.), *The New Handbook of Language and Social Psychology* (pp. 103-118) .Chichester: John Wiley&Sons Ltd.

Potter, J., & Edwards, D. (2003). Sociolinguistics, Cognitivism, and Discursive Psychology. *International Journal of English Studies*, 3 (1) , 93-109.

Potter, J., & Hepburn, A. (2005) . Disvursive Psychology as a Qualitative Approach for Analysing Interaction in Medical Settingsmaking Sense of Qualitative Research. *Medical Education* (39) : 338-344.

Potter, J., & Wetherell, M. (1987) .*Discourse and Social Psychology: Beyond*

Attitudes and Behaviour. London: Sage.

Pratt, T. C. (1998). Race and Sentencing: A Meta-Analysis of Conflicting Empirical Research Results. *Journal of Criminal Justice,* 26 (6), 513-523.

Prichett, C. H. (1948). *The Roosevelt Court*. New York: Macmillan.

Raiffa, H. (1994). The Prescriptive Orientation of Decision Making: A Synthesis of Decision Analysis, Behavioral Decision Making, and Game Theory. In S. Rios (Ed.), *Decision Theory and Decision Analysis: Trends and Challenges* (pp. 1-13). Dordrecht: Kluwer Academic Publishers.

Rawls, J. (1971). *A Theory of Justice*. MA: The Belknap Press of Harvard University Press.

Reavey, P., & Brown, S. D. (2006). Transforming Past Agency and Action in the Present: Time, Social Remembering and Child Sexual Abuse. *Theory & Psychology,* 16 (2), 179-202.

Resnik, M. D. (1987). *Choices: An Introduction to Decision Theory*. Minnesota: University of Minnesota Press.

Rigney, A. C. (1999). Questioning in Interpreted Testimony. *Forensic Linguistics,* 6 (1), 83-108.

Sacks, H. (1992). *Lectures on Conversation*. Oxford: Blackwell Publishers.

Sadock, J. (2006). Speech Acts. In L. R. Horn & G. L. Ward (Eds.), *The Handbook of Pragmatics*. London: Blackwell.

Sales, B. D. (Ed.). (1981). *The Trial Process: Perspectives in Law and Psychology*. New York: Plenum Press.

Sanborn, J. B. (1996). Factors Perceived to Affect Delinguent Dispositions in Juvenile Court: Putting the Sentencing Decision into Context. *Crime and Delinquency,* 42, 99-113.

Sanders, J., & Hamilton, V. L. (eds.) (2000). *Handbook of Justice Research in Law*. New York: Kluwer Academic Publishers.

Sbis, M. (2002). Speech Acts in Context. *Language & Communication*, 22 (4), 421-436.

Scheb, J. M., Bowen, T., & Anderson, G. (1991). Ideology, Role

Orientations, and Behavior in the State Courts of Last Resort. *American Politics Research*, 19 (3), 324.

Scheb, J. M., Ungs, T. D., & Hayes, A. L. (1989). Judicial Role Ungs, Orientations, Attitudes and Decision Making: A Research Note. *Political Research Quarterly* (42), 427-436.

Schegloff, E. A. (1992). In Another Context. In A. Duranti & C. Goodwin (Eds.), *Rethinking Context: Language as an Interactive Phenomenon* (pp. 191-227). Cambridge: Cambridge University Press.

Schegloff, E. A. (2007). *Sequence Organization in Interaction: A Primer in Conversation Analysis*. Cambridge: Cambridge University Press.

Schubert, G. (1965). *The Judicial Mind: The Attitudes and Ideologies of Supreme Court Justices*, 1946-1963. Evanston: Northwestern University Press.

Schubert, G. E., & Danelski, D. E. (1969). *Comparative Judicial Behavior: Cross-Cultural Studies of Political Decision-Making in the East and West*. Oxford: Oxford University Press.

Searle, J. R. (1969a). *Speech Acts: An Essay in the Philosophy of Language*. London: Cambridge University Press.

Segal, J. A., & Cover, A. D. (1989). Ideological Values and the Votes of US Supreme Court Justices. *American Political Science Review*, 83 (2), 557-565.

Segal, J. A., & Spaeth, H. J. (2002). *The Supreme Court and the Attitudinal Model Revisited*. Cambridge: Cambridge University Press.

Sharples, K. S. (1972). *The Legal Framework of Judicial Sentencing Policy*. Amsterdam: Amsterdam University Press.

Shuy, R. W. (2006). *Linguistics in the Courtroom: A Practical Guide*. Oxford: Oxford University Press, USA.

Sigler, M. (2000). The Story of Justice: Retribution, Mercy, and the Role of Emotions in the Capital Sentencing Process. *Law and Philosophy*, 19 (3), 339-367.

Simon, H. A. (1993). Decision Making: Rational, Nonrational, and Irrational. *Educational Administration Quarterly*, 29 (3), 392.

Simon, H. (1960). *The New Science of Management Decision.* New York: Harper & Row.

Simon, T. W. (2001). *Law and Philosophy: An Introduction with Readings* New York: McGraw Hill.

Sinclair, J. M., & Coulthard, R. M. (1975). *Towards an Analysis of Discourse: The English Used by Teachers and Pupils.* London: Oxford University Press.

Solan, L., & Tiersma, P. M. (2005). *Speaking of Crime: The Language of Criminal Justice.* Chicago, Ill.: University of Chicago Press.

Sperber, D., & Wilson, D. (1995). *Relevance: Communication and Cognition.* Oxford: Blackwell Publishers Ltd.

Spiegel, U., & Templeman, J. (1989). Economics of Discriminatory Sentencing. *Journal of Quantitative Criminology*, 5 (4), 317-332.

St. Louis, J. M. (2000). *Examination of Judicial Discretion in Sentencing of Adjudicated Juvenile Offenders.* PhD Dissertation, California School of Professional Psychology, Fresno Campus.

Staley, C. (2007). *Facial Attractiveness and the Sentencing of Male Defendants.* PhD Dissertation, Alliant International University, Calitornia.

Steffensmeier, D., & Britt, C. L. (2001). Judges, Race and Judicial Decision Making: Do Black Judges Sentence Differently? *Social Science Quarterly*, 82 (4), 749-764.

Stokoe, E., & Edwards, D. (2008). "Did You Have Permission to smash your neighbour's Door?" Silly Questions and their Answers in Police-suspect Interrogations. *Discourse Studies*, 10 (1), 89-111.

Stubbs, M. (1983). *Discourse Analysis: The Sociolinguistic Analysis of Natural Language.* Oxford: Blackwell.

Susan, E., & Jack, S. (2006). "I Think That's Not an Assumption You Ought to Make": Challenging Presuppositions in Inquiry Testimony. *Language in Society*, 35 (5), 655-676.

Swales, J. (1990). *Genre Analysis: English in Academic and Research*

Settings. Cambridge: Cambridge University Press.

Tate, C. N. (1983). The Methodology of Judicial Behavior Research: A Review and Critique. *Political Behavior*, 5 (1), 51-82.

Tate, C. N. (1981). Personal Attribute Models of the Voting Behavior of U. S. Supreme Court Justices: Liberalism in Civil Liberties and Economics Decisions, 1946-1978. *American Political Science Review*, 75 (2), 355-367.

Taylor, C. (1989). *Sources of the Self*. Harvard University Press: Cambridge, Mass.

Thomas, D. (2003). Judicial Discretion in Sentencing. In L. Gelsthorpe & N. Padfield (Eds.), *Exercising Discretion: Decision-Making in the Criminal Justice System and Beyond* (pp. 50-73). Portland: Willan Publishing.

Tiede, L. B. (2007). Delegating Discretion: Quasi Experiments on District Court Decision Making. *American Politics Research*, 35 (5), 595-620.

Tiersma, P. M. (1999). *Legal Language*. Chicago/London: University of Chicago Press.

Tomaino, J. (1997). Guess Who's Coming to Dinner? A Preliminary Model for the Satisfaction of Public Opinion as a Legitimate Aim in Sentencing. *Crime, Law and Social Change*, 27 (2), 109-119.

Toulmin, S. E. (2003). *The Uses of Argument*. Cambridge: Cambridge University Press.

Tracy, K. (2002). *Everyday Talk: Building and Reflecting Identities*. New York/London: The Guilford Press.

Trosborg, A. (1995). Statutes and Contracts: An Analysis of Legal Speech Acts in the English Language of the Law. *Journal of Pragmatics-Laying Down the Law-Discourse Analysis of Legal Institutions*, 23 (1), 31-53.

Tsui, A. B. (1994). *English Conversation*. Oxford: Oxford University Press.

Turk, A. M. (Ed.). (1997). *Introduction to Law and Society* (5th ed.). MA: Simon and Schuster Publishing.

Ungs, T. D., & Baas, L. R. (1972). Judicial Role Perceptions: A Q-Technique Study of Ohio Judges, *6* (3), 343-366.

Van Dijk, T. A. (1977). *Text and Context: Explorations in the Semantics and Pragmatics of Discourse*. London: Longman Group.

Van Dijk, T. A. (2008). *Discourse and Context: A Sociocognitive Approach*. Cambridge: Cambridge University Press.

Van Dijk, T. (2004). Political Discourse and Political Cognition. In P. Chilton & C. Schaffner (Eds.), *Politics as Text And Talk: Analytic Approaches to Political Discourse* (pp. 203-237). Amsterdam and Phiadelphia: John Benjamin.

Vojcanin, S. A (ed.). (1990). *Law, Culture, and Values: Essays in Honor of Gray Dorsey*. New Brunswick, N. J.: Transaction Publishers.

VonDoepp, P. (2008). Context-Sensitive Inquiry in Comparative Judicial Research: Lessons From the Namibian Judiciary. *Comparative Political Studies*, 41 (11), 1515-1540.

Wagenaar, W. A. (1995). Anchored Narratives: A Theory of Judicial Reasoning and Its Consequences. In G. Davies, S. Lloyd-Bostock, M. McMurran & C. Wilson (eds.), *Psychology, Law and Criminal Justice: International Developments in Research and Practice* (pp. 267-285). Berlin: Walter de Gruyter.

Walker, A. (1987). Linguistic Manipulation, Power, and the Legal Setting. In L. Kedar (Ed.), *Power through Language* (pp. 55-76). Norwood, NJ: Ablex.

Watson, D. R. (1983). The Presentation of Victim and Motive in Discourse: The Case of Police Interrogations and Interviews. *Victimology*, 8 (1/2), 31-52.

West, R. (1988). Jurisprudence and Gender. *Jurisprudence and Gender*. 55 (1), 1-72.

Wetherell, M. (1998). Positioning and Interpretative Repertoires: Conversation Analysis and Post-Structuralism in Dialogue. *Discourse & Society*, 9 (3), 387-412.

Wetherell, M. (2007). A Step Too Far: Discursive Psychology, Linguistic Ethnography and Questions of Identity. *Journal of Sociolinguistics*, 11 (5), 661-681.

Wetherell, M., & Potter, J. (1989). Narrative Characters and Accounting for Violence. In J. Shotter and K. J. Gergen (Ed.), *Text of Identity* (pp. 206-219). London: Sage.

Wittgenstein, L. (1997). *Philosophische Untersuchungen/Philosophical Investigations*. Oxford: Blackwell Publishers Ltd.

Wood, L. A., & MacMartin, C. (2007). Constructing Remorse: Judges'Sentencing Decisions in Child Sexual Assault Cases. *Journal of Language and Social Psychology*, 26 (4), 343-362.

Woodbury, H. (1984). The Strategic Use of Questions in Court. *Semiotica*, 48 (3/4), 197-228.

Wooffitt, R., & Clark, C. (1998). Mobilizing Discourse and Social Identities in Knowledge Talk. In C. Antaki & S. Widdicombe (Eds.), *Identities in Talk* (pp. 107-120). London: Sage Publications.

Wroblewski, J. (1988). Response to P. J. Van Den Hoven and P. Ingram: Analytical and Semiotic Approaches to Justification of Legal Decision. *International Journal for the Semiotics of Law*, 1 (1), 71-78.

Wróblewski, J. (1990). Principles, Values, and Rules in Legal Decision-Making and the Dimensions of Legal Rationality. *Ratio Juris*, 3 (1), 130-147.

Wu, Z. (2007). *Examining Good Character as a Mitigating Factor in Canadian Sentencing*. PhD Dissertation, Queen's University, Kingston, Ontario, Canada.

Zajacova, A. (2002). The Background of Discourse Analysis: A New Paradigm in Social Psychology. *Journal of Social Distress and the Homeless*, 11 (1), 25-40.

Zimmerman, D. H. (1998). Identity, Context and Interaction. In C. Antaki & S. Widdicombe (Eds.), *Identities in Talk* (pp. 87-106). London: Sage Publications.

Zimmerman, D. H., & Pollner, M. (1970). Understanding Everyday Life: Toward the Reconstruction of Sociological Knowledge. In J. D. Douglas (Ed.), *Understanding Everyday Life: Toward the Reconstruction of Sociological*

Knowledge (pp. 80-103) .London: Routledge.

Zorn, Christopher J. and Bowie, Jennifer Barnes. *An Empirical Analysis of Hierarchy Effects in Judicial Decision Making* (June 30, 2007). Available at SSRN: http: //ssrn. com/abstract = 987862.

(Cai) 蔡晖．(2003) .法官职业素质: 从经验型到知识型．*人民司法* (10), 1.

(Fu) 付建平．(2001) .法官判决中的竞争性因素．*法学*(3), 12-16.

(Gao & Jiang) 高其才; 姜振业．(2006) .判决是如何形成的: 乡土社会语境中的法官判决模式研究．*云南大学学报*, 19 (2), 92-99.

(He) 贺卫方．(2002) .中国的法院改革与司法独立——一个参与者的观察与反思．*科学中国人*(5), 17-19.

(Hu) 胡海娟．(2004) .法庭话语研究综论．*广东外语外贸大学学报, 15* (1), 8-11.

(Huai) 怀效锋．(2006) .*法官行为与职业伦理*. 北京: 法律出版社.

(Huang) 黄竹胜．(2002) .论司法行为理性化及其制度性条件．*当代法学*(3), 29-33.

(Li) 李辰星．(2013) .司法行为规范化的构建路径．*中南民族大学学报(人文社会科学版)* (2), 108-111.

(Li) 李奕．(2005) .*法官自由裁量权论*．博士毕业论文．长春: 吉林大学．

(Liao) 廖美珍．(2003) .*法庭问答及其互动研究*. 北京: 法律出版社.

(Liao) 廖美珍．(2006) .论法学的语言转向．*社会科学在线* (2), 200-204.

(Lin) 林珣．(2006) .中国法官职业化的悖论．*经济与社会发展, 4* (7), 94-98.

(Qian) 钱卫清．(2008) .*法官决策论—影响司法过程的力量*. 北京: 北京大学出版社．

(Qu) 瞿琨．(2006) .论法官角色与公正司法．*学术界*(1), 79-84.

(Qu) 曲颖．(1999) .论法官素质．*人民司法*(11), 12-14.

(the National People's Congress) 全国人民代表大会．(2001) .中华人民共

和国法官法．中华人民共和国．

(the National People's Congress) 全国人民代表大会．(2004)．中华人民共和国宪法．中华人民共和国．

(the National People's Congress) 全国人民代表大会．(2006)．中华人民共和国人民法院组织法．中华人民共和国．

(the National People's Congress) 全国人民代表大会．(2007)．中华人民共和国民事诉讼法．中华人民共和国．

(Shen) 沈德咏．(2004)．新时期中国司法改革进程(纲要)．*人民司法*(6), 4-6.

(Su) 苏力．(2004)．*也许正在发生: 转型中国的法学*. 北京: 法律出版社．

(Sun & Xiong) 孙笑侠; 熊静波．(2007)．判决与民意—兼比较考察中美法官如何对待民意．*政法论坛, 23* (5), 47-56.

(Tian) 田力男．(2013)．论公诉审查程序中法官角色的改革．*中国刑事法杂志*(05), 78-85.

(Wang) 王纳新．(2005)．*法官的思维—司法认知的基本规律*. 北京: 法律出版社．

(Wu) 吴英姿．(2008)．*法官角色与司法行为*. 北京: 中国大百科全书出版社．

(Wu) 吴宗杰．(2004)．论证中的话语混杂外语测试的社会分析．*外国语*(5), 48-55.

(Xia) 夏克勤．(2001)．中国法官职业化的必由之路—以法官选任制替代审判长选任制．*法学*(4), 11-13.

(Xiao) 肖扬．(2002)．法院、法官与司法改革．中国人民大学"大法官讲坛"讲演．

(Xu) 徐阳．(2012)．"舆情再审": 司法决策的困境与出路．*中国法学*(2), 180-191.

(Yang) 杨立新．(2014)．国家治理现代化与司法改革．*法制与社会发展*(5), 66-67.

(Yu) 于晓青．(2012)．法官的法理认同及裁判说理．*法学*(8), 76-86.

(Zhang) 张其山 . (2014) .我国基层法院的司法决策探析 . *山东社会科学*(8) , 164-169.

(Zhang) 詹森林 . (2005) . *民事法理与判决研究*. 北京: 北京大学出版社 .

(Zhang) 张玮 . (1999) .法官独立审判与程序性司法: 关于审判管理体制改革的两个主要问题 . *法学论坛*(5) , 13-21.

(Zhang) 张新红 . (2000) .汉语立法语篇的言语行为分析 . *现代外语, 23* (3) , 283-295.

(Zhang) 张谊生 . (2004) .试论"由"字被动句: 兼论由字句和被字句的区别 . *语言科学, 3* (3) , 38-53.

(Zhong & Huang) 钟彩顺; 黄永平 . (2009) .基于后维特根斯坦语言哲学的法律语言学研究 . *广东外语外贸大学学报, 20* (1) , 73-77.

(the Supreme People's Court) 最高人民法院 . (2005) .法官行为规范(试行) . 中华人民共和国 .

Appendices

1. General Information on the Dataset *

1. Observed Cases

Case no.	Time	Division	Case
1	Oct. 2007	L	Du…vs. Village Committee (death compensation)
2	Nov. 2007	L	Liu vs. Zeng (the rights for a divorced parent to visit the child)
3	Nov. 2007	M	…Real Estate Company vs. …Civil Construction Company
4	Dec. 2007	L	Cui…vs. …Business Mansion
5	Dec. 2007	I	Yang…vs. Zhang… (real estate dispute)
6	Feb. 2008	M	Ding…vs. China's Stock Supervisory Committee
7	April 2008	L	Jin…and Wang… (petition for a change of custody)
8	Mar. 2008	L	Zhao…vs. Jian… (dispute over a heritage)
9	Aug. 2008	L	Yu…vs. Shen… (dispute over a heritage)
10	Sep. 2008	L	Liu…vs. Yang… (a business contract)

2. Sampled Judgments from CLIPS

Case no.	Division	Nature of the case
C. F. L. 1	Tort	Accident injury
C. F. L. 2	Intellectual Property	Infringement of a software copyright
C. F. M 3	Intellectual Property	Infringement of a patent
C. F. L. 4	Divorce	Appealing for divorce
C. F. L. 5	Contract	A business dispute between a laundry and a customer
C. F. L. 6	Tort	Disposal of the deceased body
C. S. L. 7	Tort	Death caused by medical negligence
C. F. L. 8	Tort	Malpractice in food service

续表

Case no.	Division	Nature of the case
C. F. L. 9	Tort	Damages caused by traffic accident
C. F. L. 10	Contract	Cost of a shared wall between neighbors

* C: civil; F: first instance; S: second instance; L: court of the local level; M: court of the intermediary level

3. Transcription Conventions

[ ]	Square brackets mark the start and end of overlapping speech.
_ _	Underscoring indicates some form of stress, via pitch and/or amplitude. A short underscore indicates lighter stress than does a long underscore.
Bold	Bold marks speech that is obviously louder than surrounding speech.
(0. 4)	Numbers in parentheses indicate elapsed time by tenths of a second.
—	Dashes indicate a short, untimed interval without talk.
:	Colons indicate elongation of the prior sound; the more colons, the more elongation.
-	Hyphens mark a cut-off of the preceding sound.
?	Question marks signal stronger, questioning intonation, irrespective of grammar.
↓↑	Arrows indicate shifts into especially high or low pitch.
=	Equal signs indicate no break or gap.
,	The comma marks continuation, the speaker has not finished, intonationally it is a fall-rise or weak rising intonation.
.	Periods (full stops) mark falling, stopping intonation (final contour), irrespective of grammar.
°Word°	Degree signs bracketing an utterance or utterance-part indicate that the sounds are softer than the surrounding talk.
><	Right/left carats bracketing an utterance or utterance-part indicate that the bracketed material is speeded up, compared to the surrounding talk.
<>	Left/right carats bracketing an utterance or utterance-part indicate that the bracketed material is slowed down, compared to the surrounding talk.
()	Empty parentheses indicate that the transcriber was unable to get what was said.
(word)	Parenthesized words and speaker designations are especially dubious.
(())	Doubled parentheses contain transcriber's descriptions.